Ayu Watanabe

L♥DK

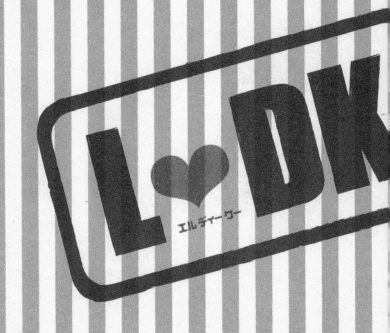

エルディーケー

6

L♥DK
Ayu Watanabe
6

c o n t e n t s

#21 The North Wind & The Sun 3

#22 Can't Go Back To How Things Were 41

#23 Gentle Hands 83

#24 Fighting Hosts 123

Special Sexy Bonus Story 163

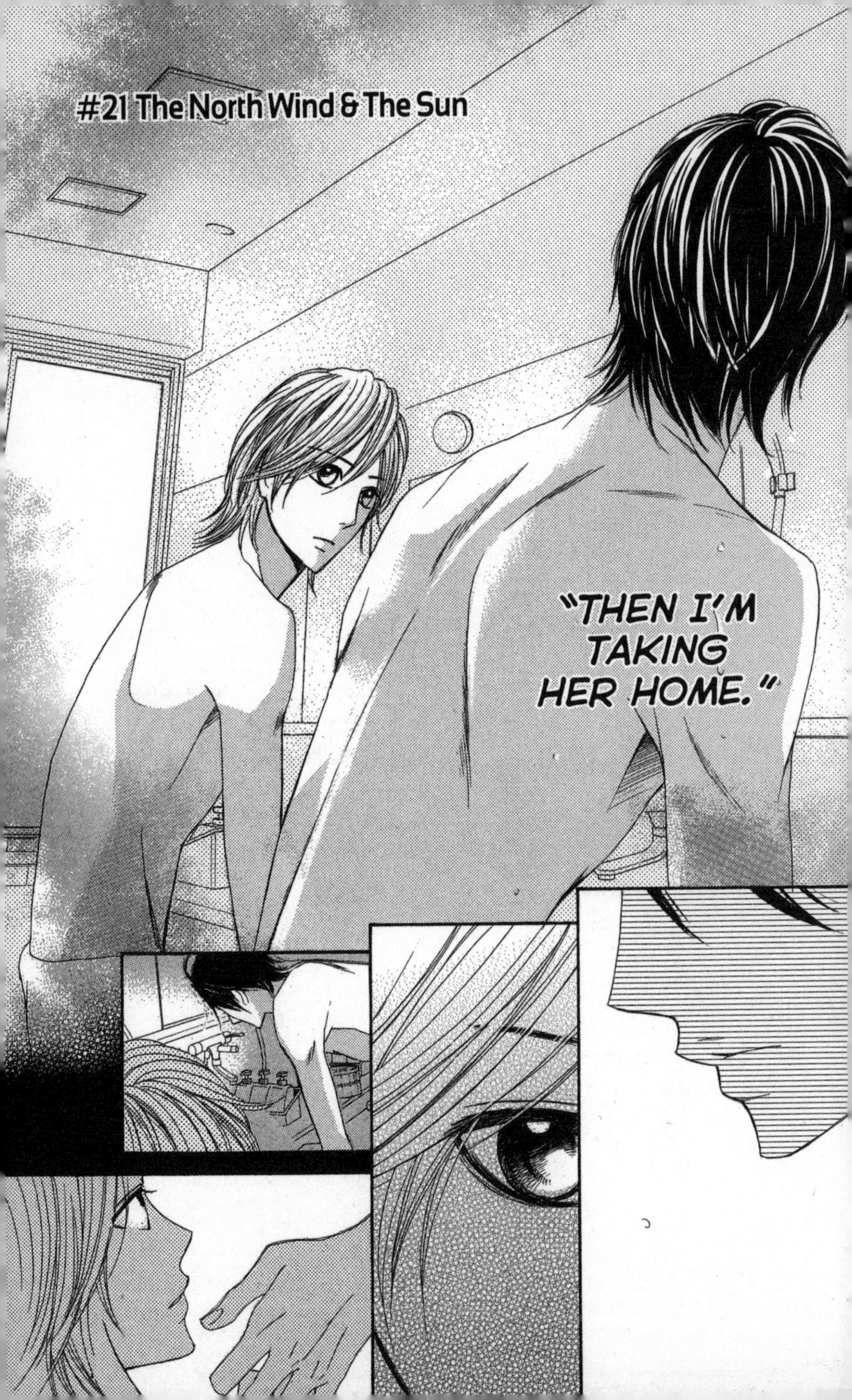
#21 The North Wind & The Sun
"THEN I'M TAKING HER HOME."

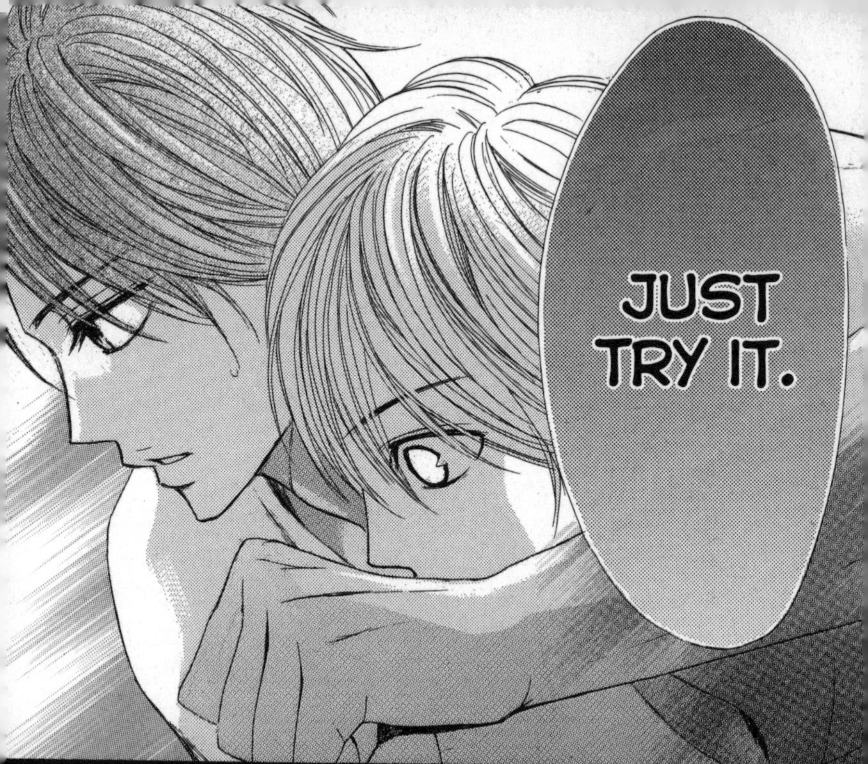
JUST TRY IT.

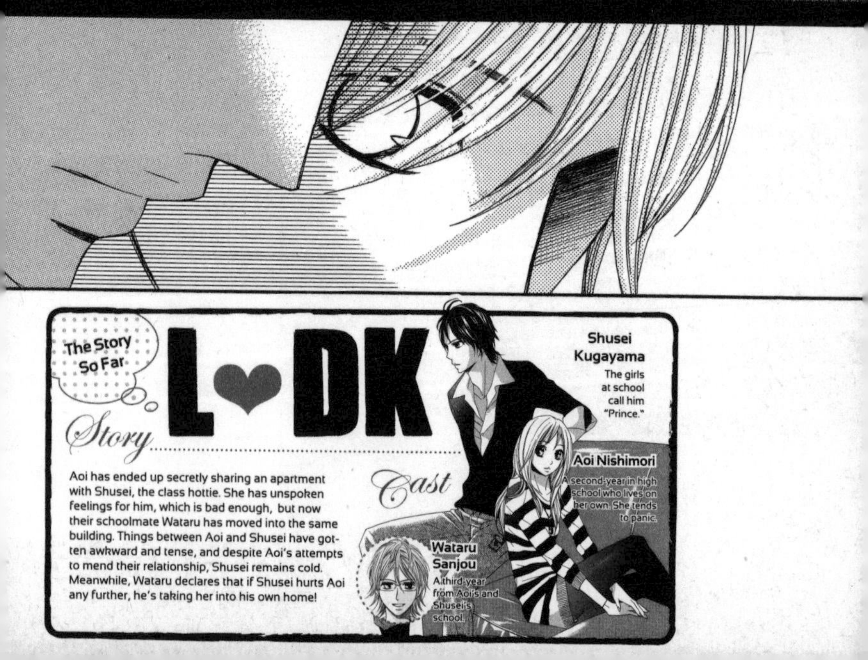

The Story So Far

L♥DK

Story

Aoi has ended up secretly sharing an apartment with Shusei, the class hottie. She has unspoken feelings for him, which is bad enough, but now their schoolmate Wataru has moved into the same building. Things between Aoi and Shusei have gotten awkward and tense, and despite Aoi's attempts to mend their relationship, Shusei remains cold. Meanwhile, Wataru declares that if Shusei hurts Aoi any further, he's taking her into his own home!

Cast

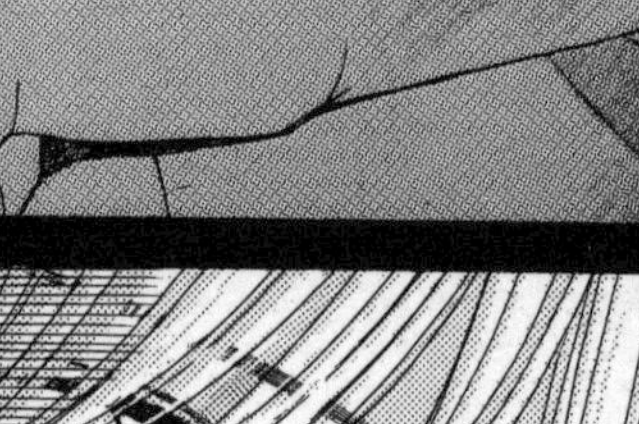

Shusei Kugayama
The girls at school call him "Prince."

Aoi Nishimori
A second-year in high school who lives on her own. She tends to panic.

Wataru Sanjou
A third-year from Aoi's and Shusei's school.

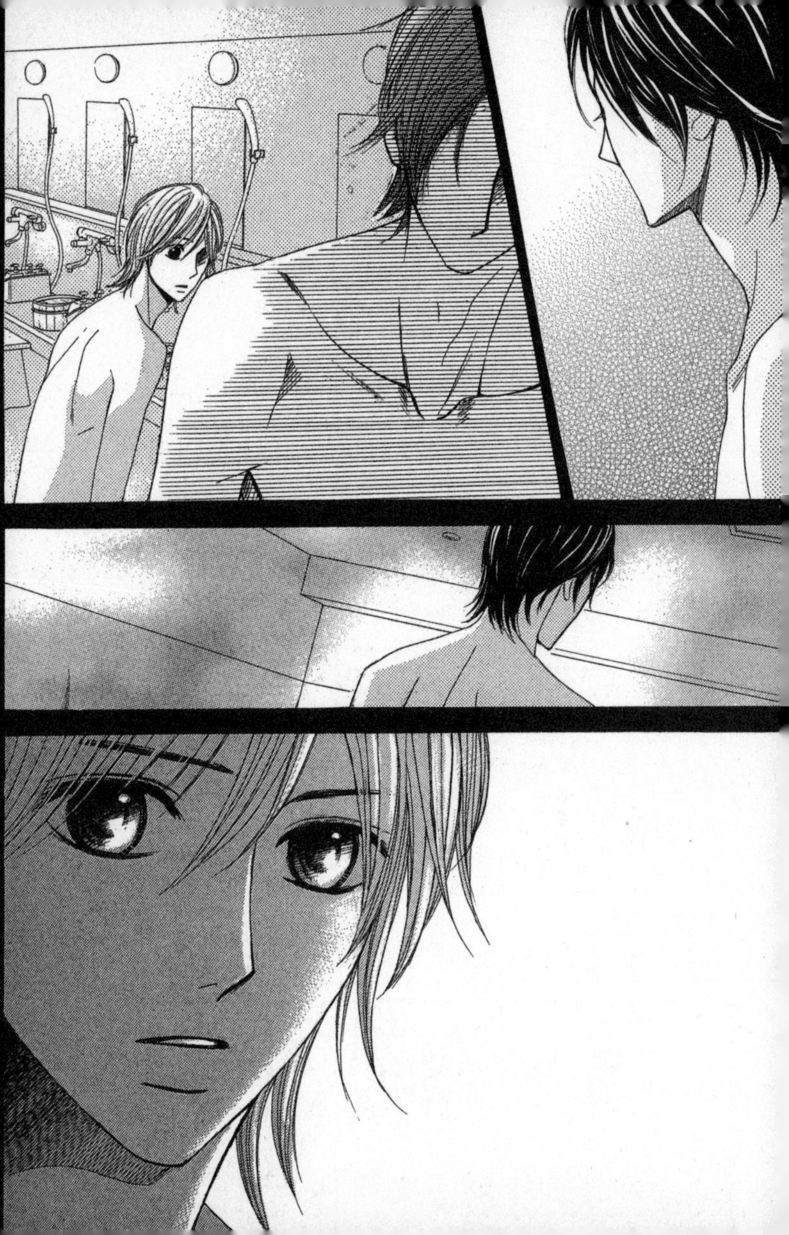

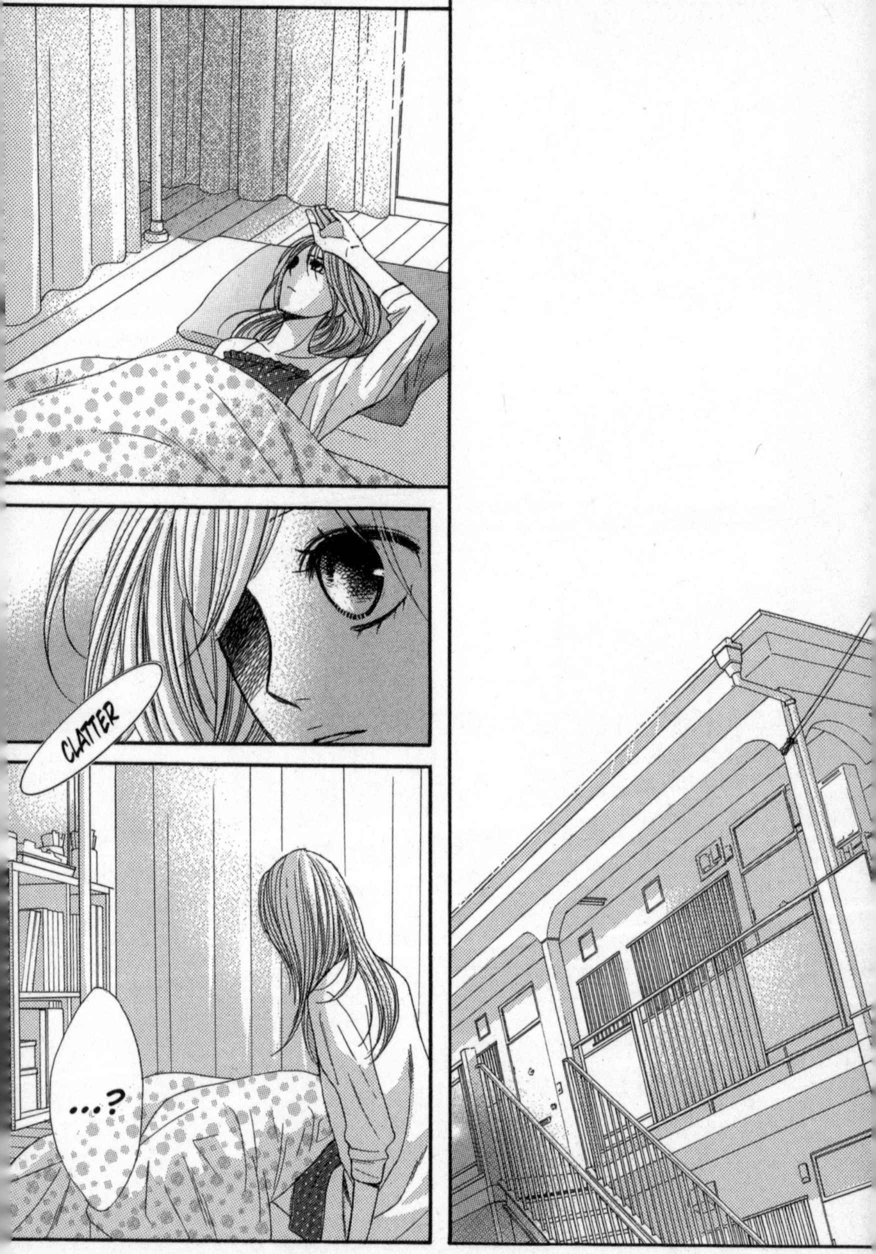
CLATTER
...?

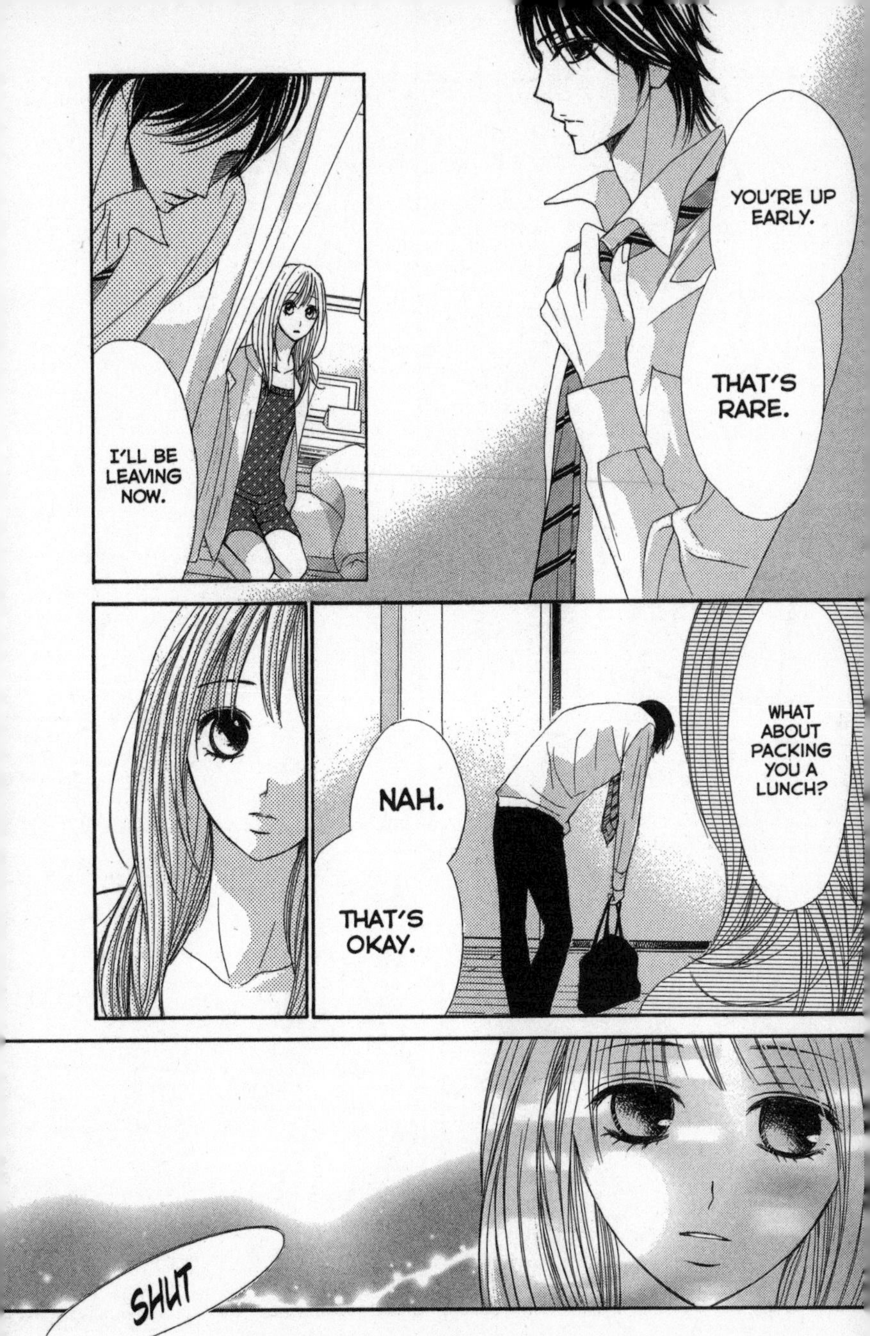
YOU'RE UP EARLY.
THAT'S RARE.
I'LL BE LEAVING NOW.
WHAT ABOUT PACKING YOU A LUNCH?
NAH.
THAT'S OKAY.
SHUT

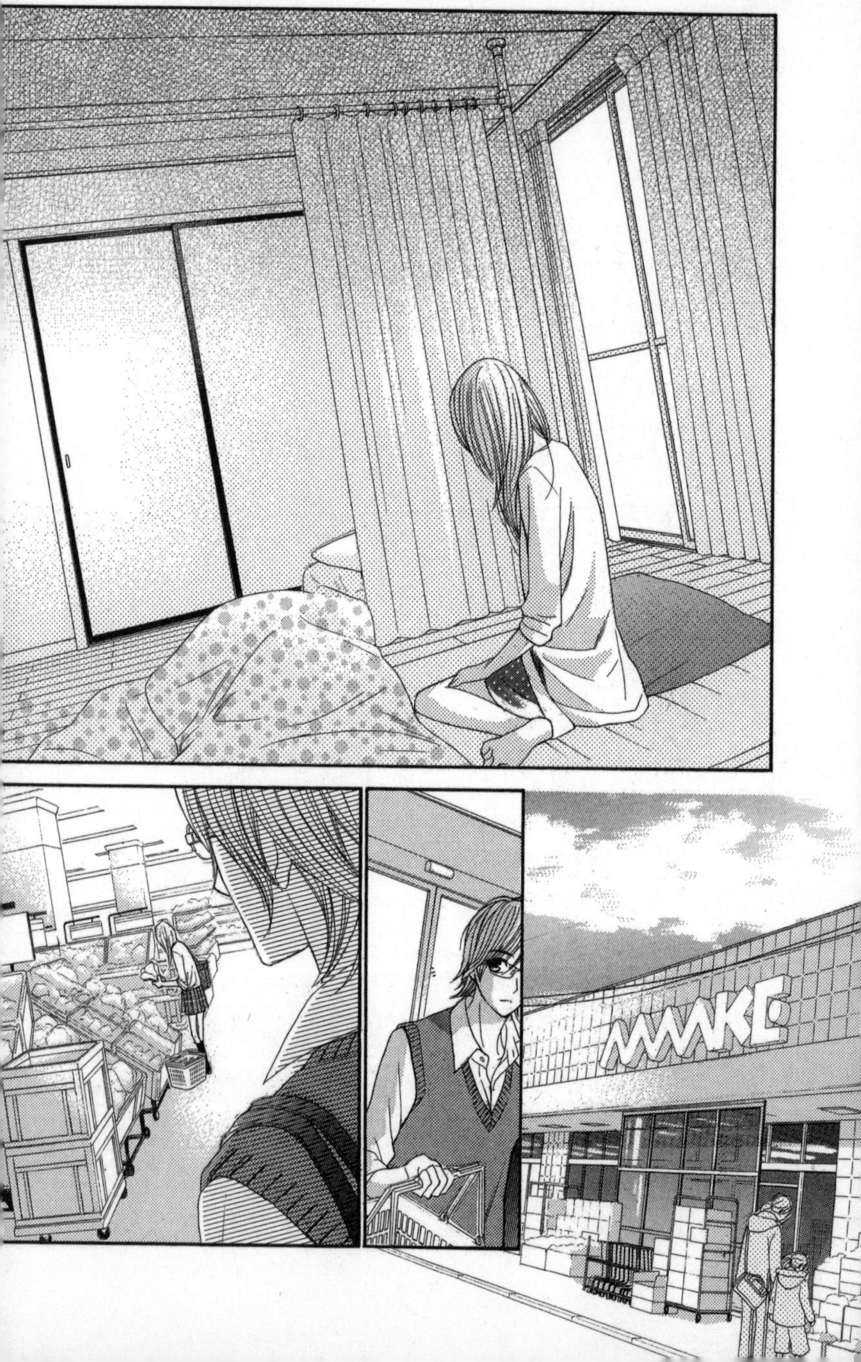

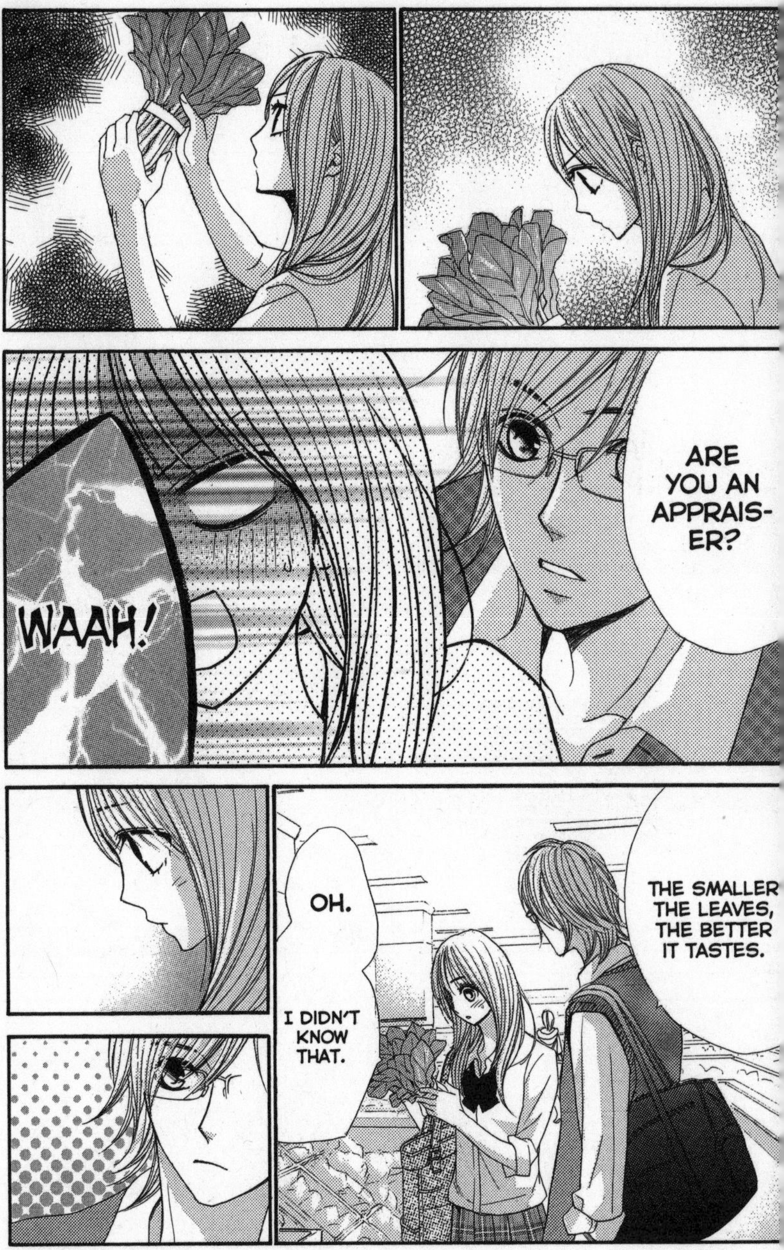
ARE YOU AN APPRAIS-ER?
WAAH!
THE SMALLER THE LEAVES, THE BETTER IT TASTES.
OH.
I DIDN'T KNOW THAT.

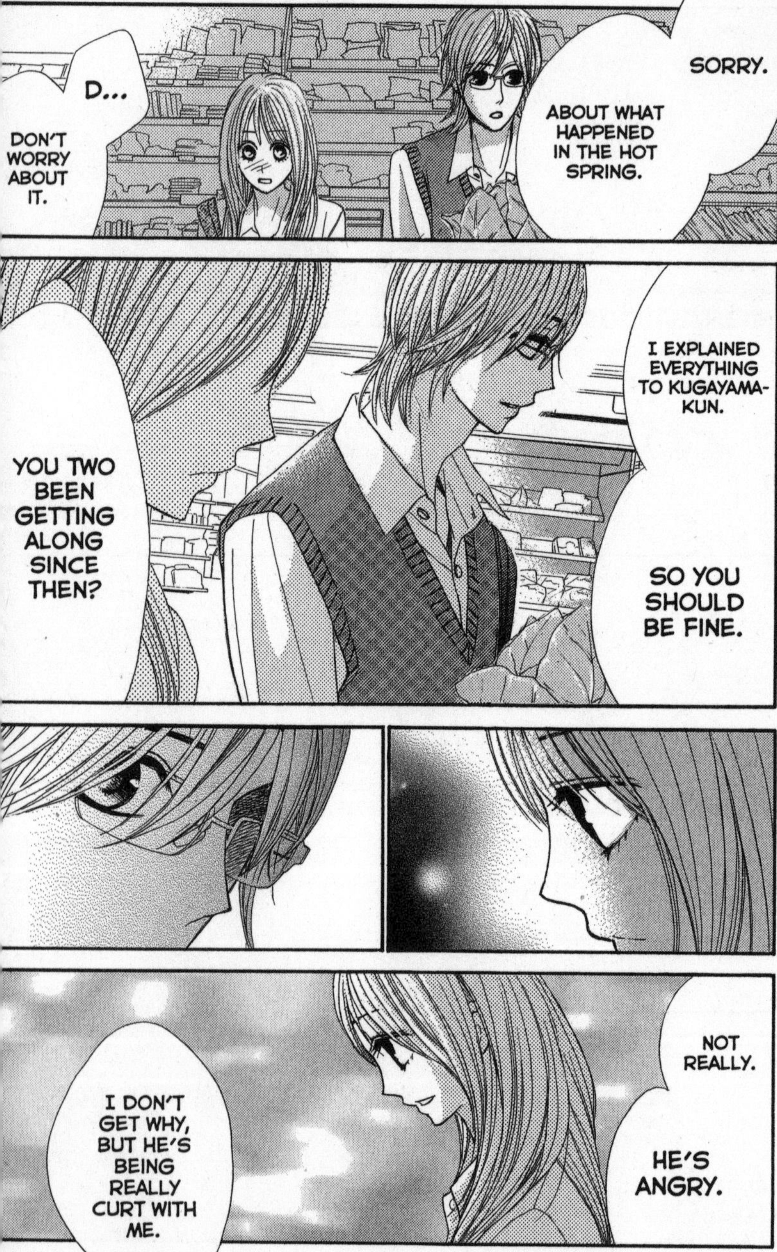
SORRY.
ABOUT WHAT HAPPENED IN THE HOT SPRING.
D...
DON'T WORRY ABOUT IT.
I EXPLAINED EVERYTHING TO KUGAYAMA-KUN.
SO YOU SHOULD BE FINE.
YOU TWO BEEN GETTING ALONG SINCE THEN?
NOT REALLY.
HE'S ANGRY.
I DON'T GET WHY, BUT HE'S BEING REALLY CURT WITH ME.

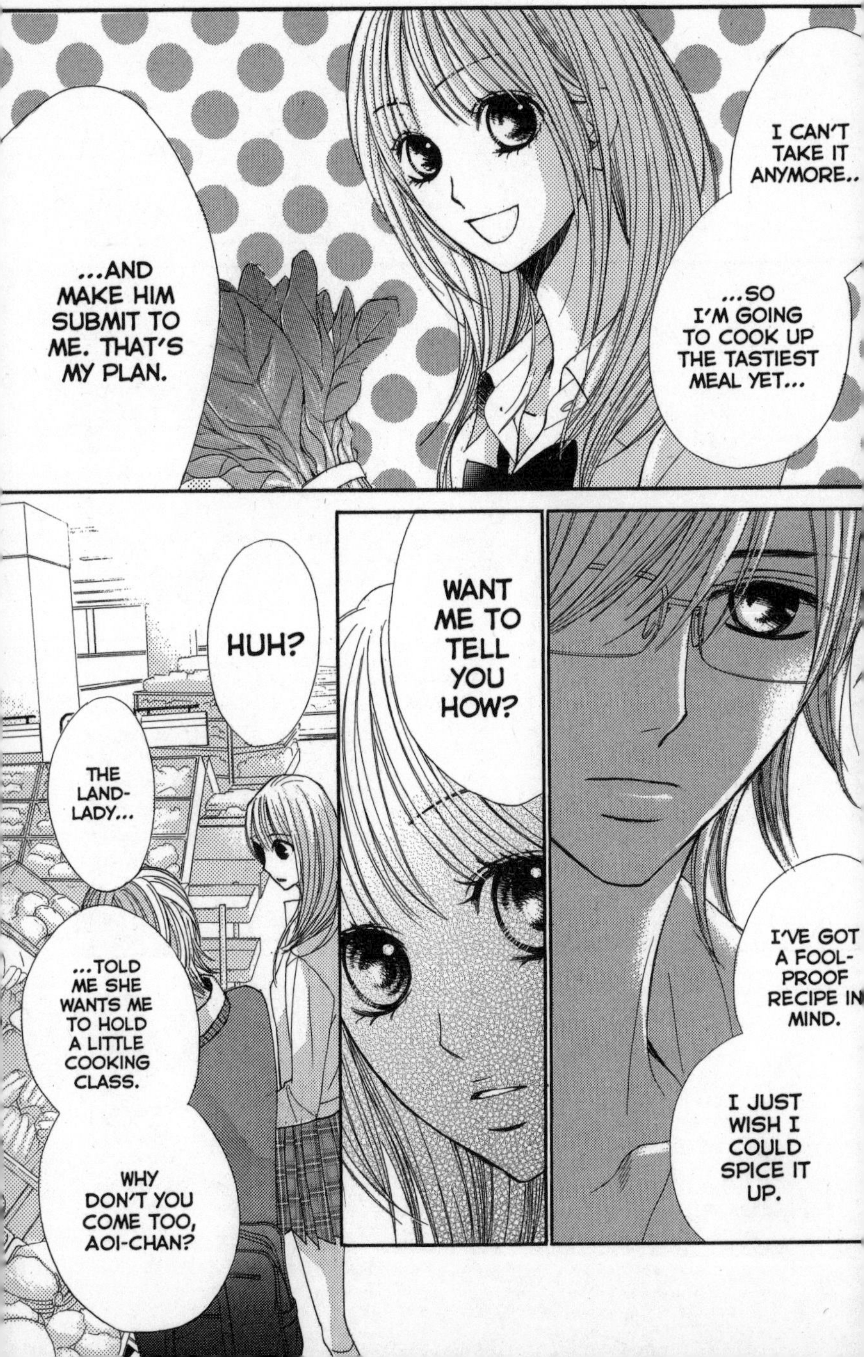
I CAN'T TAKE IT ANYMORE..
...SO I'M GOING TO COOK UP THE TASTIEST MEAL YET...
...AND MAKE HIM SUBMIT TO ME. THAT'S MY PLAN.
I'VE GOT A FOOL-PROOF RECIPE IN MIND.
I JUST WISH I COULD SPICE IT UP.
WANT ME TO TELL YOU HOW?
HUH?
THE LAND-LADY...
...TOLD ME SHE WANTS ME TO HOLD A LITTLE COOKING CLASS.
WHY DON'T YOU COME TOO, AOI-CHAN?

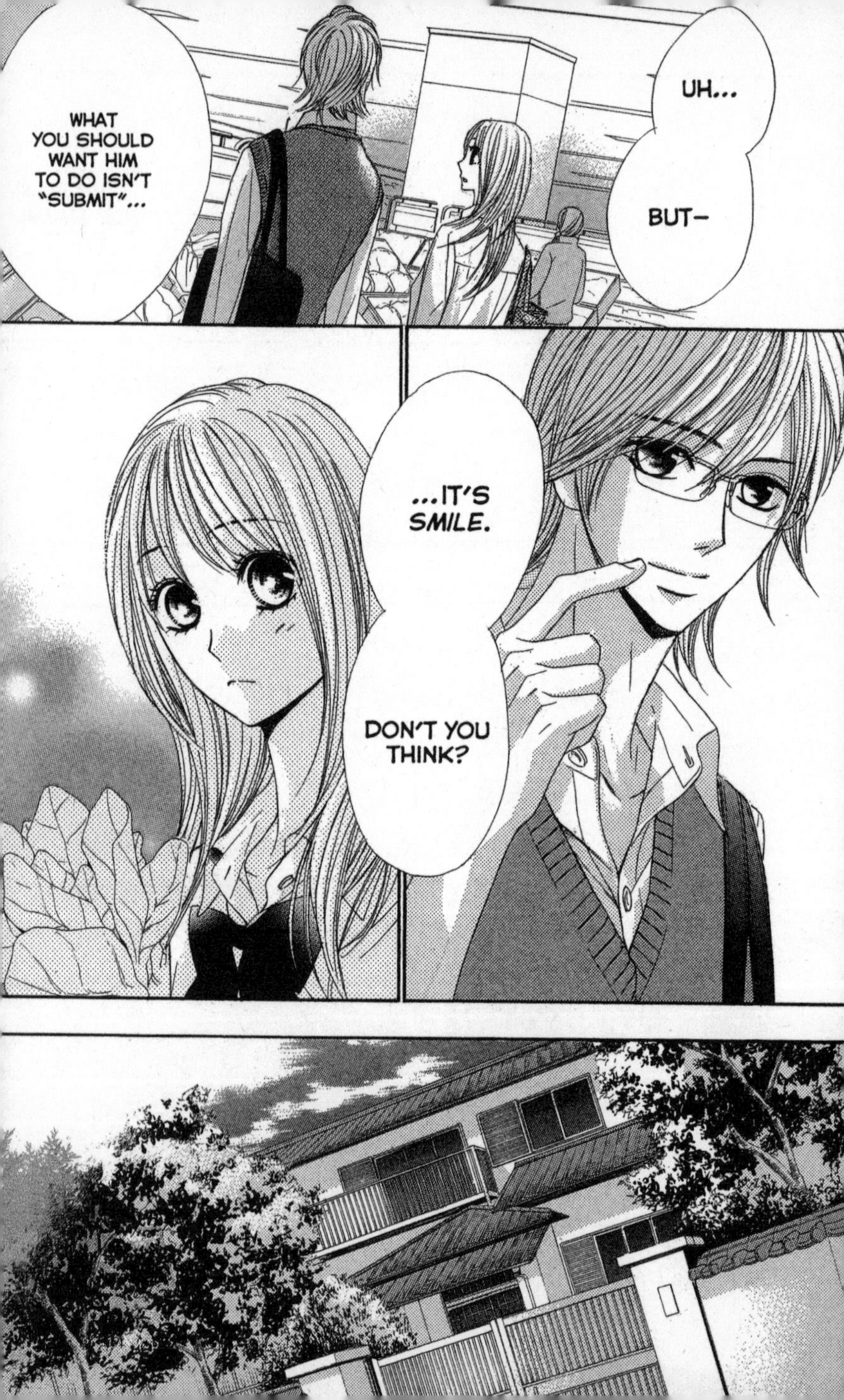
UH...
BUT–
WHAT YOU SHOULD WANT HIM TO DO ISN'T "SUBMIT"...
...IT'S SMILE.
DON'T YOU THINK?

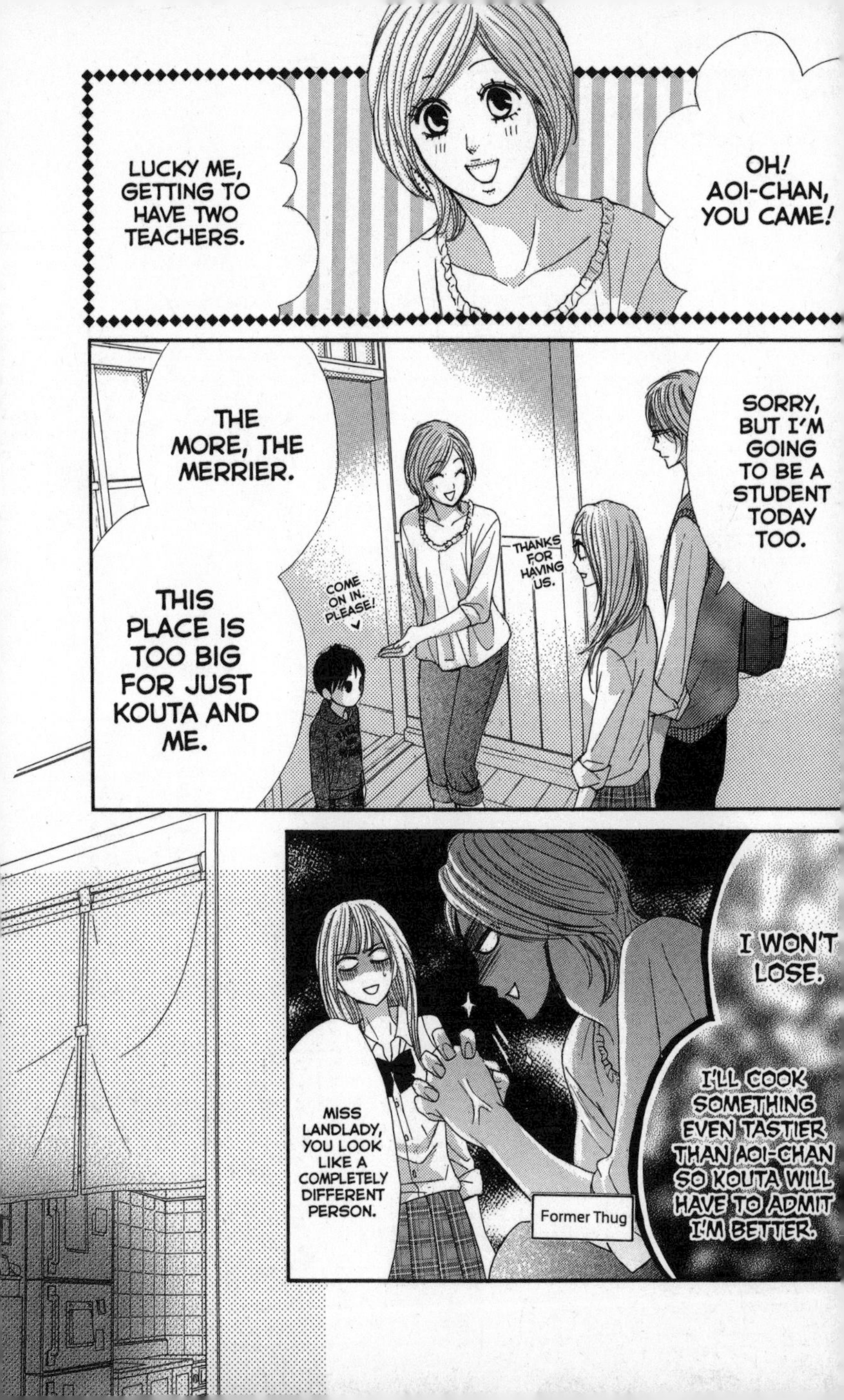
OH! AOI-CHAN, YOU CAME!
LUCKY ME, GETTING TO HAVE TWO TEACHERS.
SORRY, BUT I'M GOING TO BE A STUDENT TODAY TOO.
THANKS FOR HAVING US.
THE MORE, THE MERRIER.
COME ON IN. PLEASE!
THIS PLACE IS TOO BIG FOR JUST KOUTA AND ME.
I WON'T LOSE.
I'LL COOK SOMETHING EVEN TASTIER THAN AOI-CHAN SO KOUTA WILL HAVE TO ADMIT I'M BETTER.
Former Thug
MISS LANDLADY, YOU LOOK LIKE A COMPLETELY DIFFERENT PERSON.

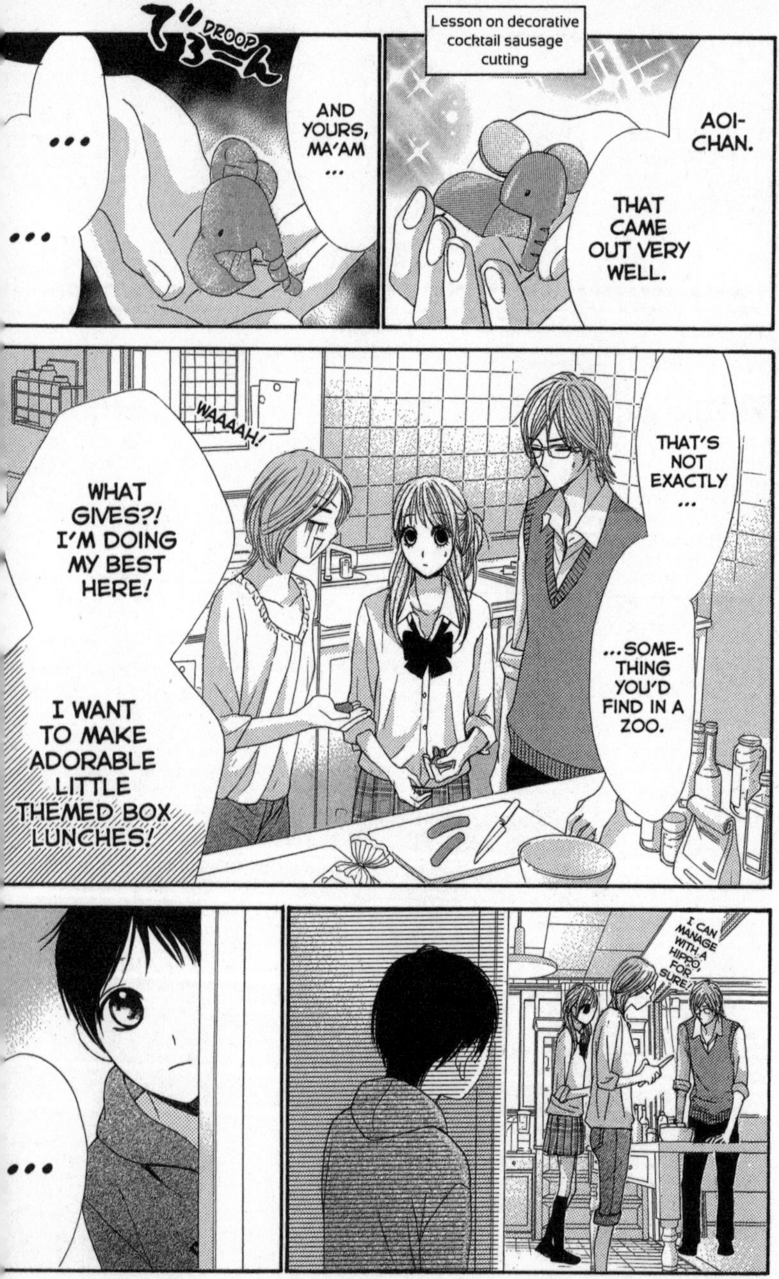
Lesson on decorative cocktail sausage cutting
AOI-CHAN.
THAT CAME OUT VERY WELL.
AND YOURS, MA'AM ...
DROOP
...
...
THAT'S NOT EXACTLY ...
...SOME-THING YOU'D FIND IN A ZOO.
WAAAAH!
WHAT GIVES?! I'M DOING MY BEST HERE!
I WANT TO MAKE ADORABLE LITTLE THEMED BOX LUNCHES!
I CAN MANAGE WITH A HIPPO, FOR SURE!
...

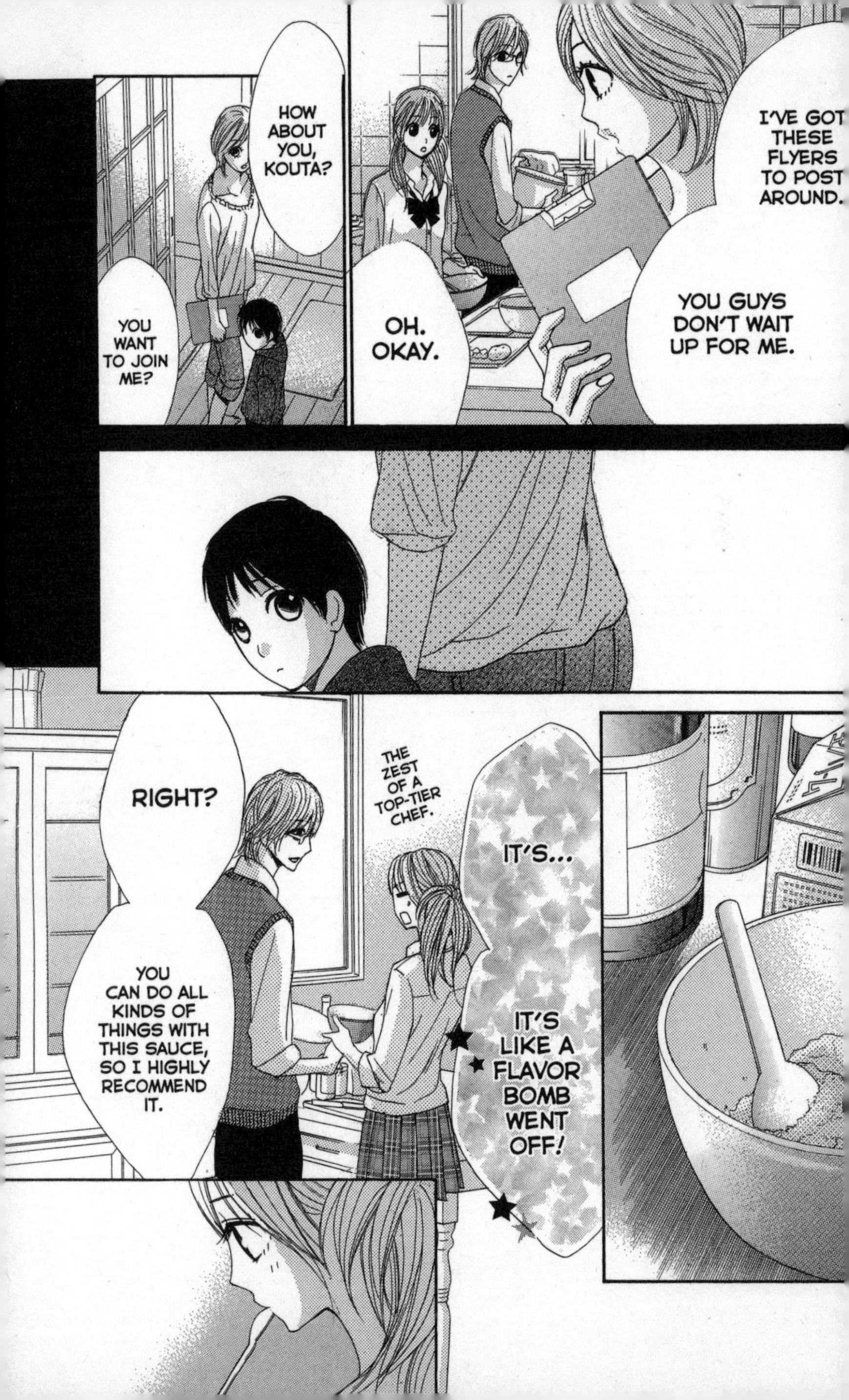
I'VE GOT THESE FLYERS TO POST AROUND.
YOU GUYS DON'T WAIT UP FOR ME.
OH. OKAY.
HOW ABOUT YOU, KOUTA?
YOU WANT TO JOIN ME?
IT'S...
IT'S LIKE A FLAVOR BOMB WENT OFF!
THE ZEST OF A TOP-TIER CHEF.
RIGHT?
YOU CAN DO ALL KINDS OF THINGS WITH THIS SAUCE, SO I HIGHLY RECOMMEND IT.

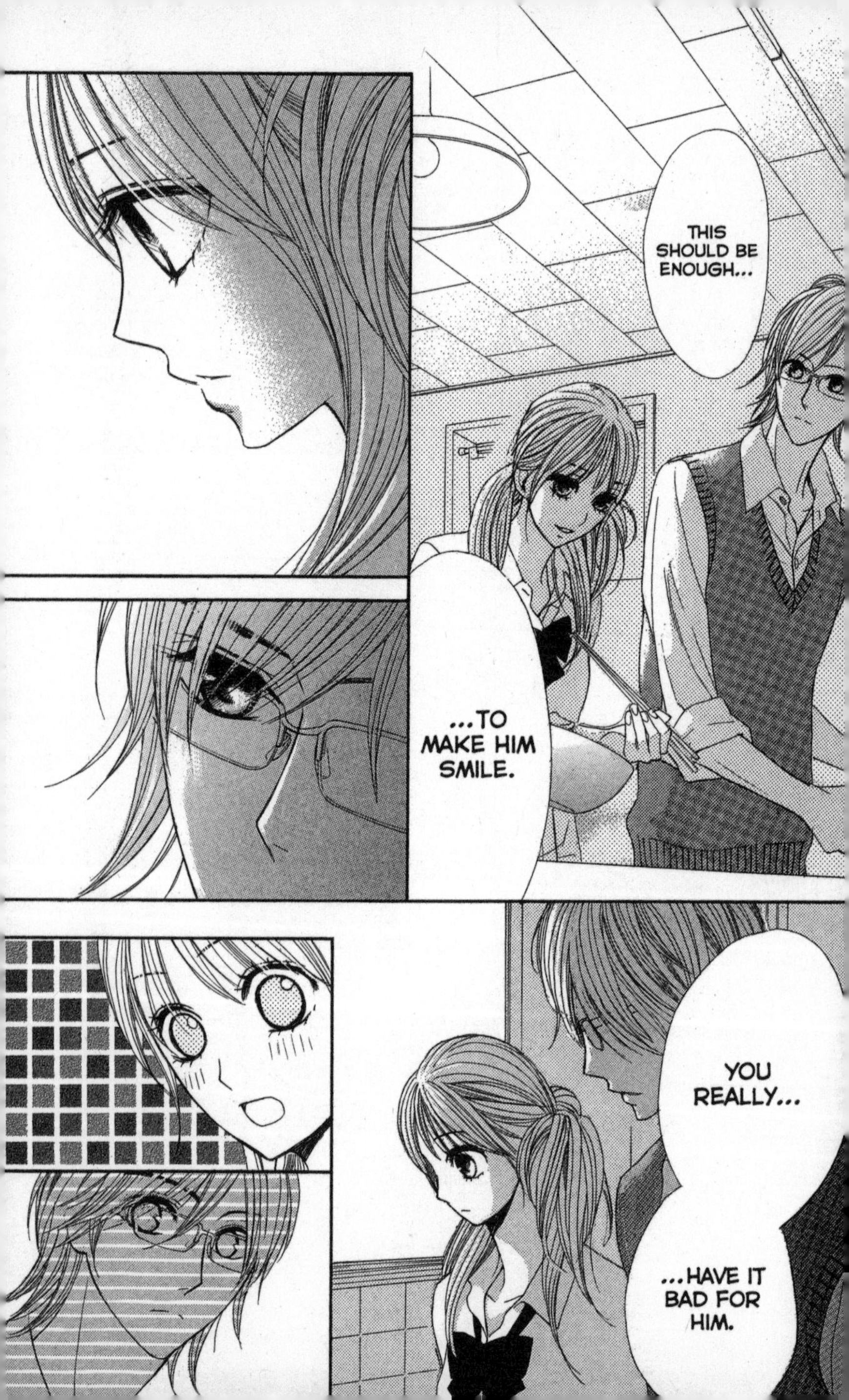
THIS SHOULD BE ENOUGH...
...TO MAKE HIM SMILE.
YOU REALLY...
...HAVE IT BAD FOR HIM.

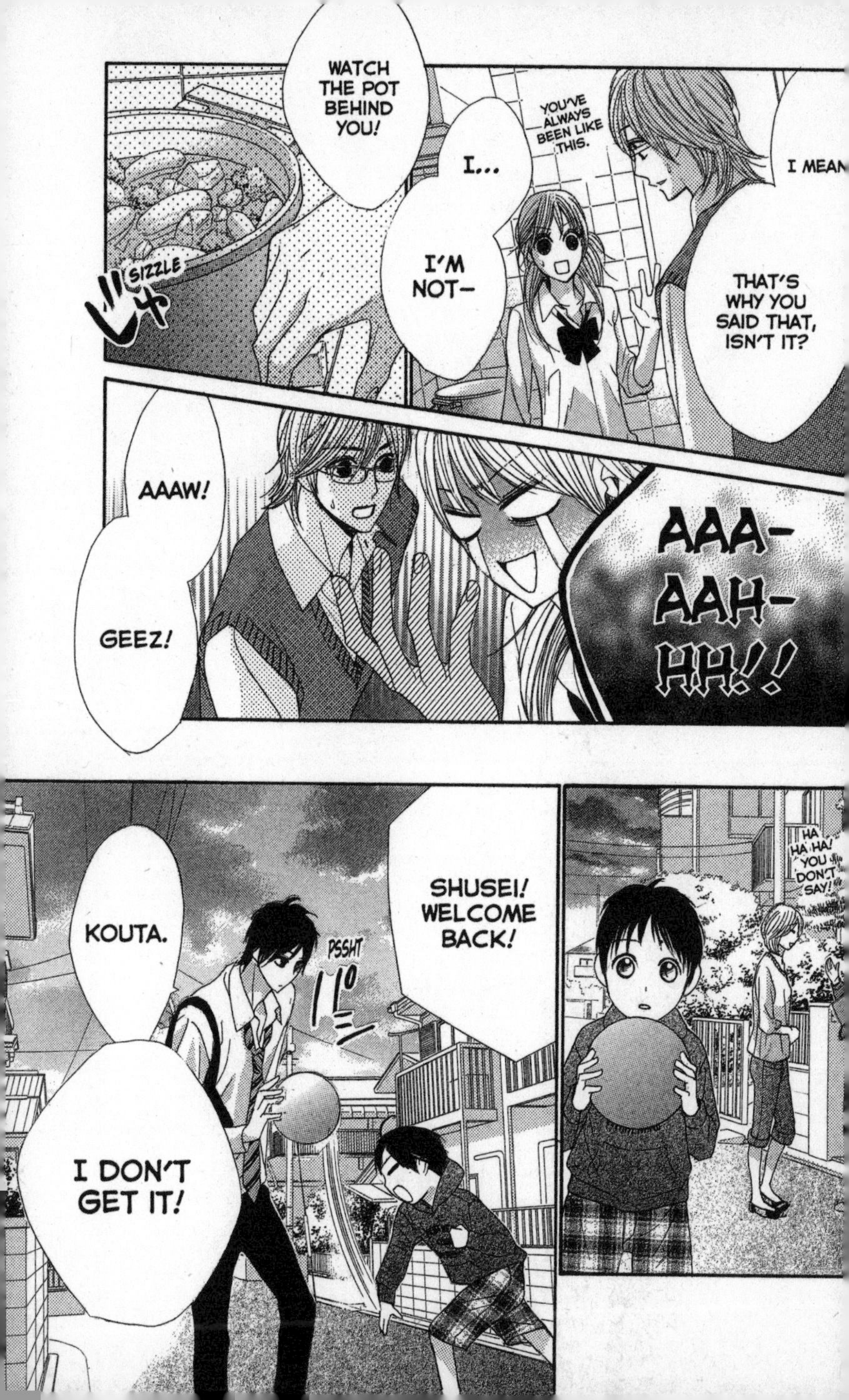
I MEAN
THAT'S WHY YOU SAID THAT, ISN'T IT?
YOU'VE ALWAYS BEEN LIKE THIS.
I...
I'M NOT-
WATCH THE POT BEHIND YOU!
SIZZLE
AAA-AAH-HH!!
AAAW!
GEEZ!
HA HA HA! YOU DON'T SAY!
SHUSEI! WELCOME BACK!
PSSHT
KOUTA.
I DON'T GET IT!

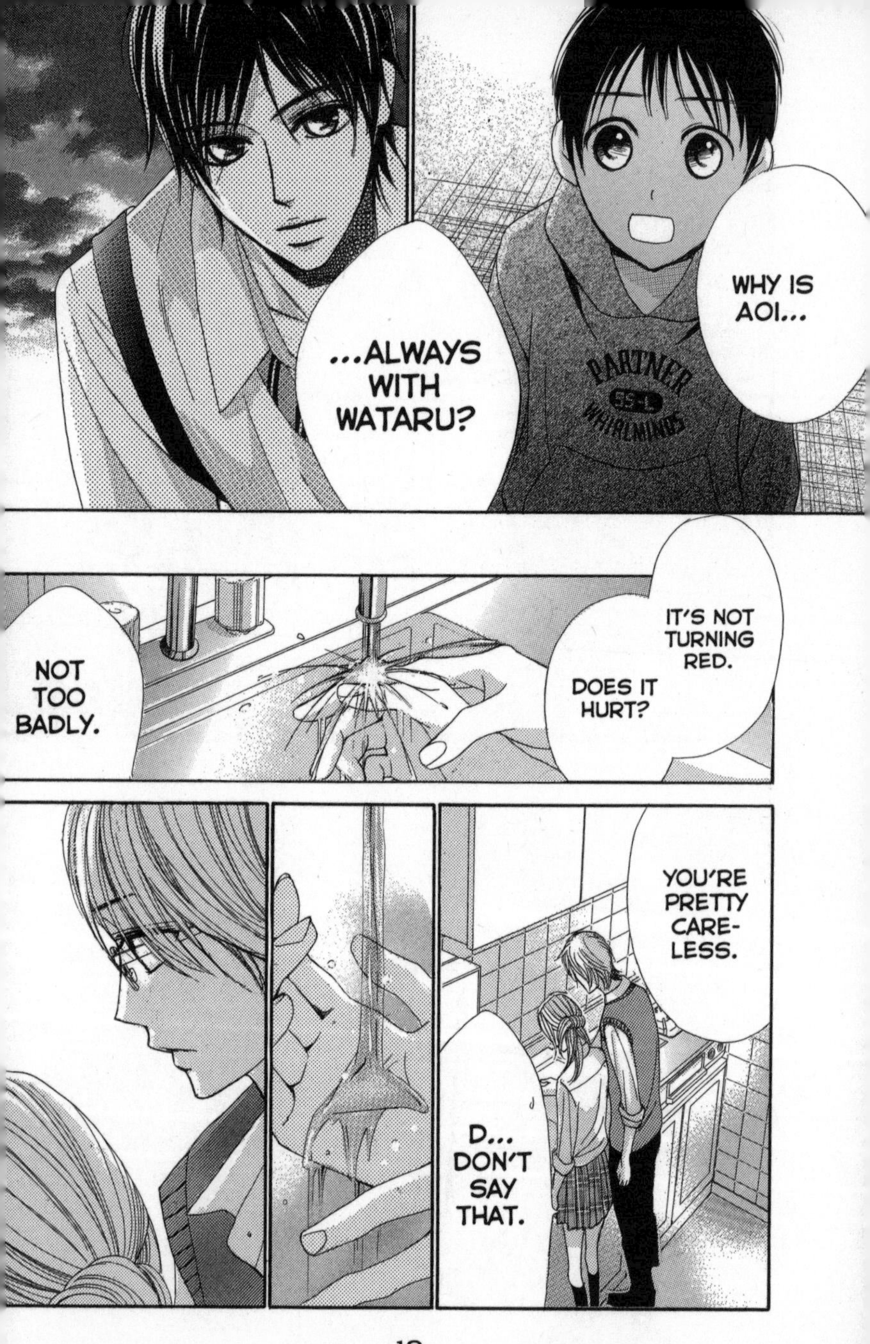
WHY IS AOI...
...ALWAYS WITH WATARU?
IT'S NOT TURNING RED.
DOES IT HURT?
NOT TOO BADLY.
YOU'RE PRETTY CARE-LESS.
D... DON'T SAY THAT.

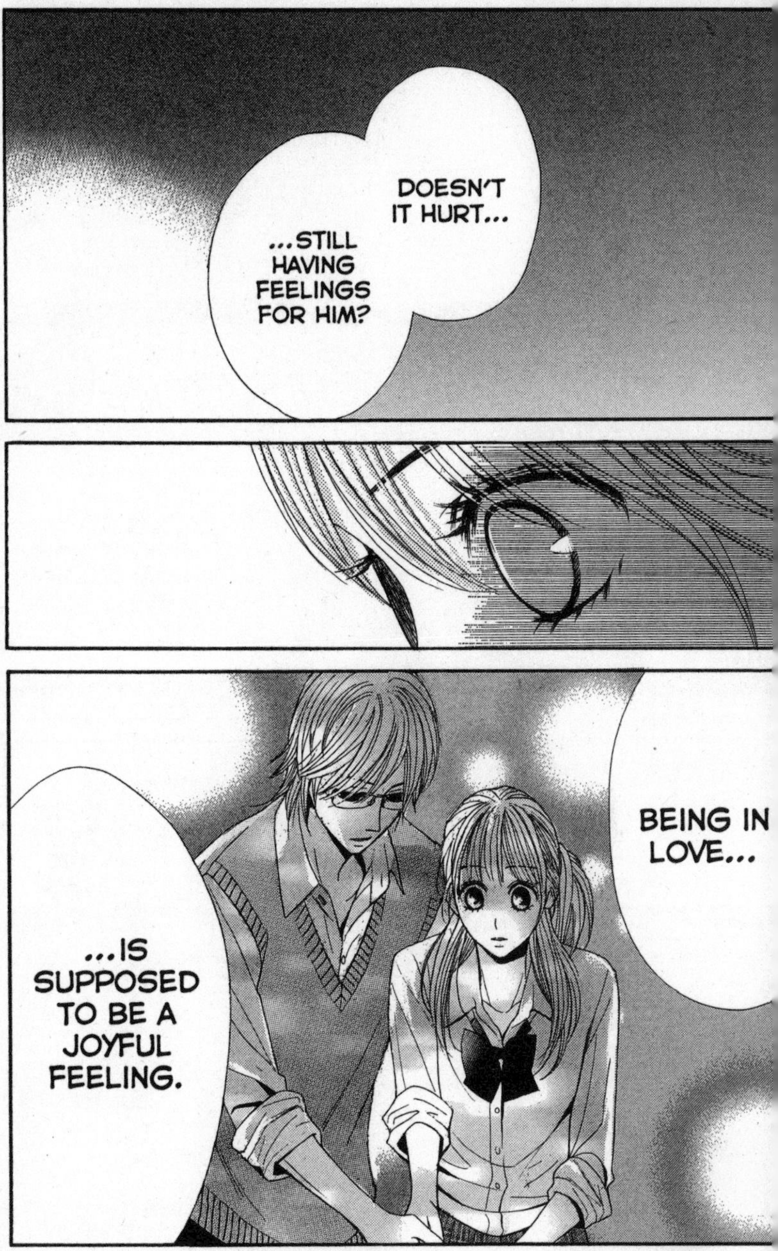
DOESN'T IT HURT...
...STILL HAVING FEELINGS FOR HIM?
BEING IN LOVE...
...IS SUPPOSED TO BE A JOYFUL FEELING.

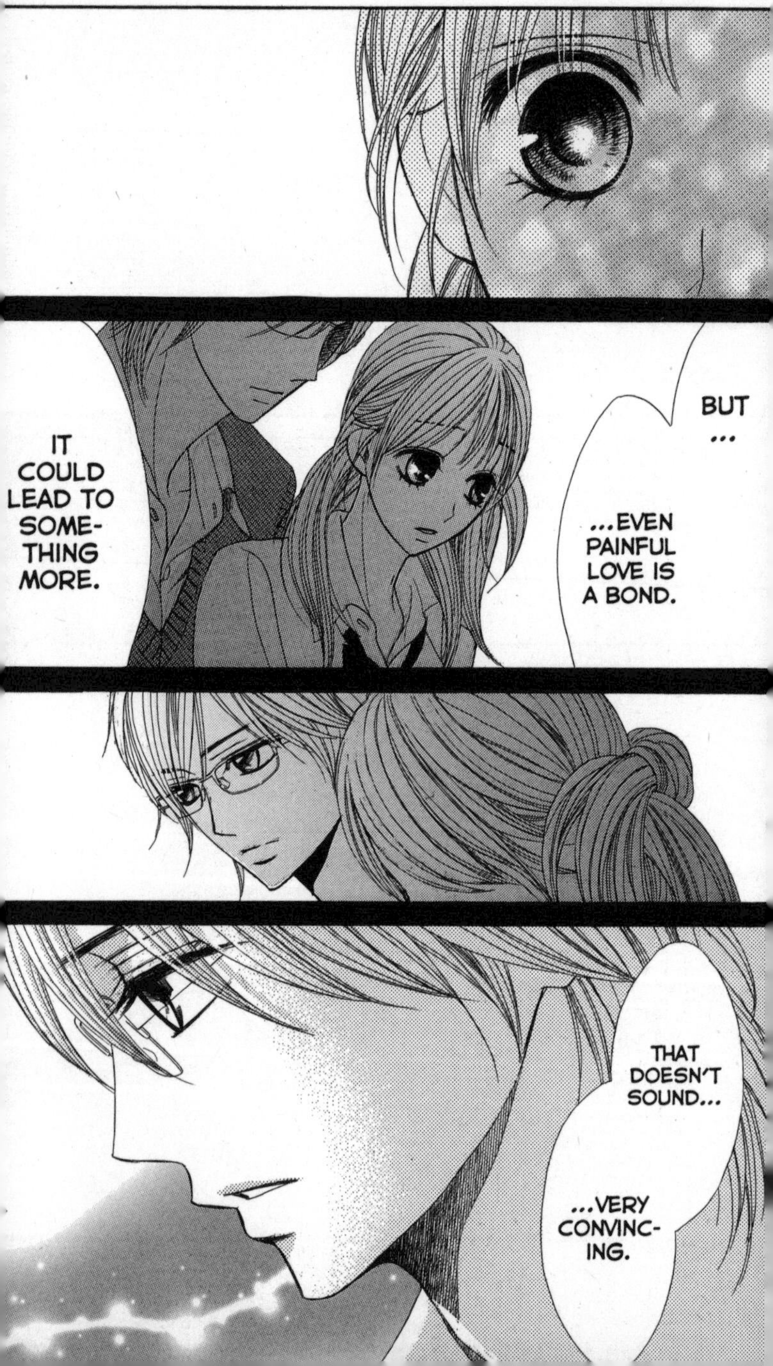
BUT ...
...EVEN PAINFUL LOVE IS A BOND.
IT COULD LEAD TO SOME-THING MORE.
THAT DOESN'T SOUND...
...VERY CONVINC-ING.

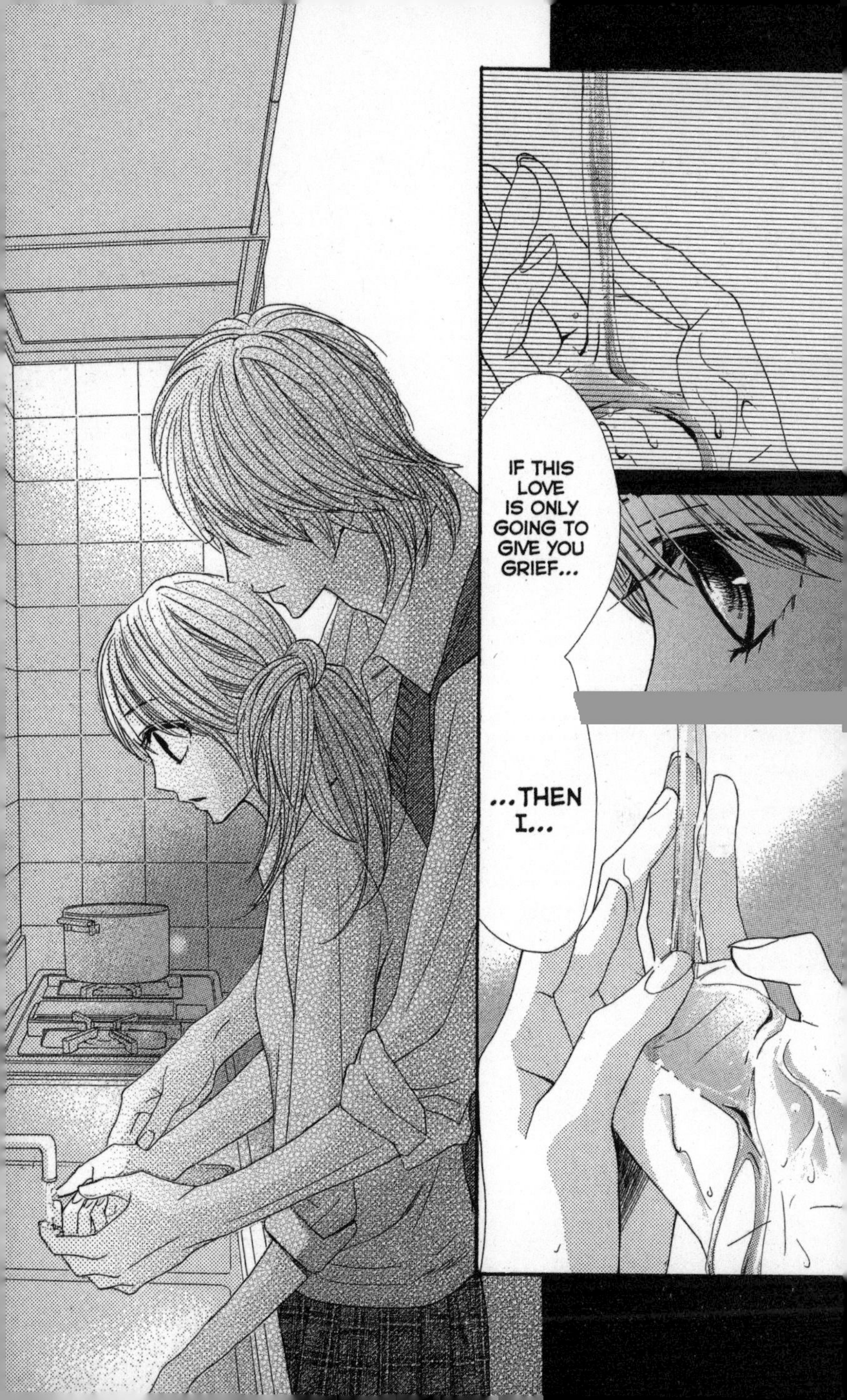
IF THIS LOVE IS ONLY GOING TO GIVE YOU GRIEF...
...THEN I...

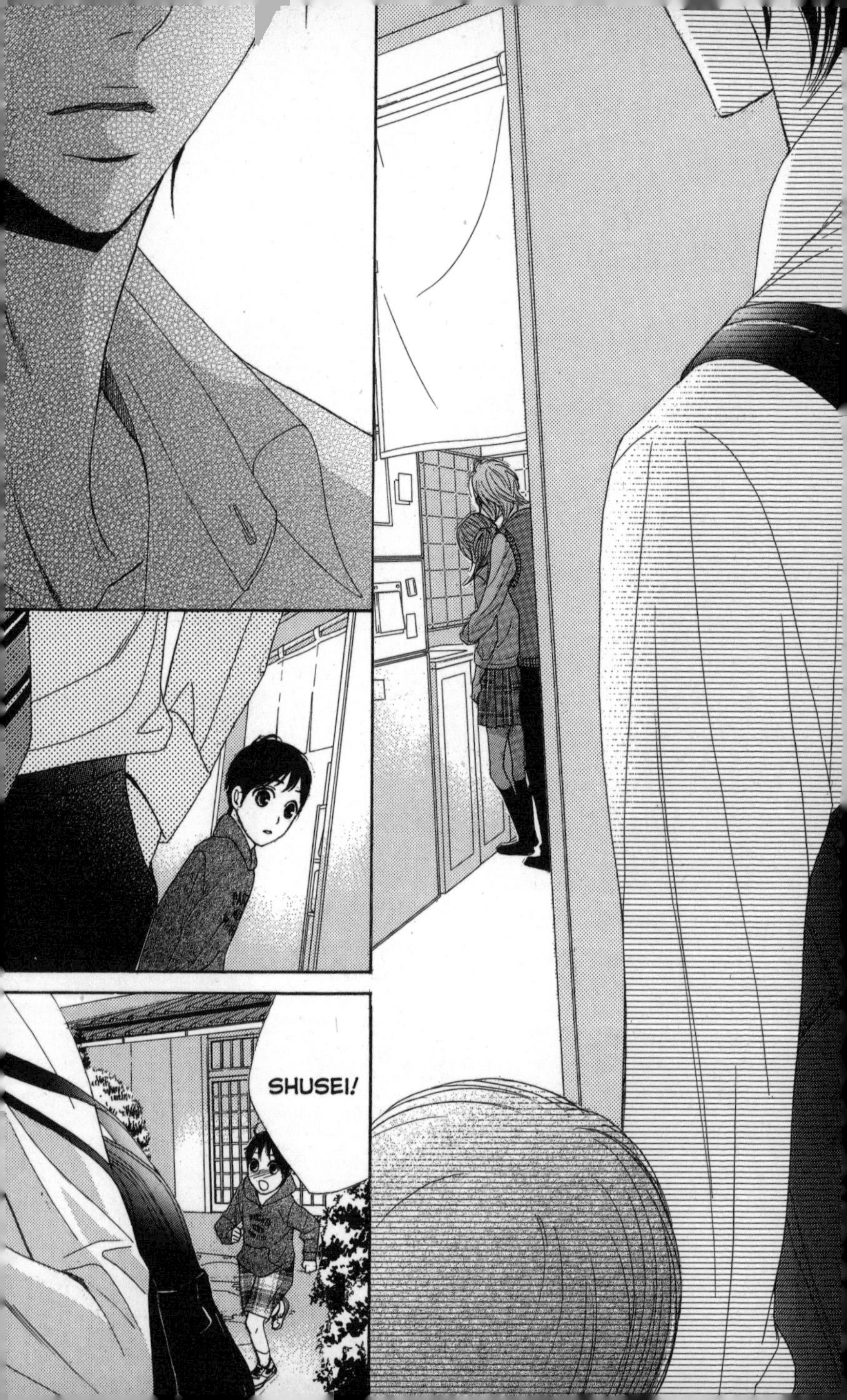
SHUSEI!

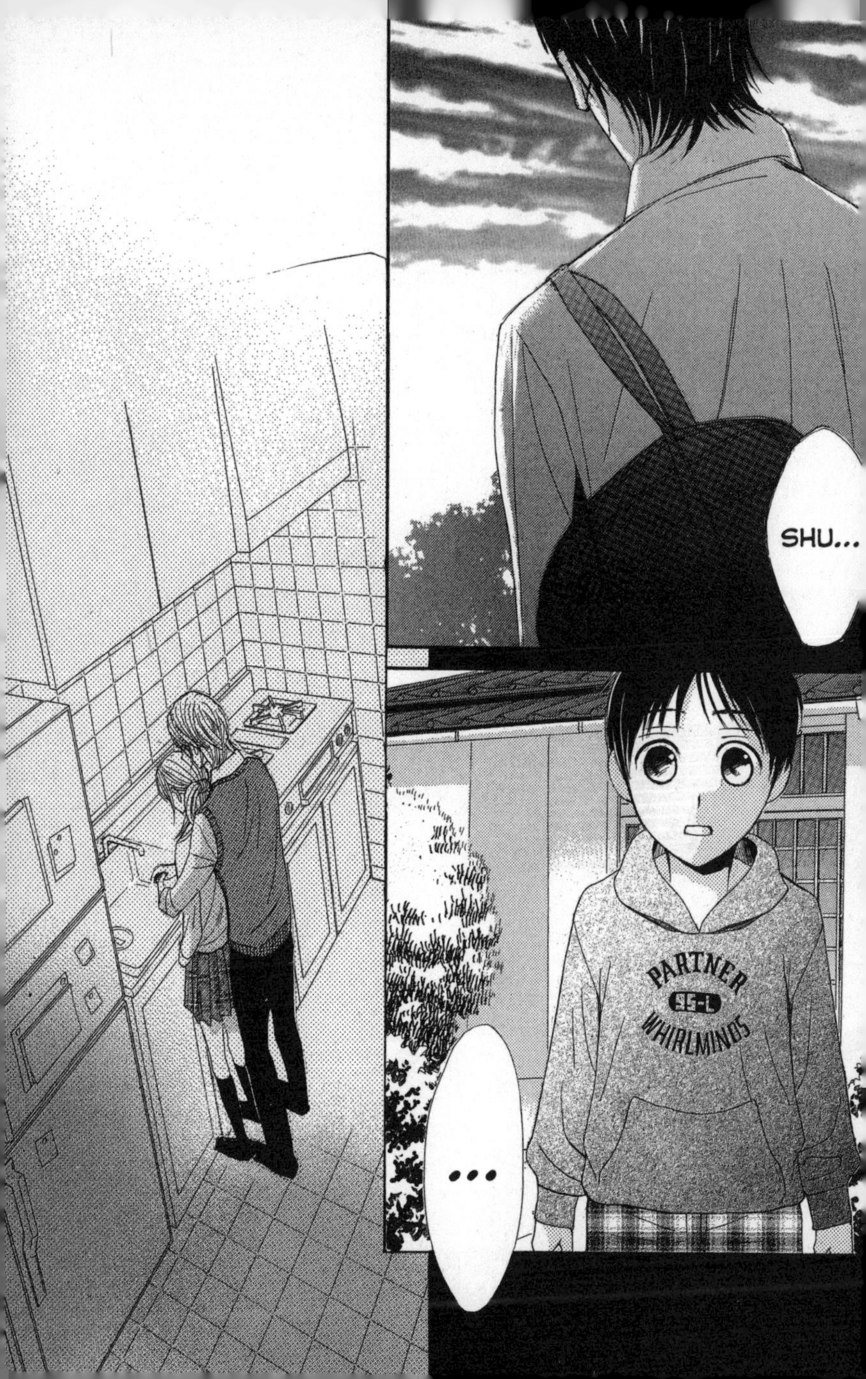
SHU...
...

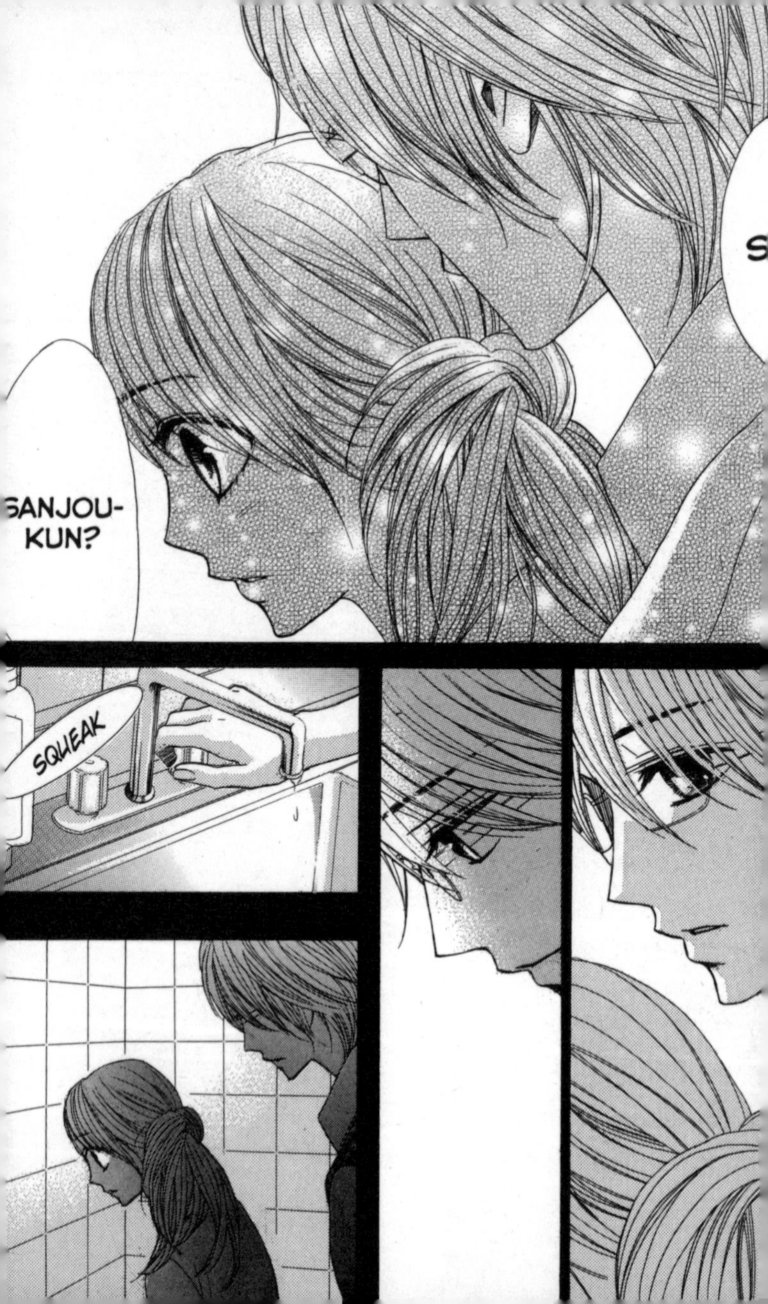
SANJOU-KUN?
SQUEAK

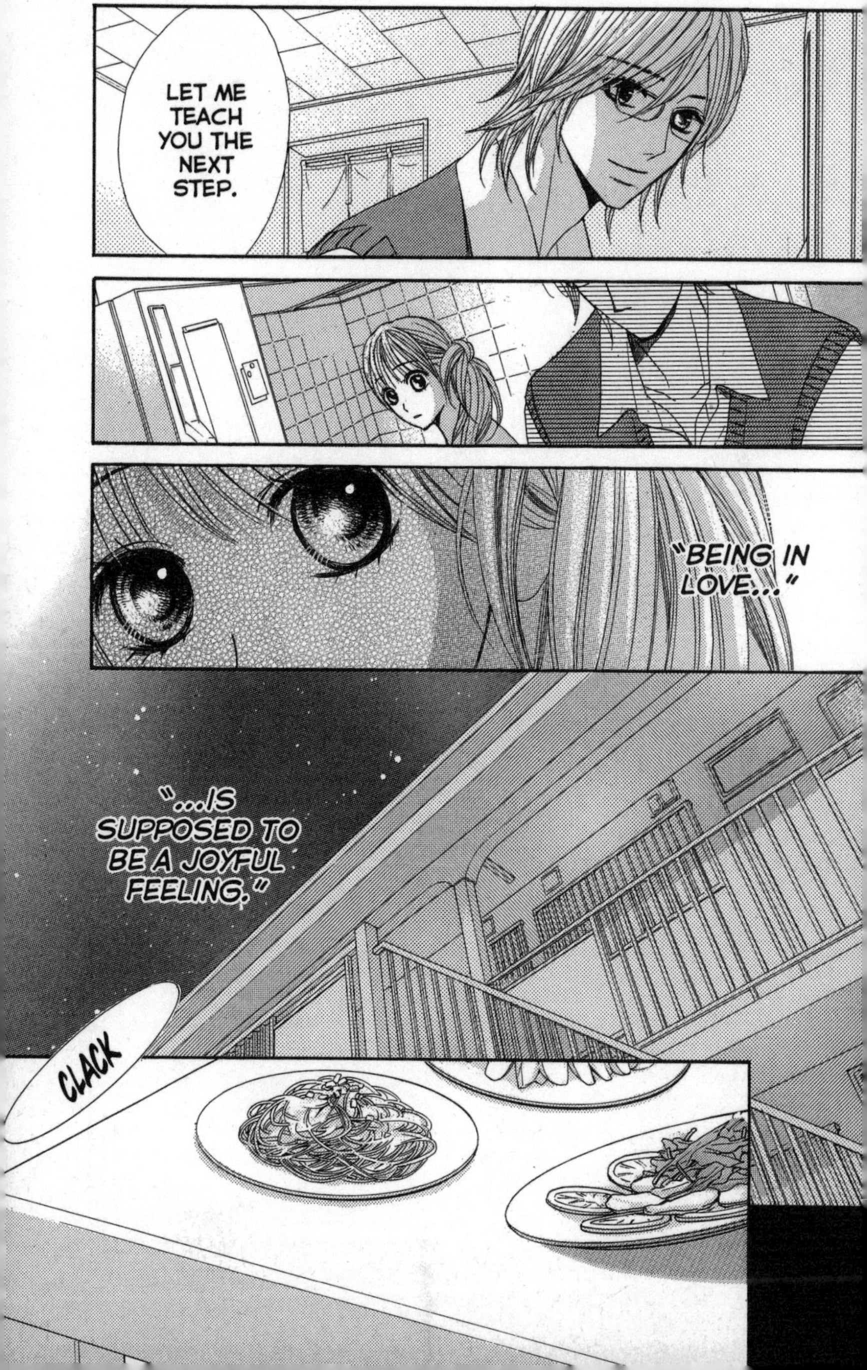
LET ME TEACH YOU THE NEXT STEP.
"BEING IN LOVE..."
"...IS SUPPOSED TO BE A JOYFUL FEELING."
CLACK

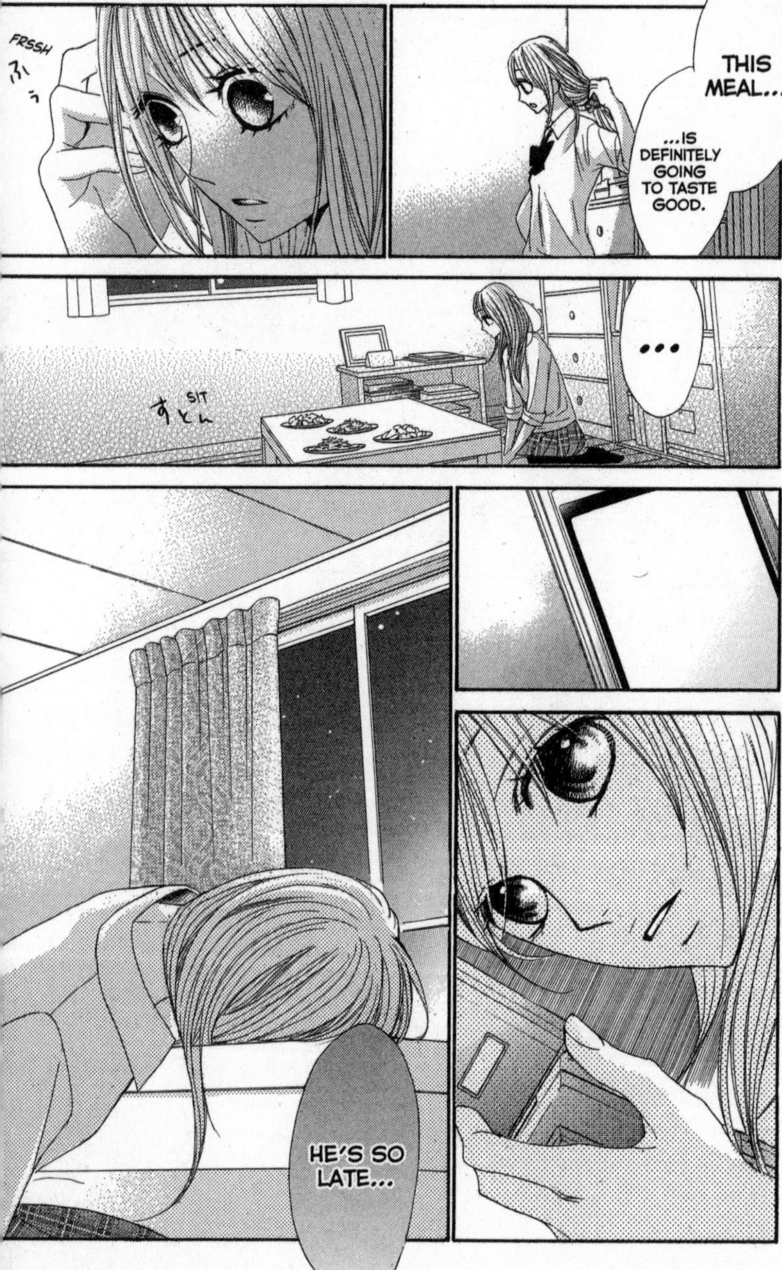
THIS MEAL...
...IS DEFINITELY GOING TO TASTE GOOD.
FRSSH
ふぅ
...
SIT
すとん
HE'S SO LATE...

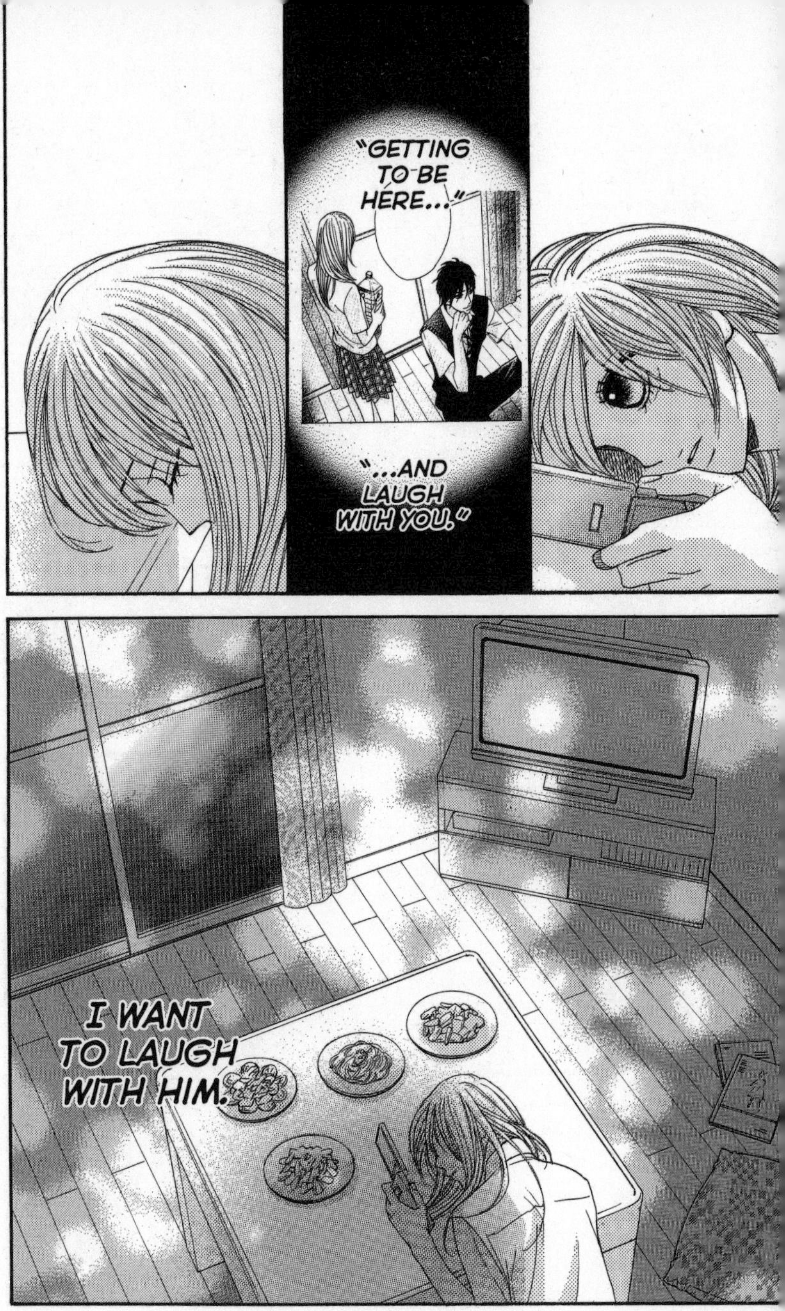
"GETTING TO BE HERE..."
"...AND LAUGH WITH YOU."
I WANT TO LAUGH WITH HIM.

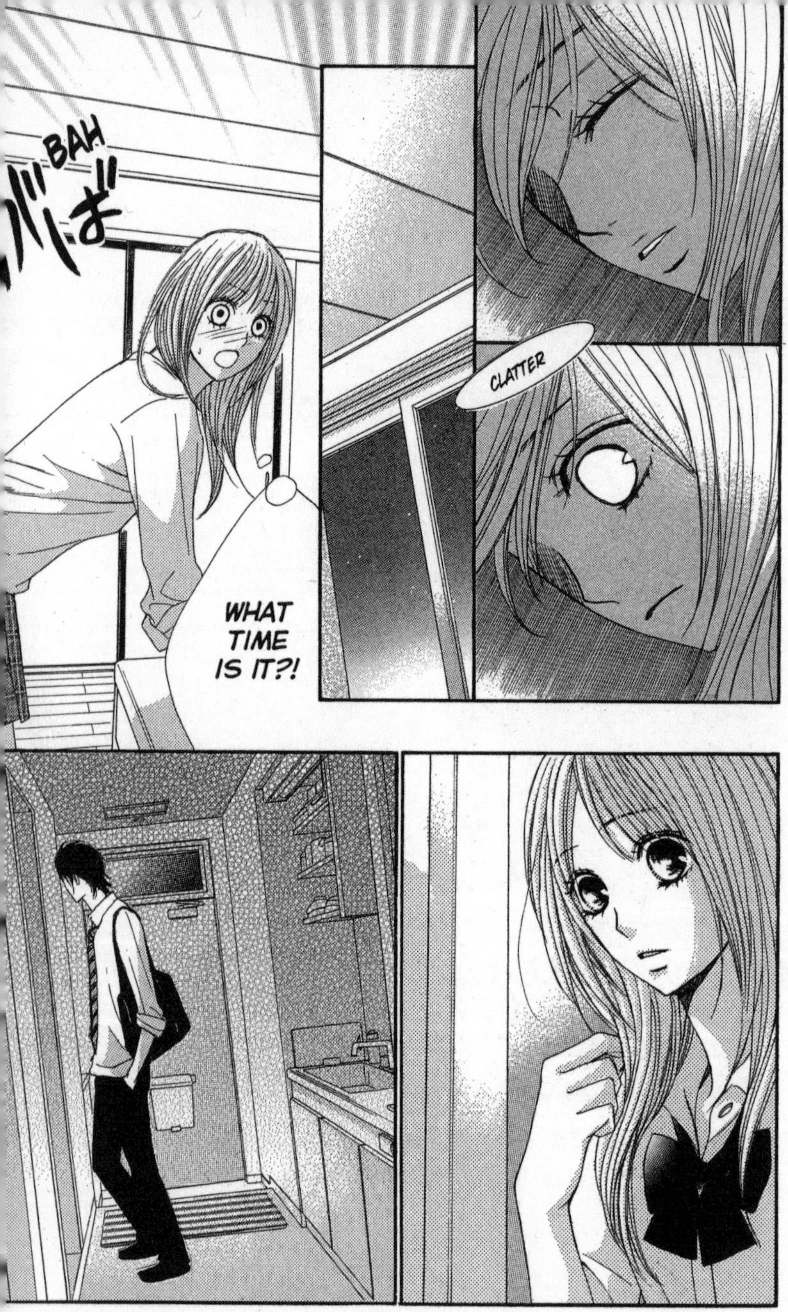
CLATTER
BAH
WHAT TIME IS IT?!

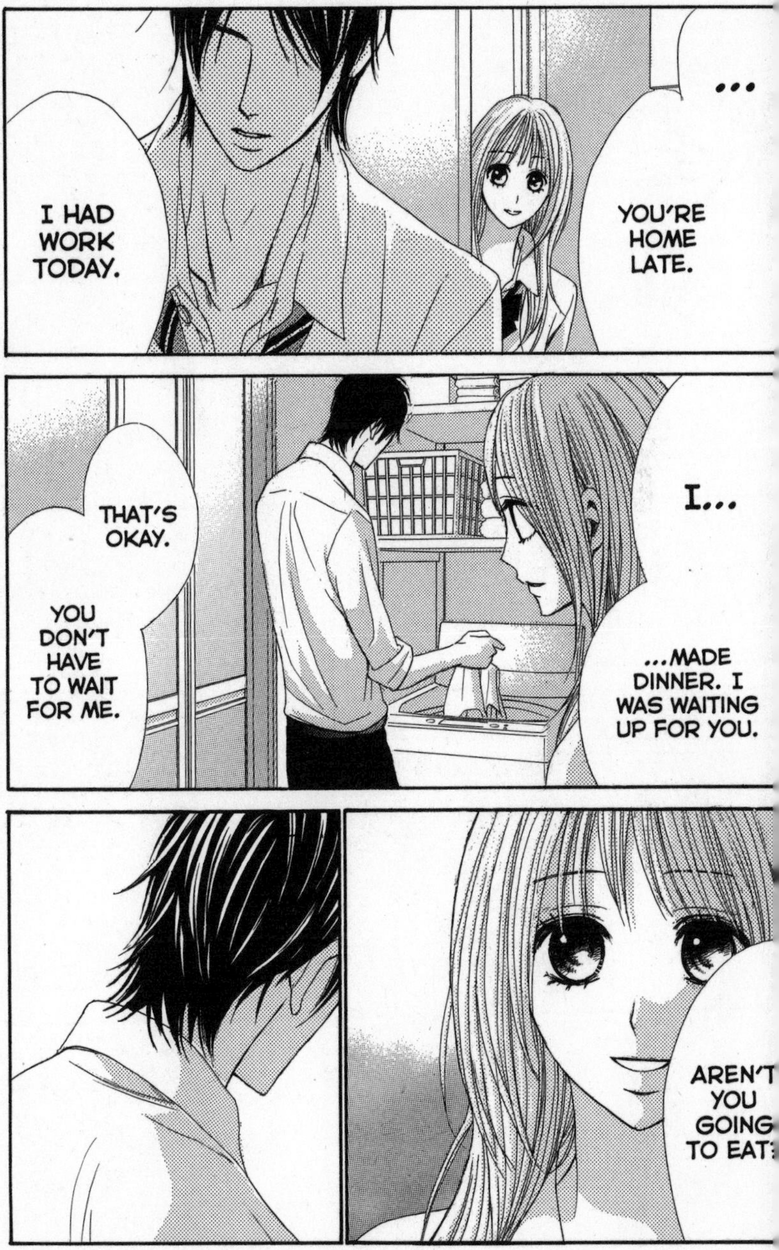
...
YOU'RE HOME LATE.
I HAD WORK TODAY.
I...
...MADE DINNER. I WAS WAITING UP FOR YOU.
THAT'S OKAY.
YOU DON'T HAVE TO WAIT FOR ME.
AREN'T YOU GOING TO EAT?

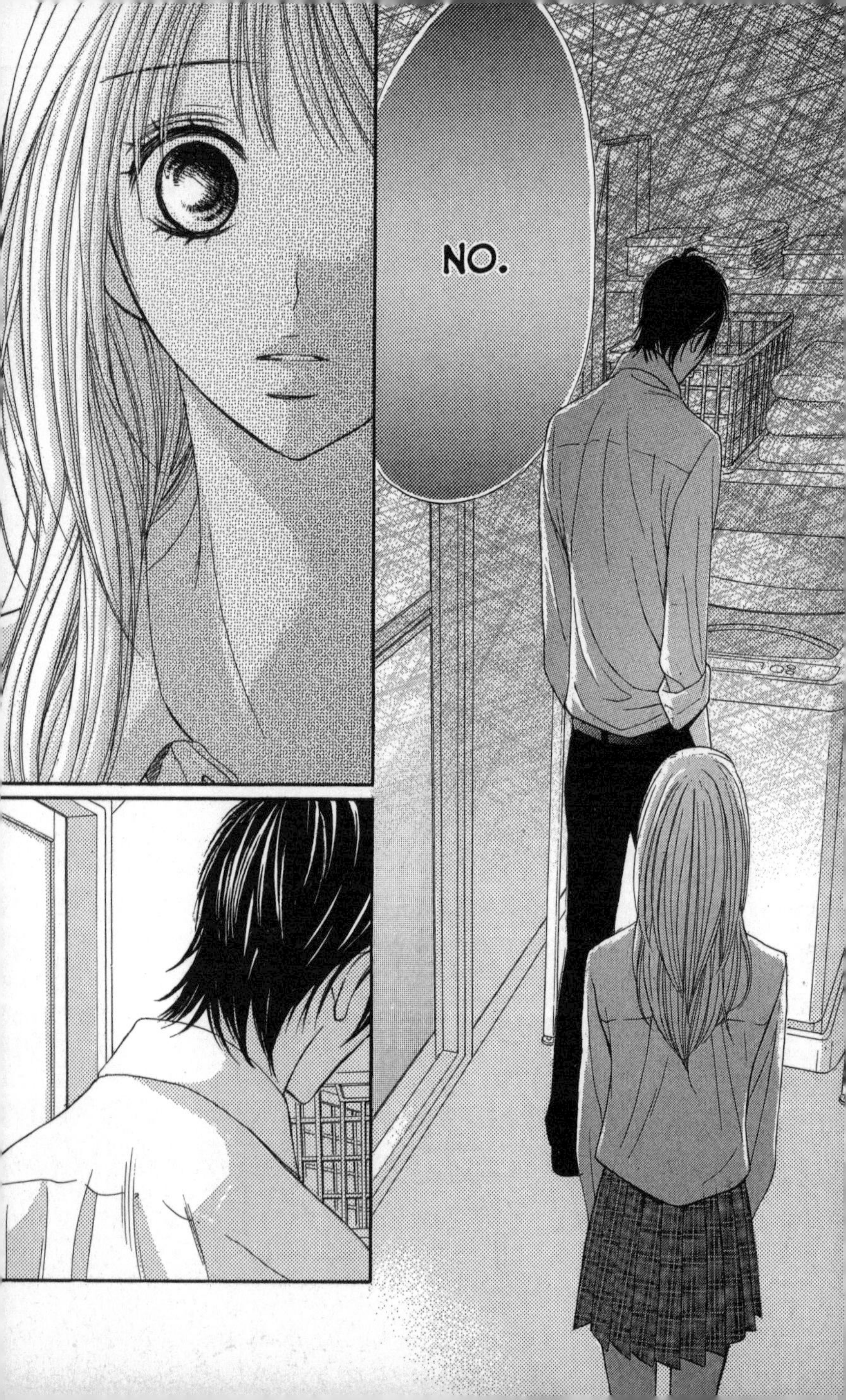
NO.

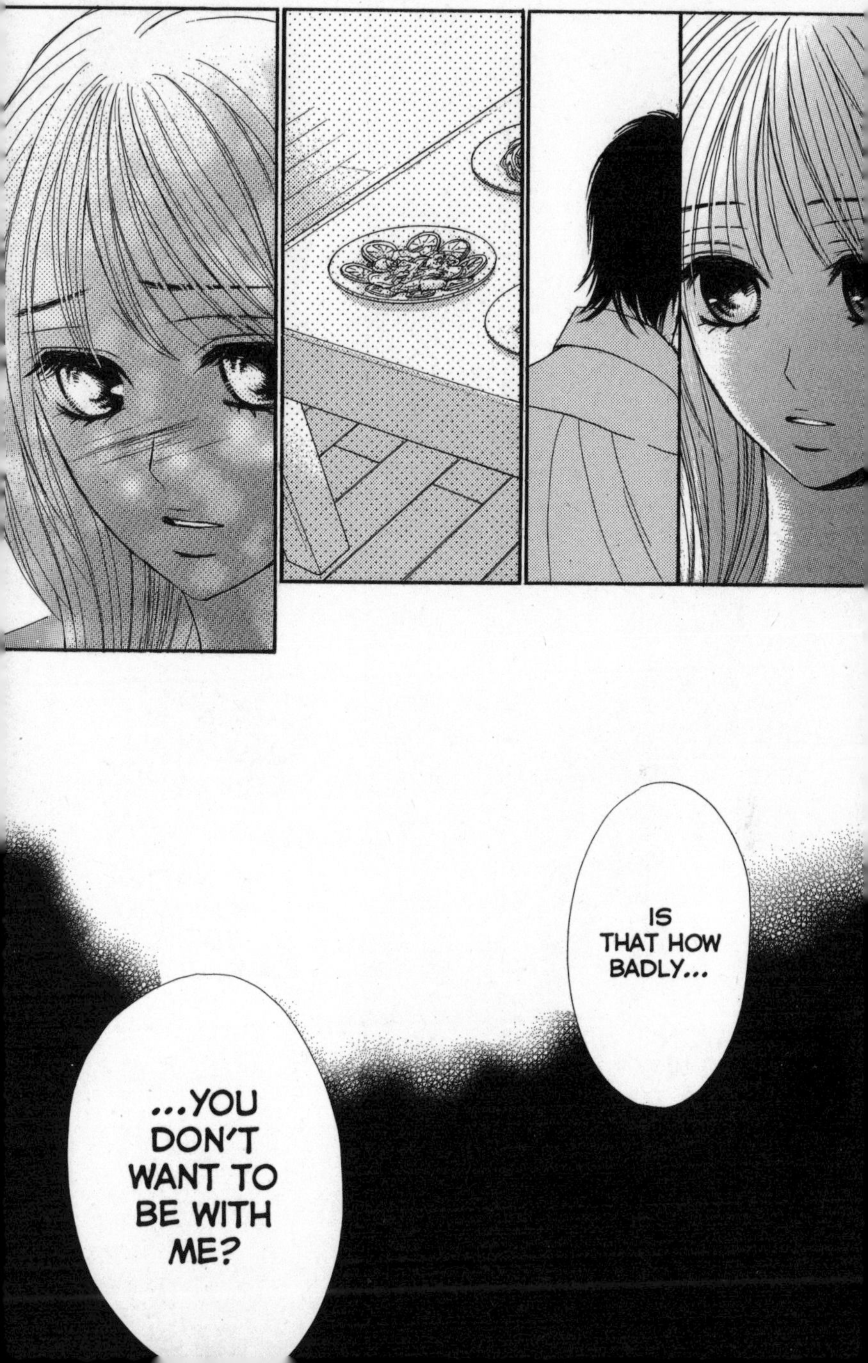
IS THAT HOW BADLY...
...YOU DON'T WANT TO BE WITH ME?

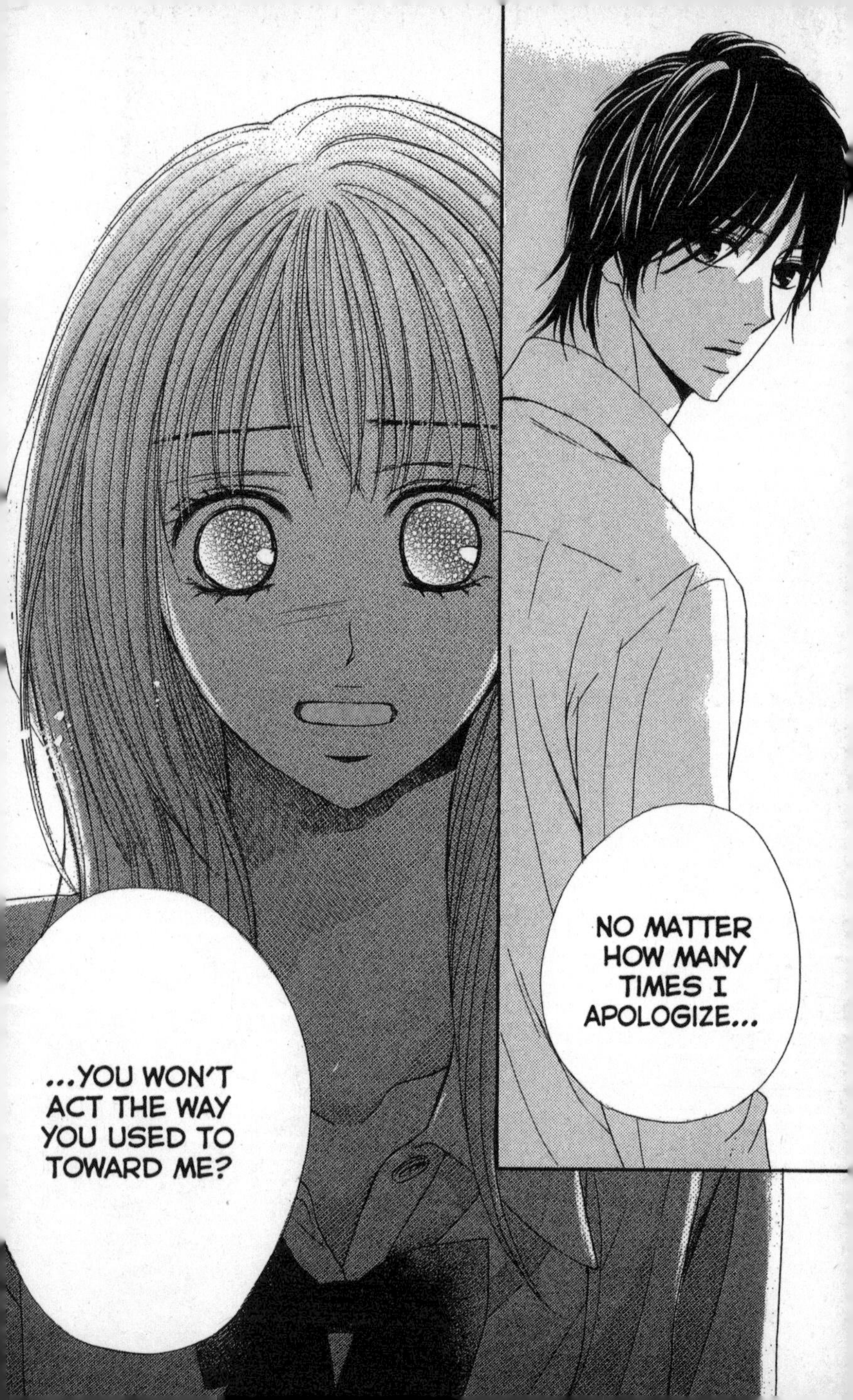
NO MATTER HOW MANY TIMES I APOLOGIZE...
...YOU WON'T ACT THE WAY YOU USED TO TOWARD ME?

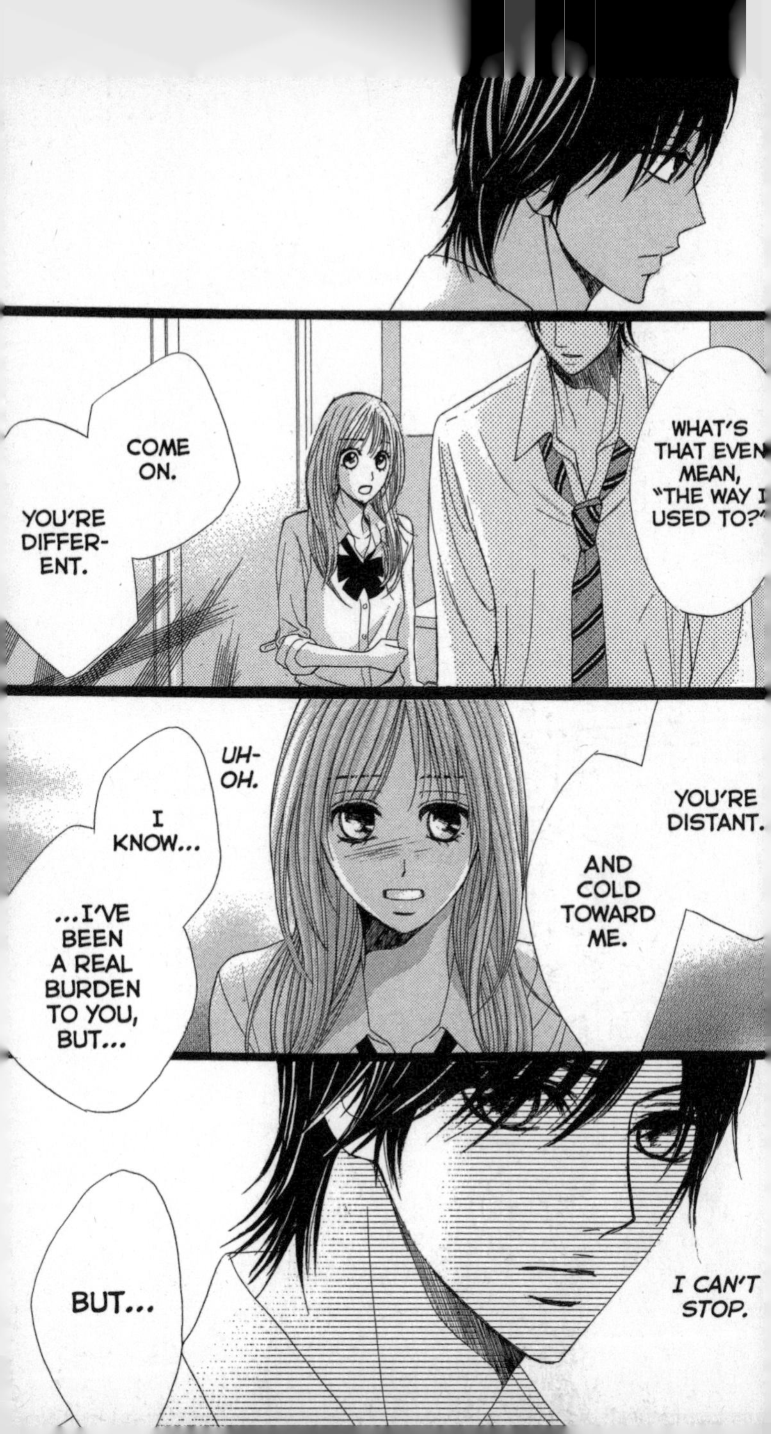
WHAT'S THAT EVEN MEAN, "THE WAY I USED TO?"
COME ON. YOU'RE DIFFER-ENT.
YOU'RE DISTANT.
AND COLD TOWARD ME.
UH-OH.
I KNOW... ...I'VE BEEN A REAL BURDEN TO YOU, BUT...
I CAN'T STOP.
BUT...

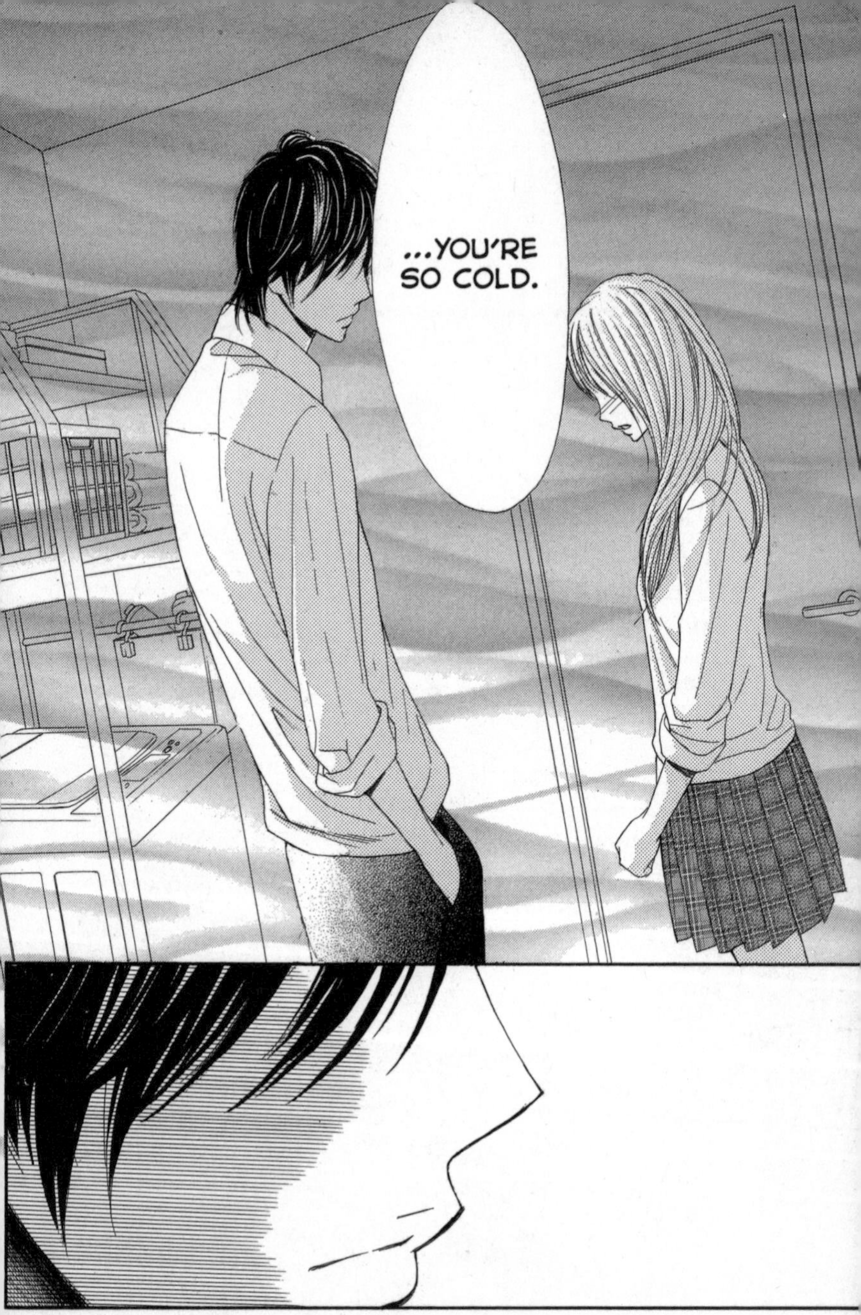
...YOU'RE SO COLD.

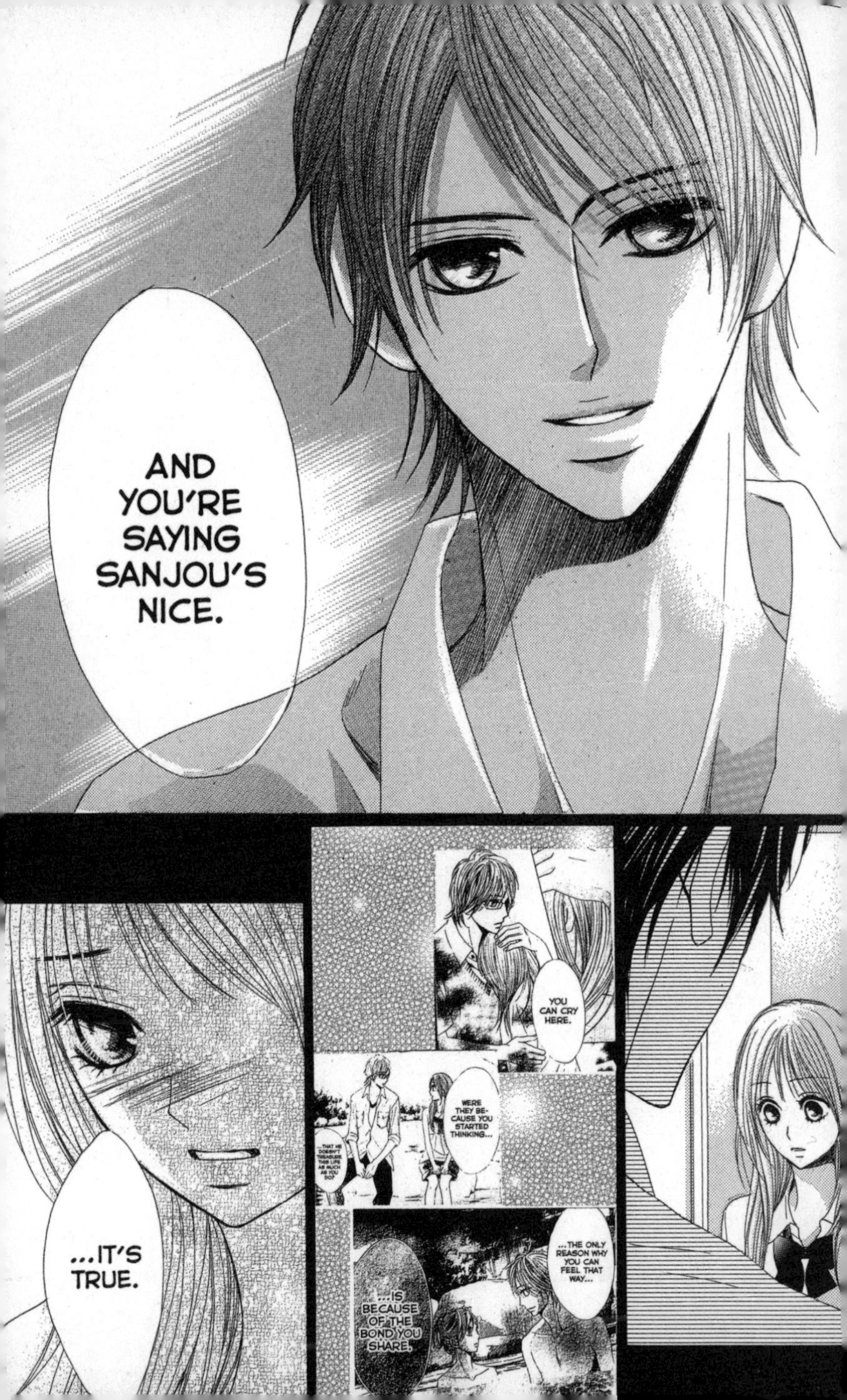
AND YOU'RE SAYING SANJOU'S NICE.
YOU CAN CRY HERE.
WERE THEY BECAUSE YOU STARTED THINKING...
...THAT HE DOESN'T TREASURE THIS LIFE AS MUCH AS YOU DO?
...THE ONLY REASON WHY YOU CAN FEEL THAT WAY...
...IS BECAUSE OF THE BOND YOU SHARE.
...IT'S TRUE.

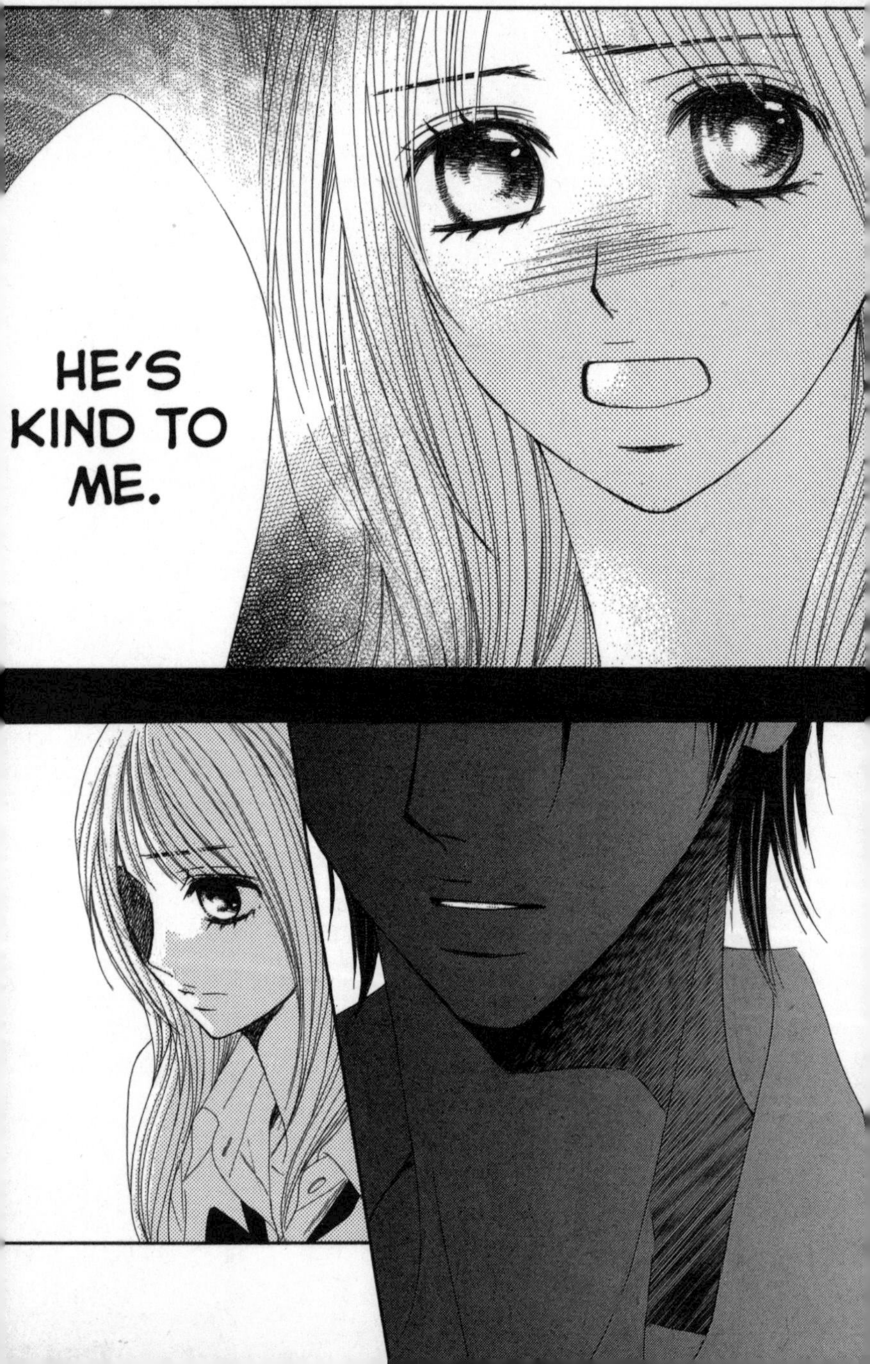
HE'S KIND TO ME.

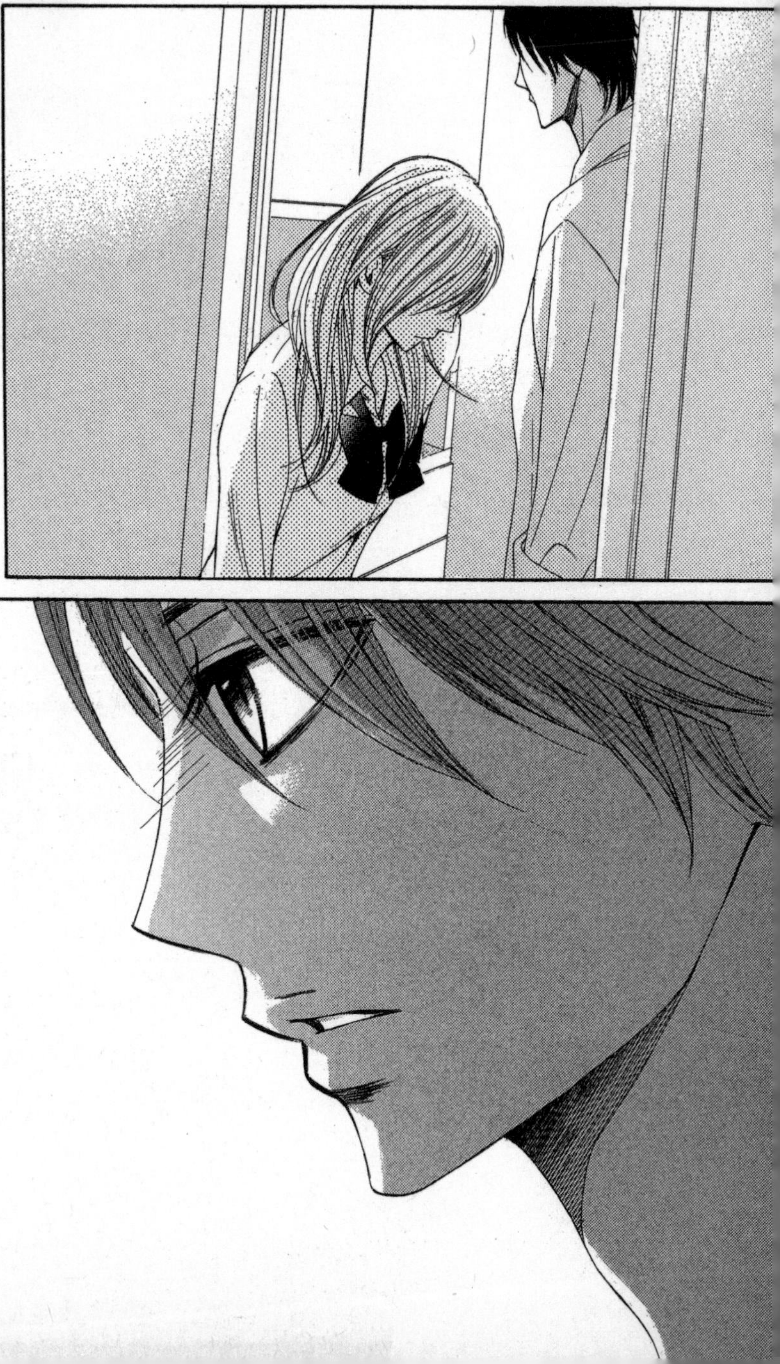

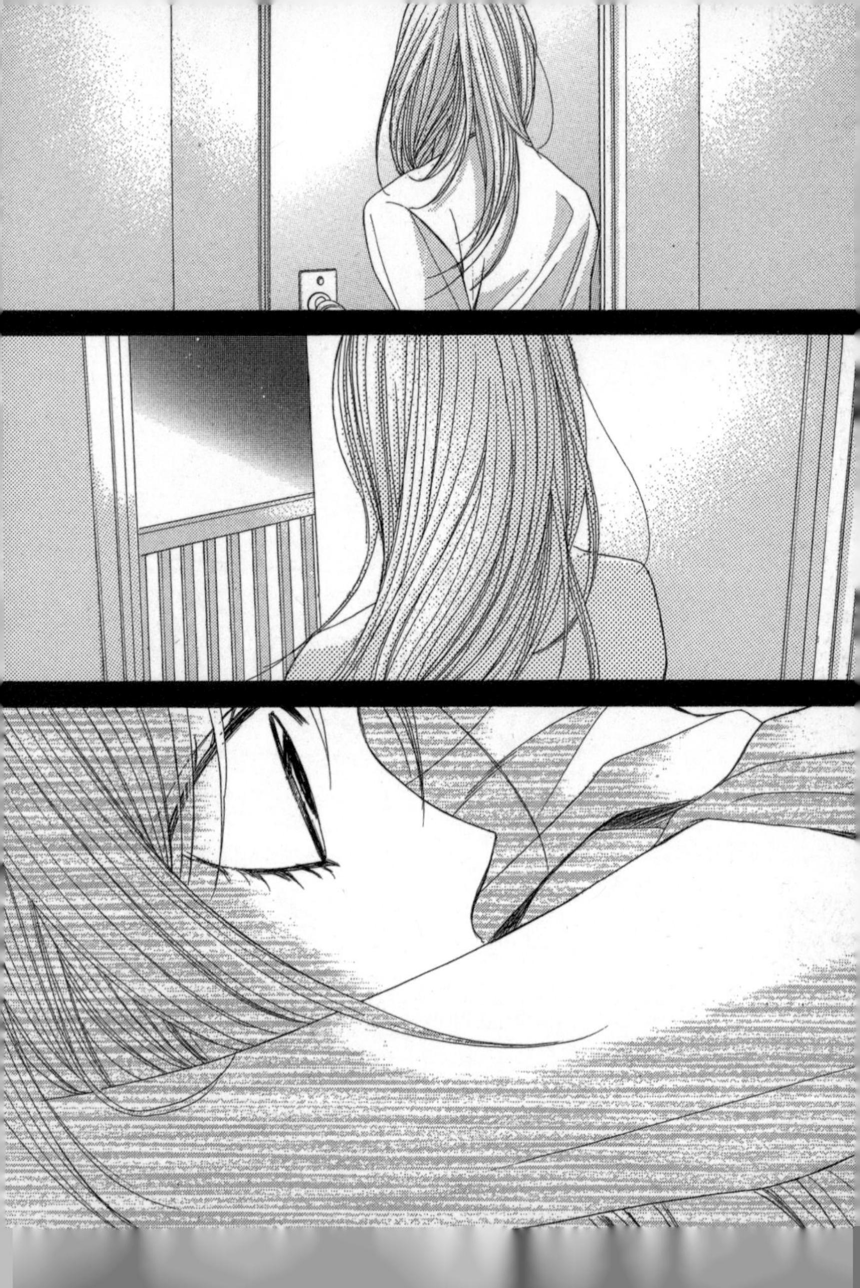

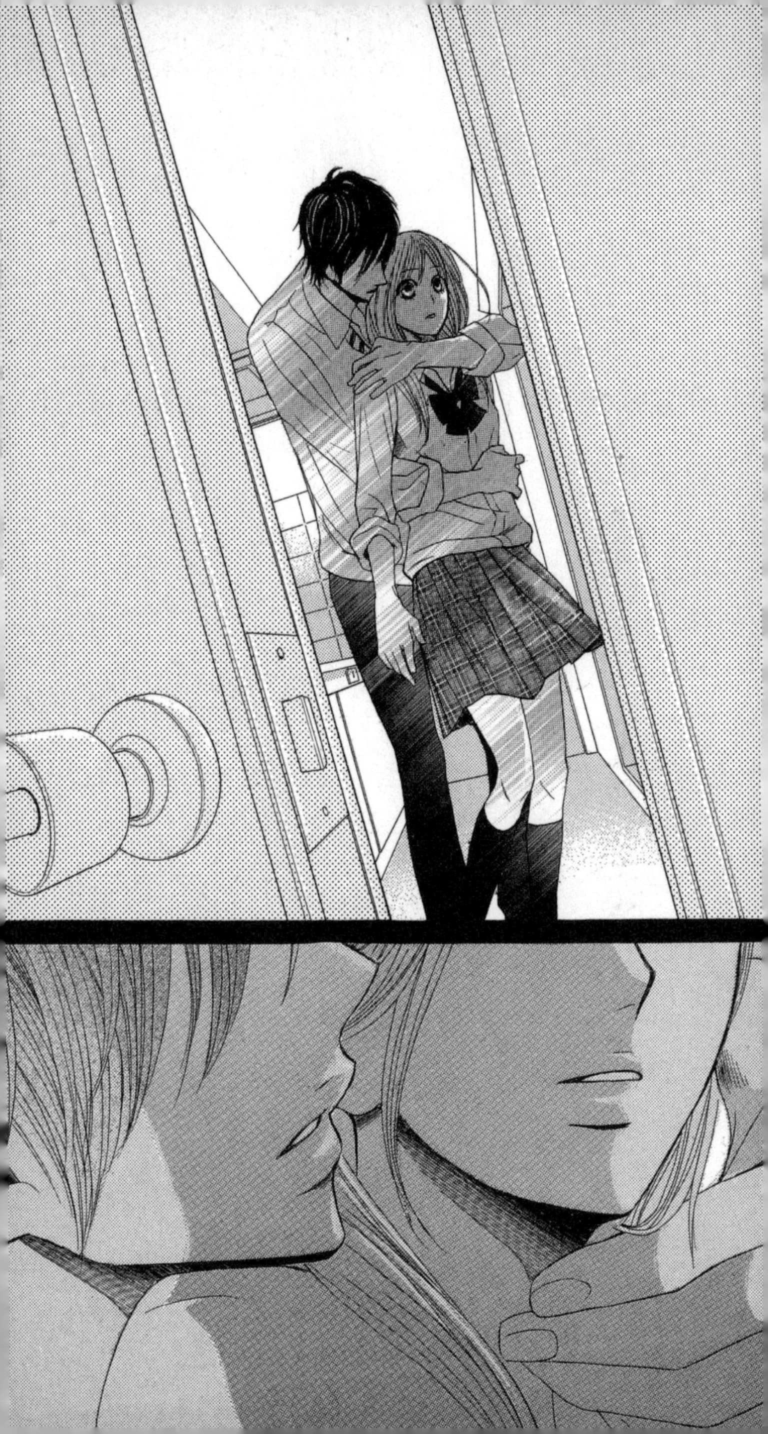

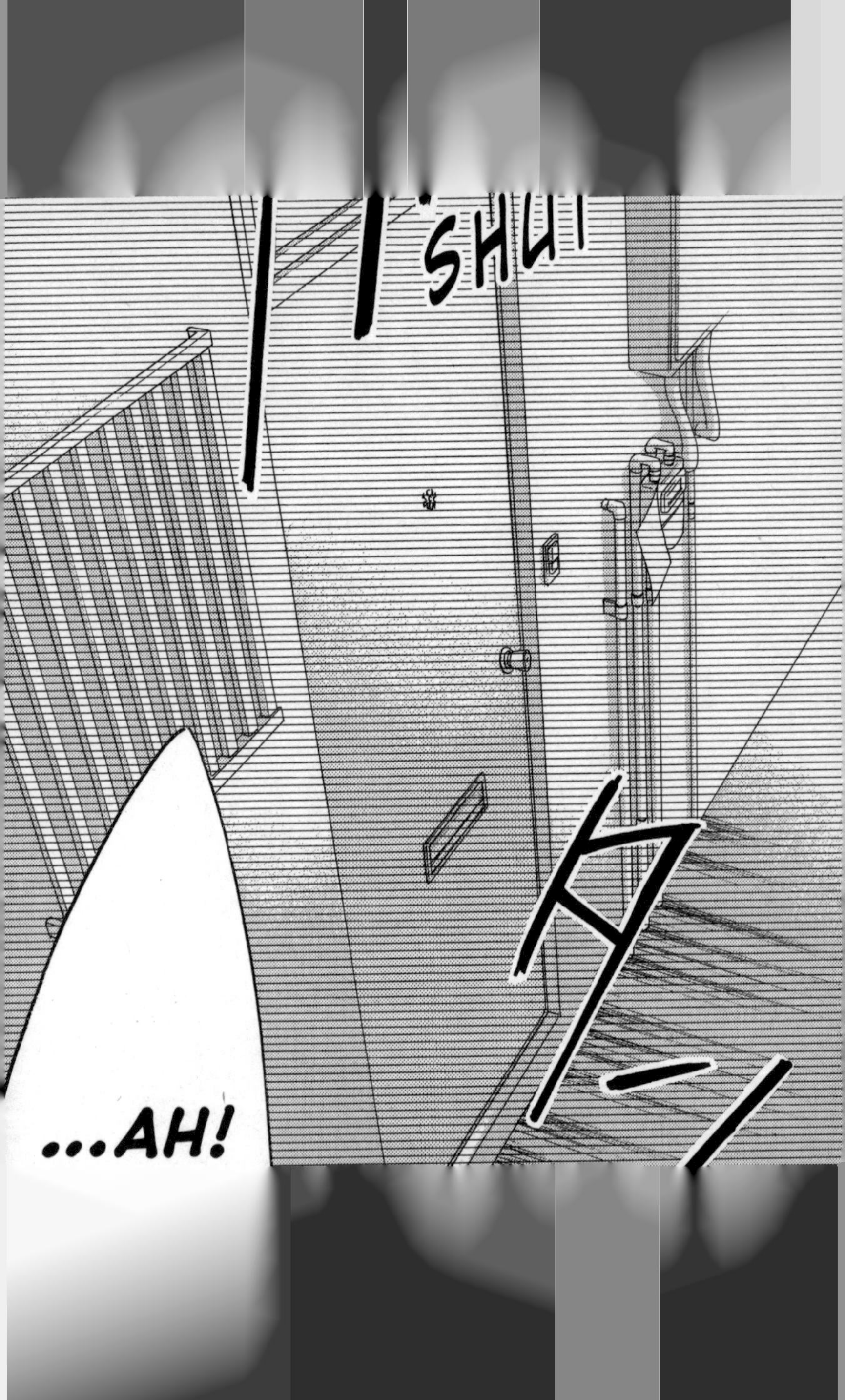
SHUT
KA-
...AH!

#22 Can't Go Back To How Things Were

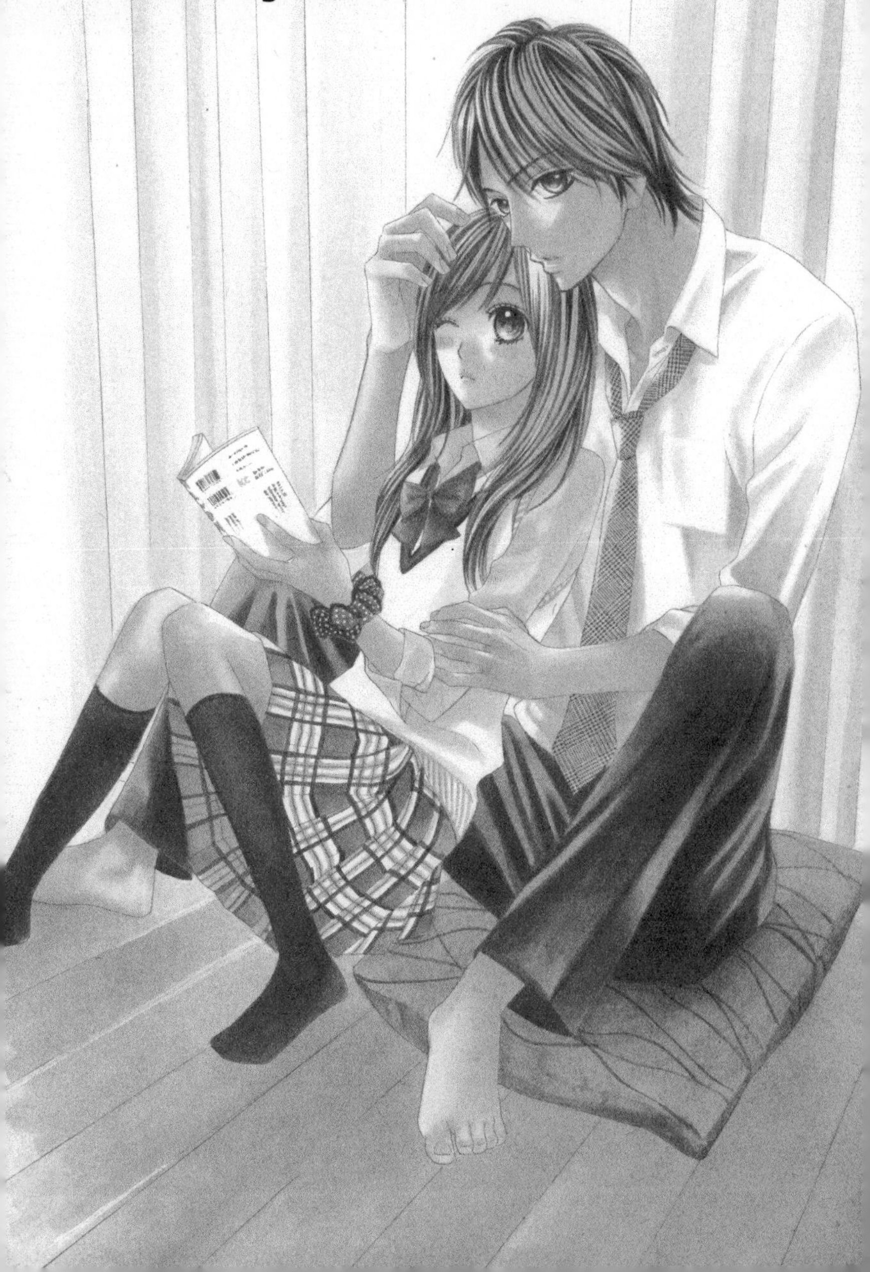

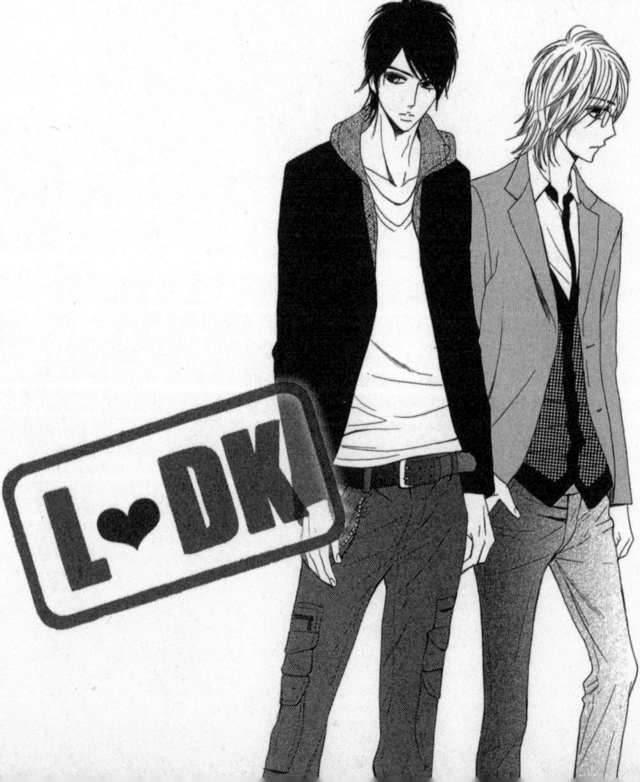
L♥DK

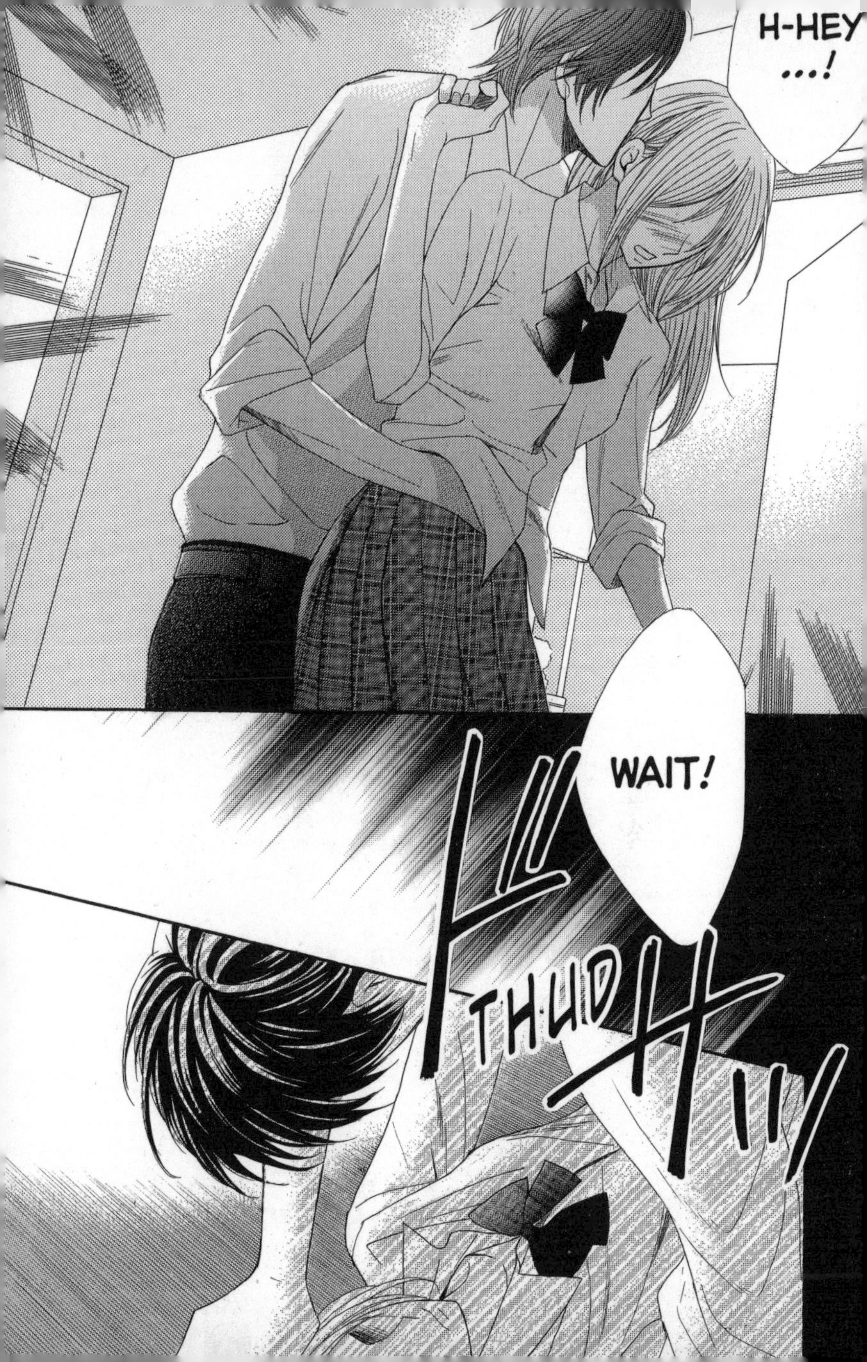
H-HEY ...!
WAIT!
THUD

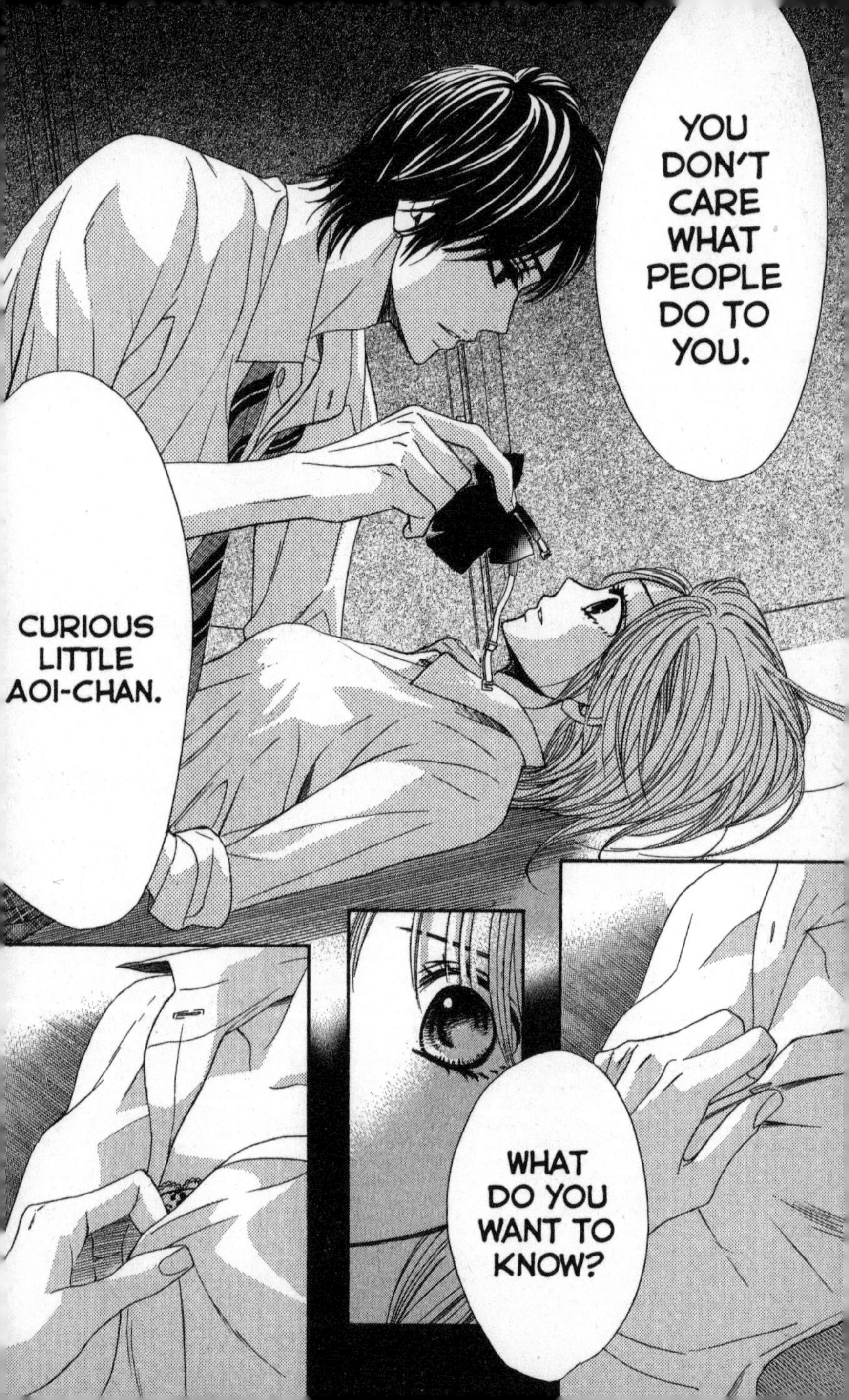
YOU DON'T CARE WHAT PEOPLE DO TO YOU.
CURIOUS LITTLE AOI-CHAN.
WHAT DO YOU WANT TO KNOW?

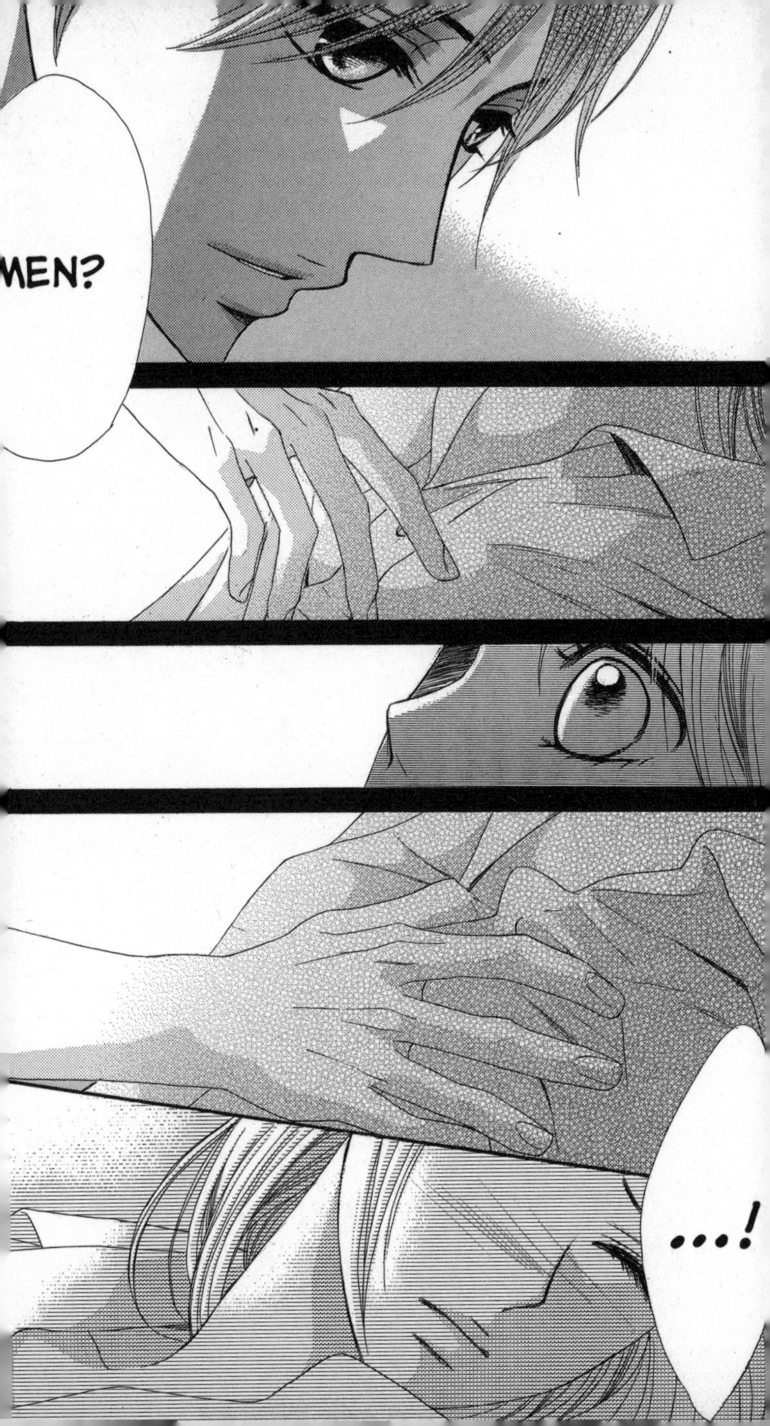
MEN?
...!

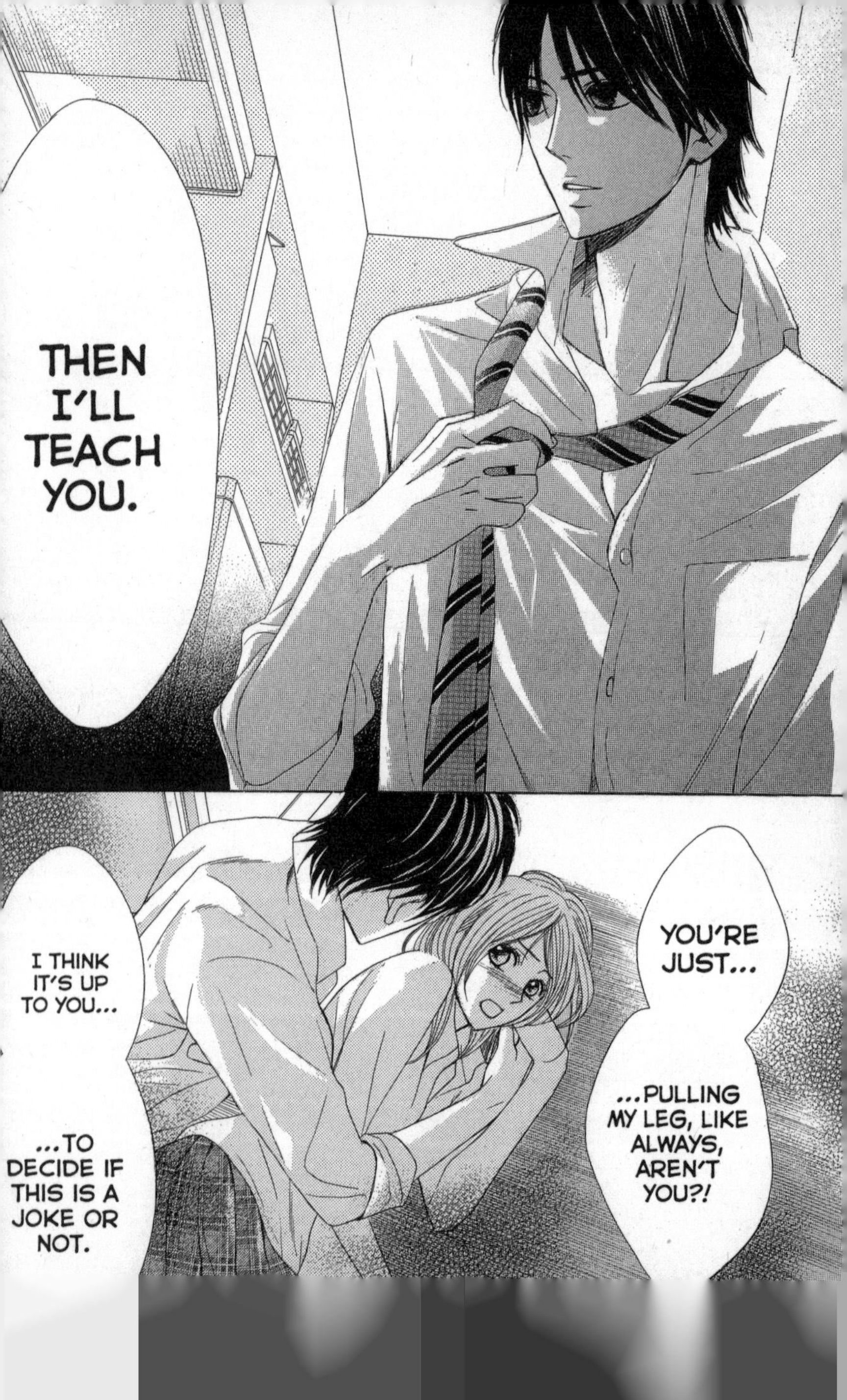
THEN I'LL TEACH YOU.
YOU'RE JUST...
...PULLING MY LEG, LIKE ALWAYS, AREN'T YOU?!
I THINK IT'S UP TO YOU...
...TO DECIDE IF THIS IS A JOKE OR NOT.

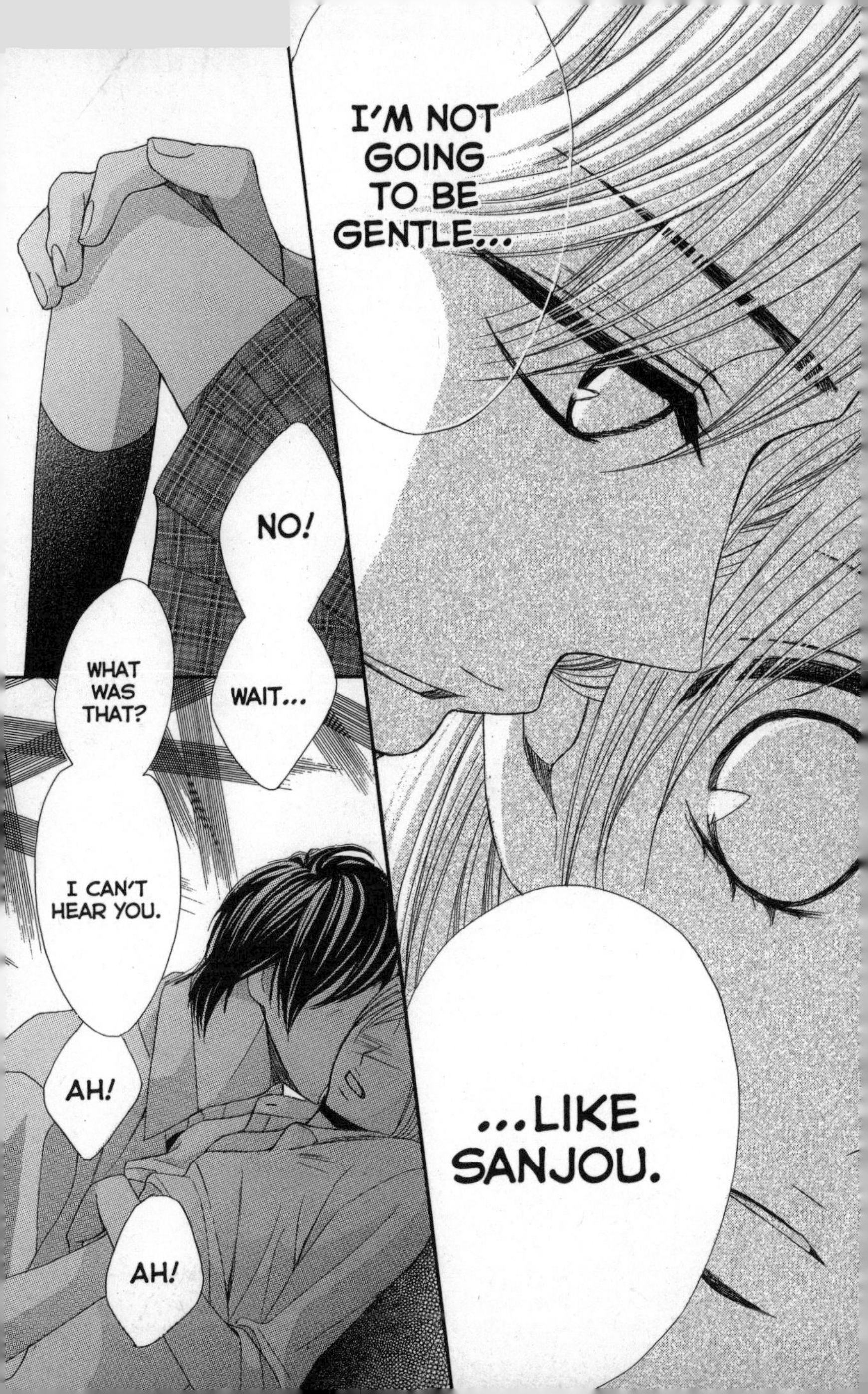
I'M NOT GOING TO BE GENTLE...
...LIKE SANJOU.
NO!
WAIT...
WHAT WAS THAT?
I CAN'T HEAR YOU.
AH!
AH!

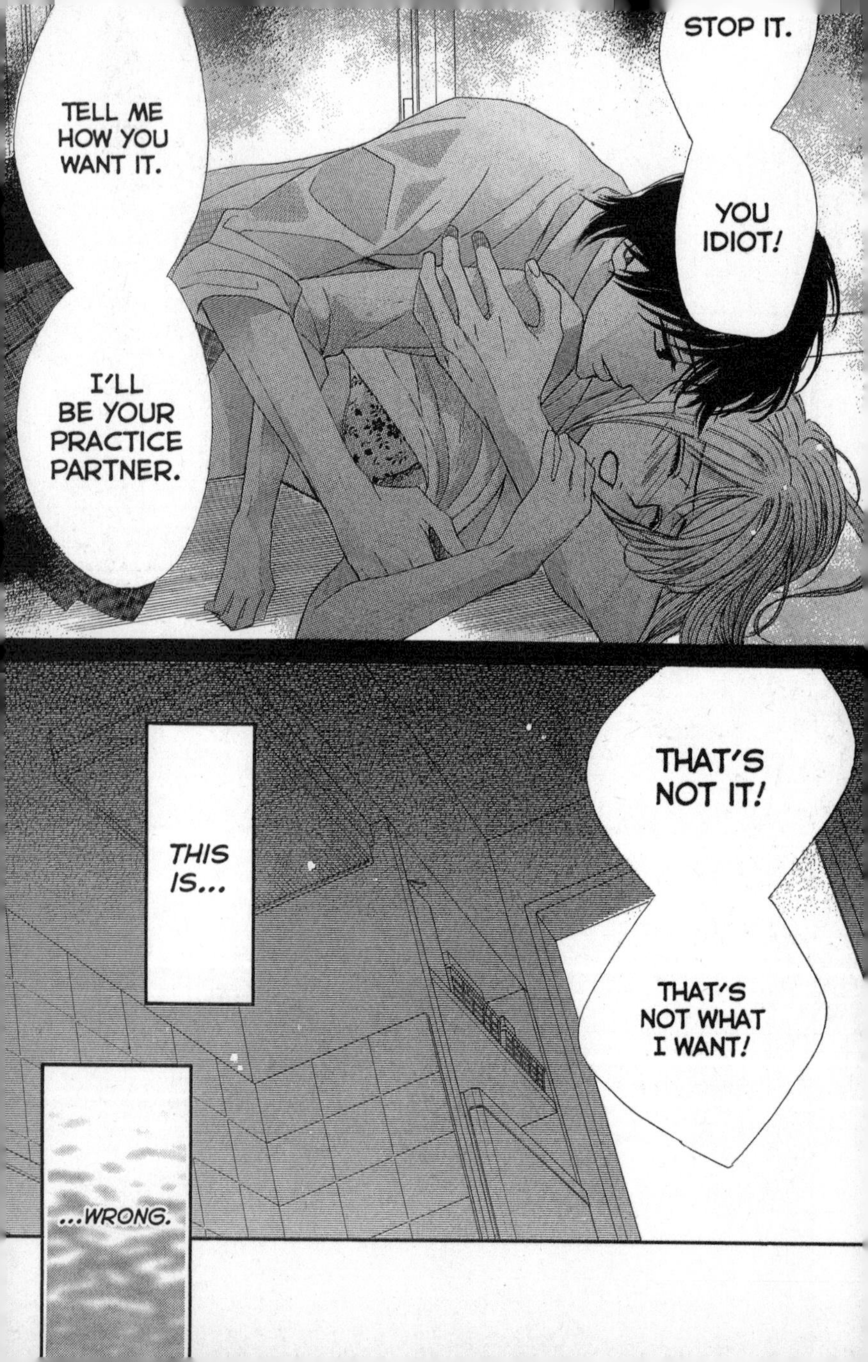
STOP IT.
YOU IDIOT!
TELL ME HOW YOU WANT IT.
I'LL BE YOUR PRACTICE PARTNER.
THAT'S NOT IT!
THAT'S NOT WHAT I WANT!
THIS IS...
...WRONG.

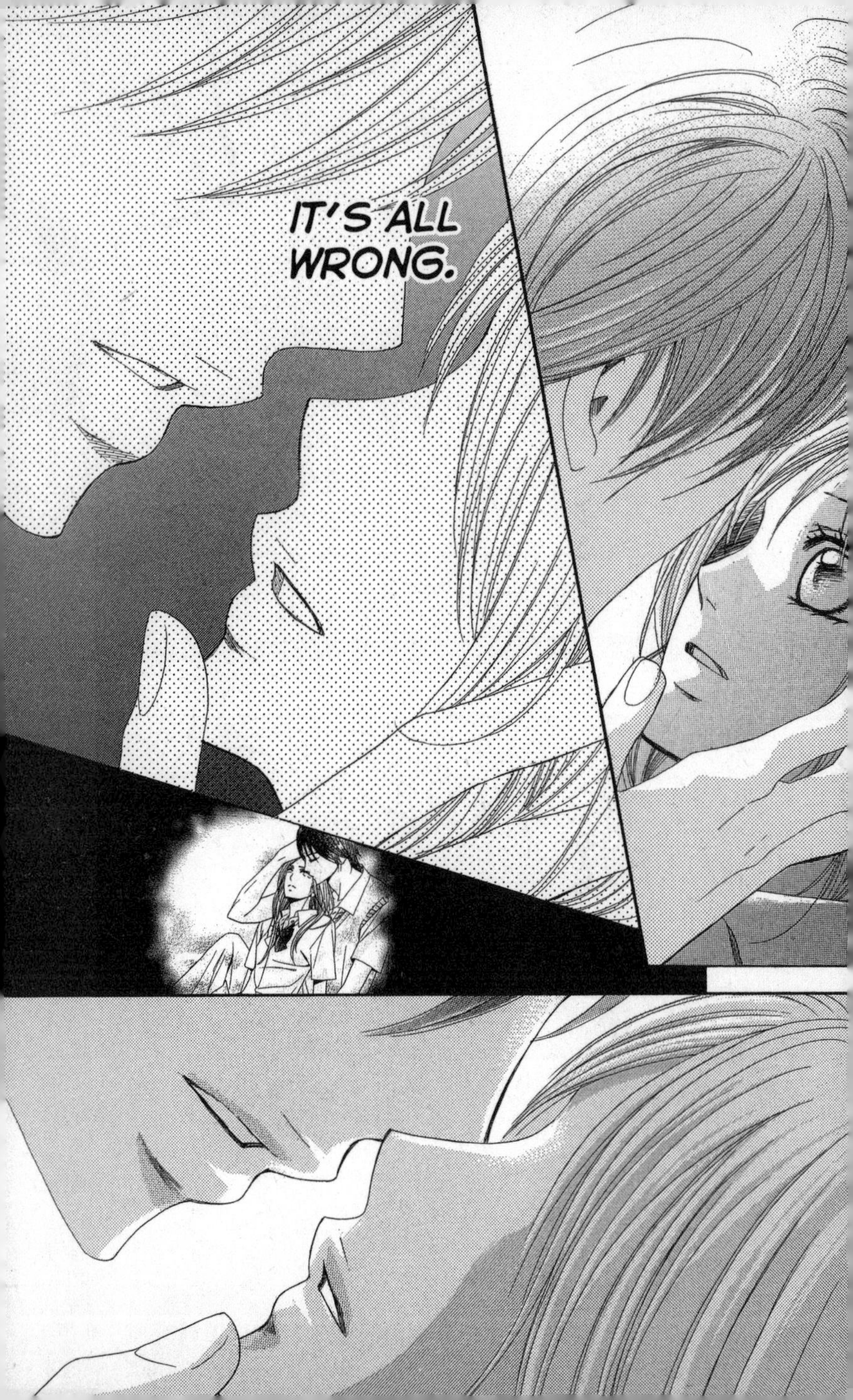
IT'S ALL WRONG.

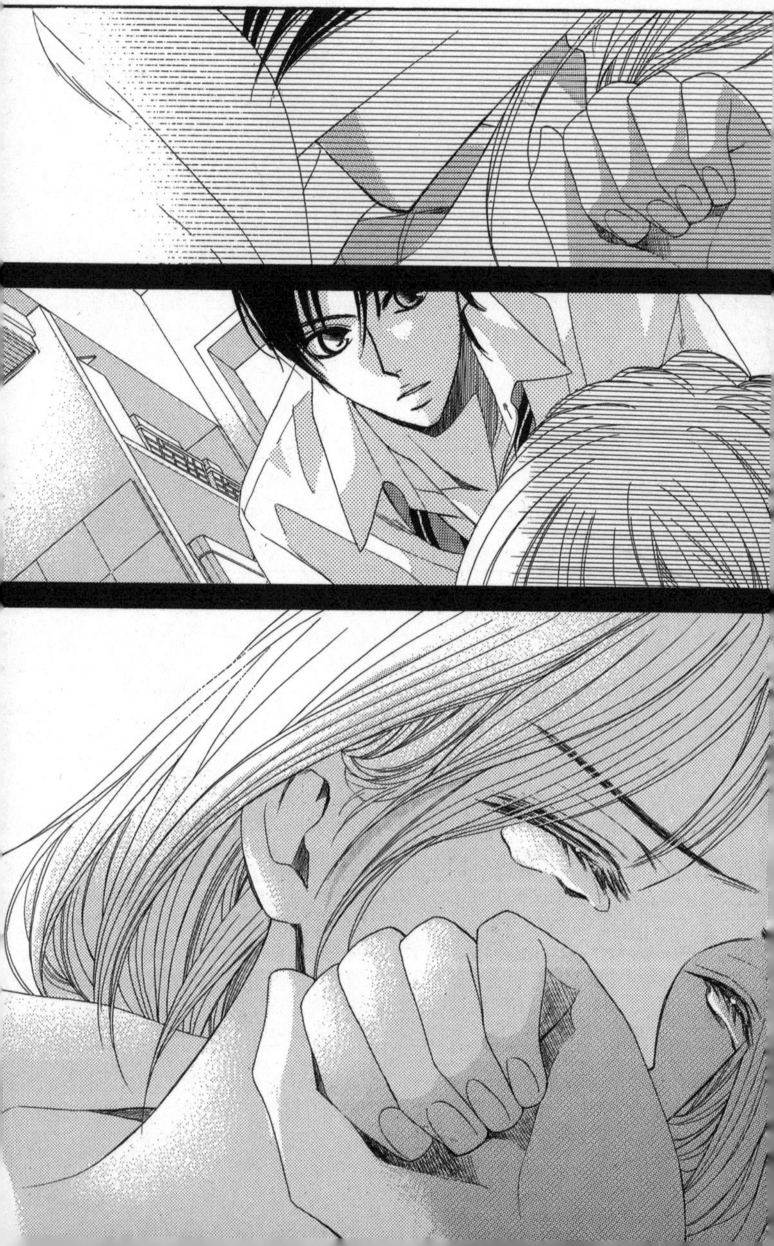

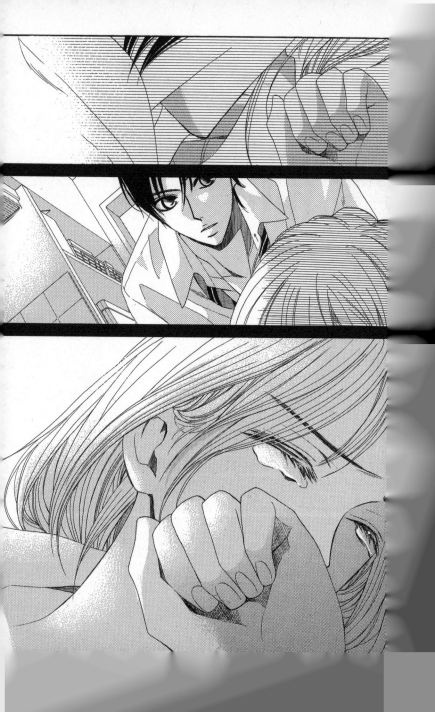

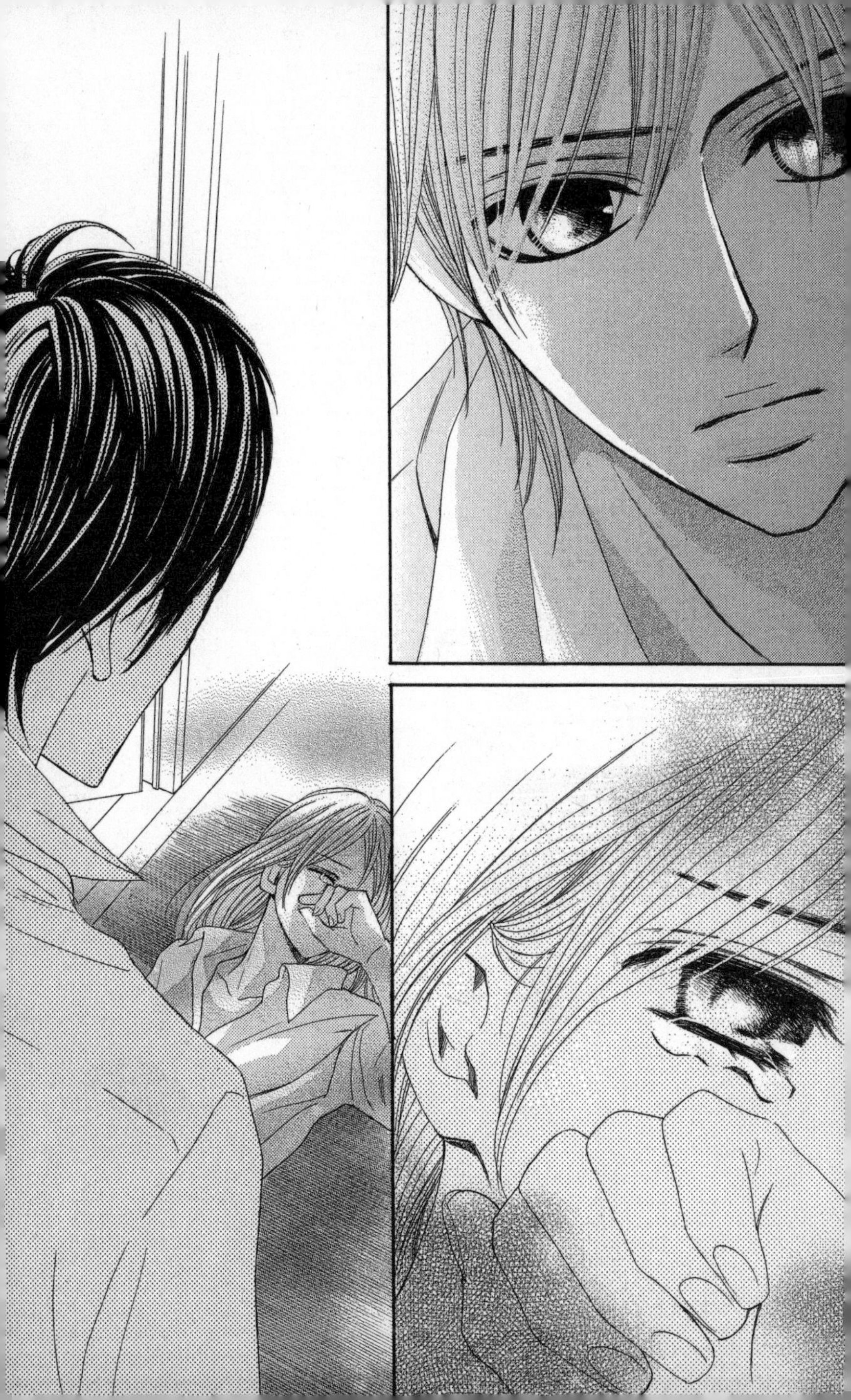

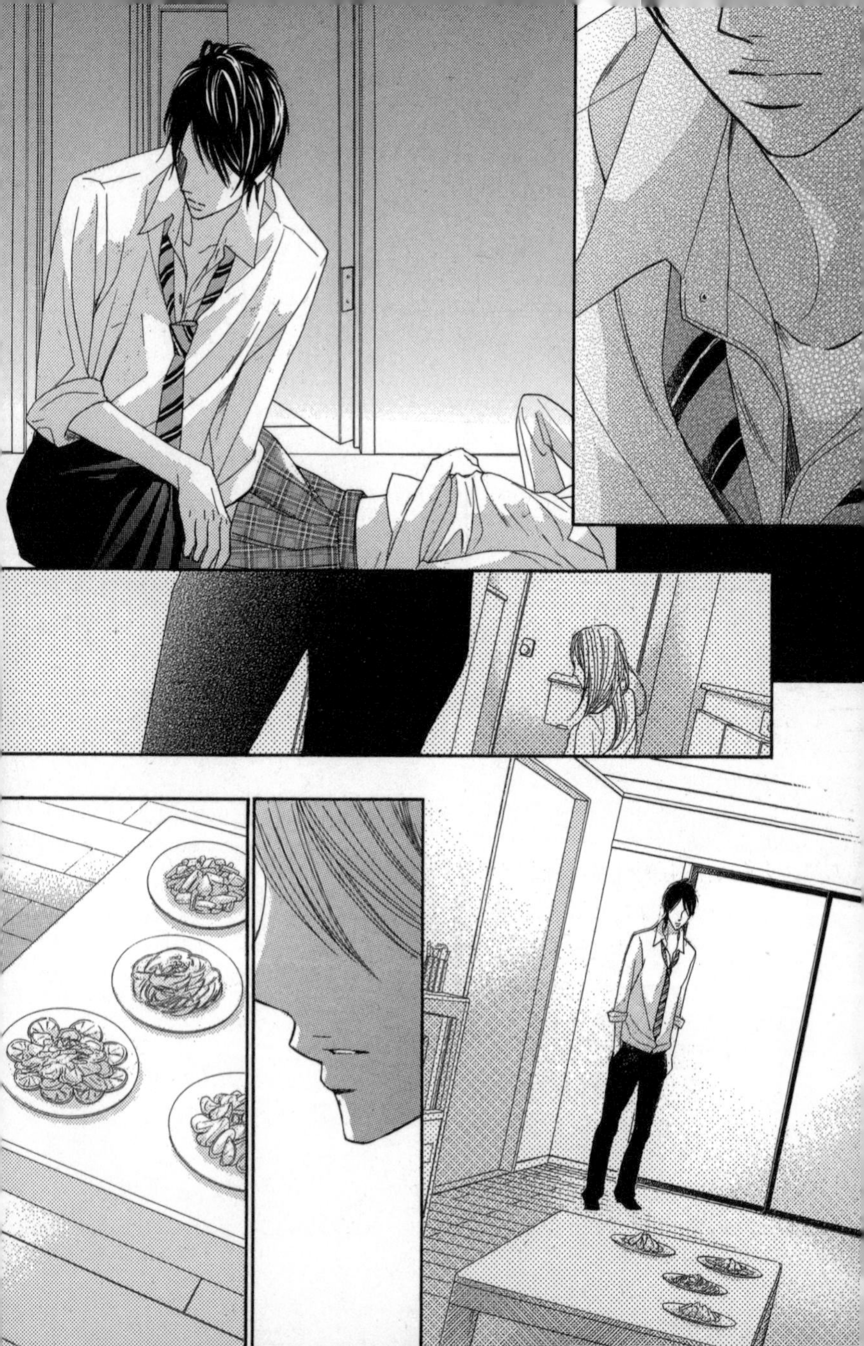

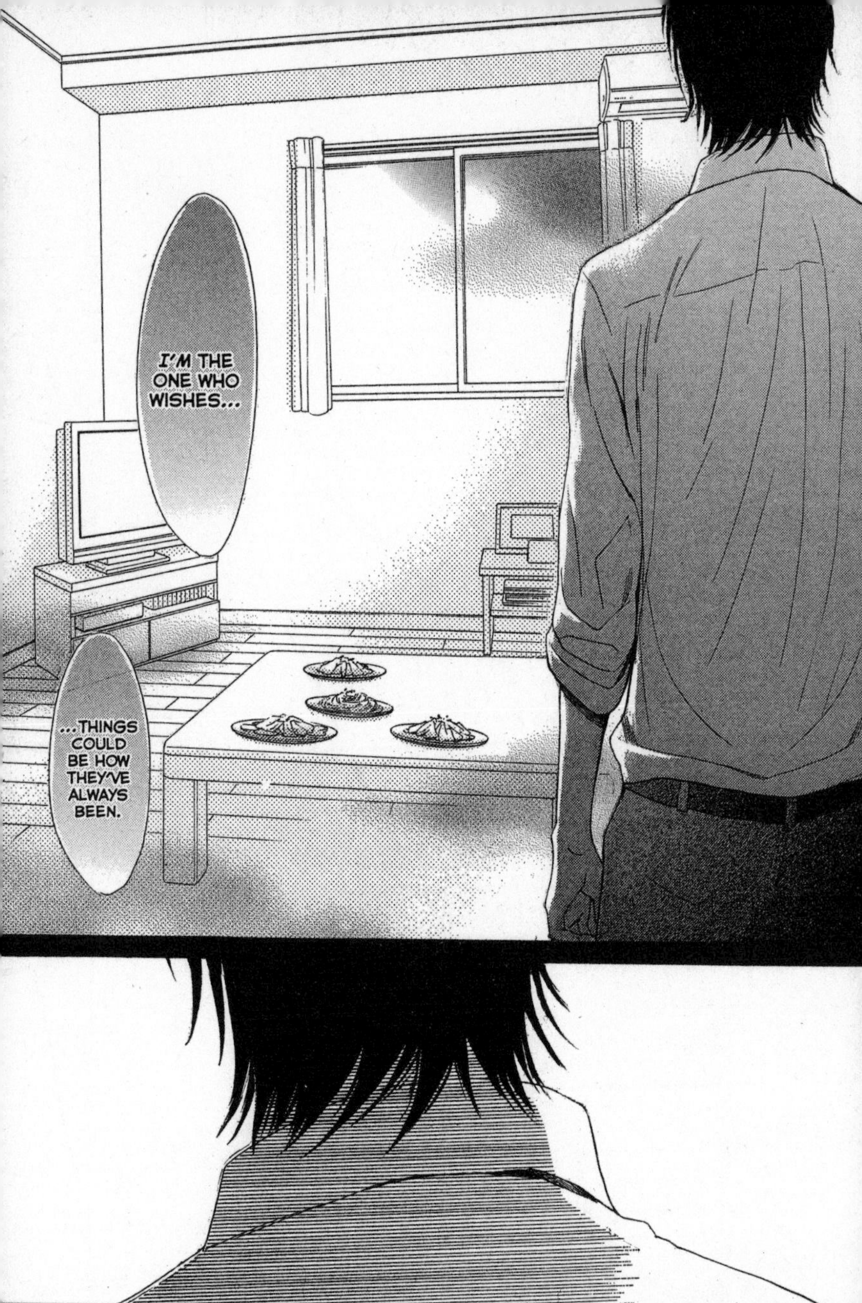
I'M THE ONE WHO WISHES...
...THINGS COULD BE HOW THEY'VE ALWAYS BEEN.

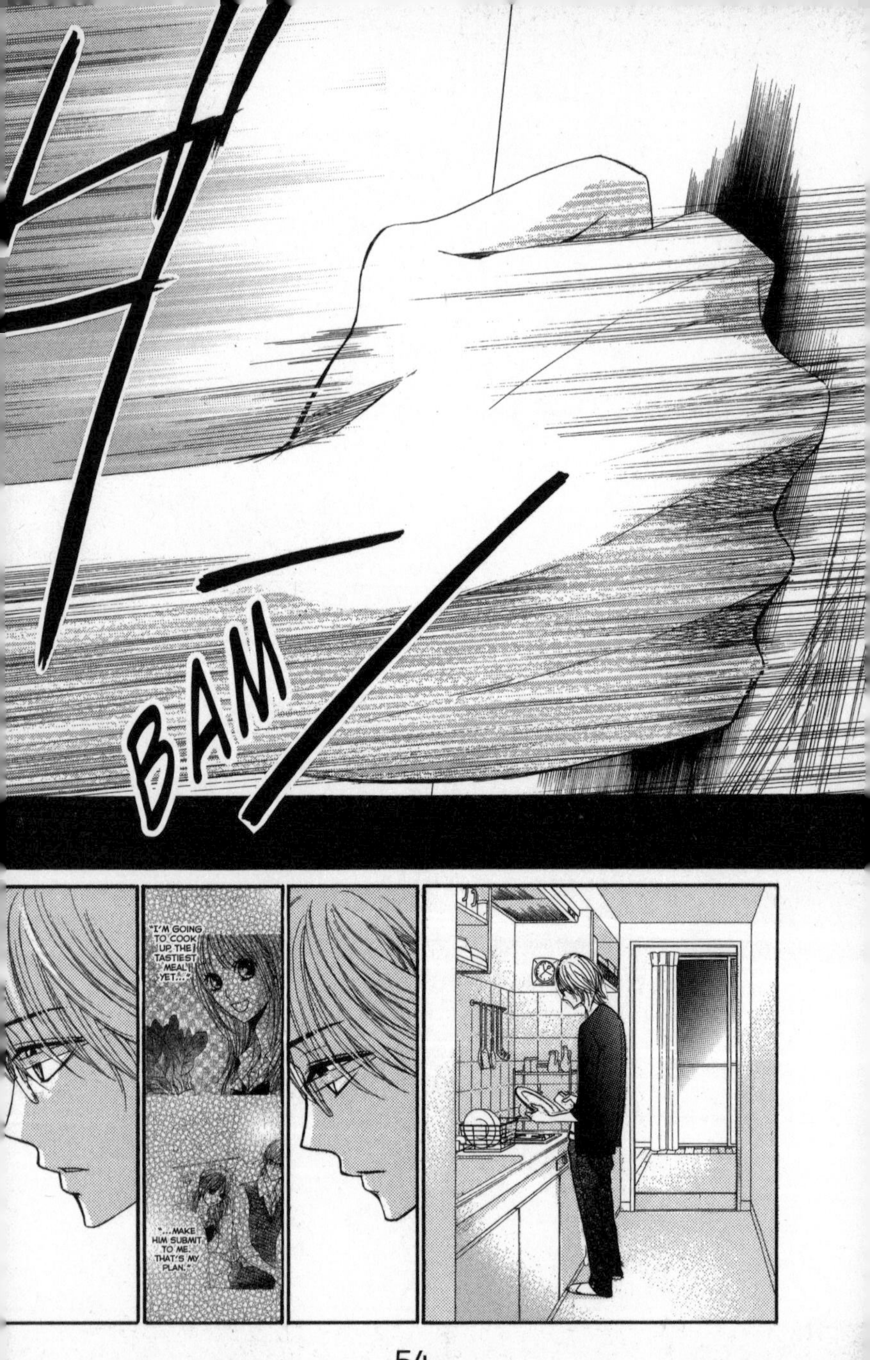
BAM
"I'M GOING TO COOK UP THE TASTIEST MEAL YET..."
"...MAKE HIM SUBMIT TO ME. THAT'S MY PLAN."

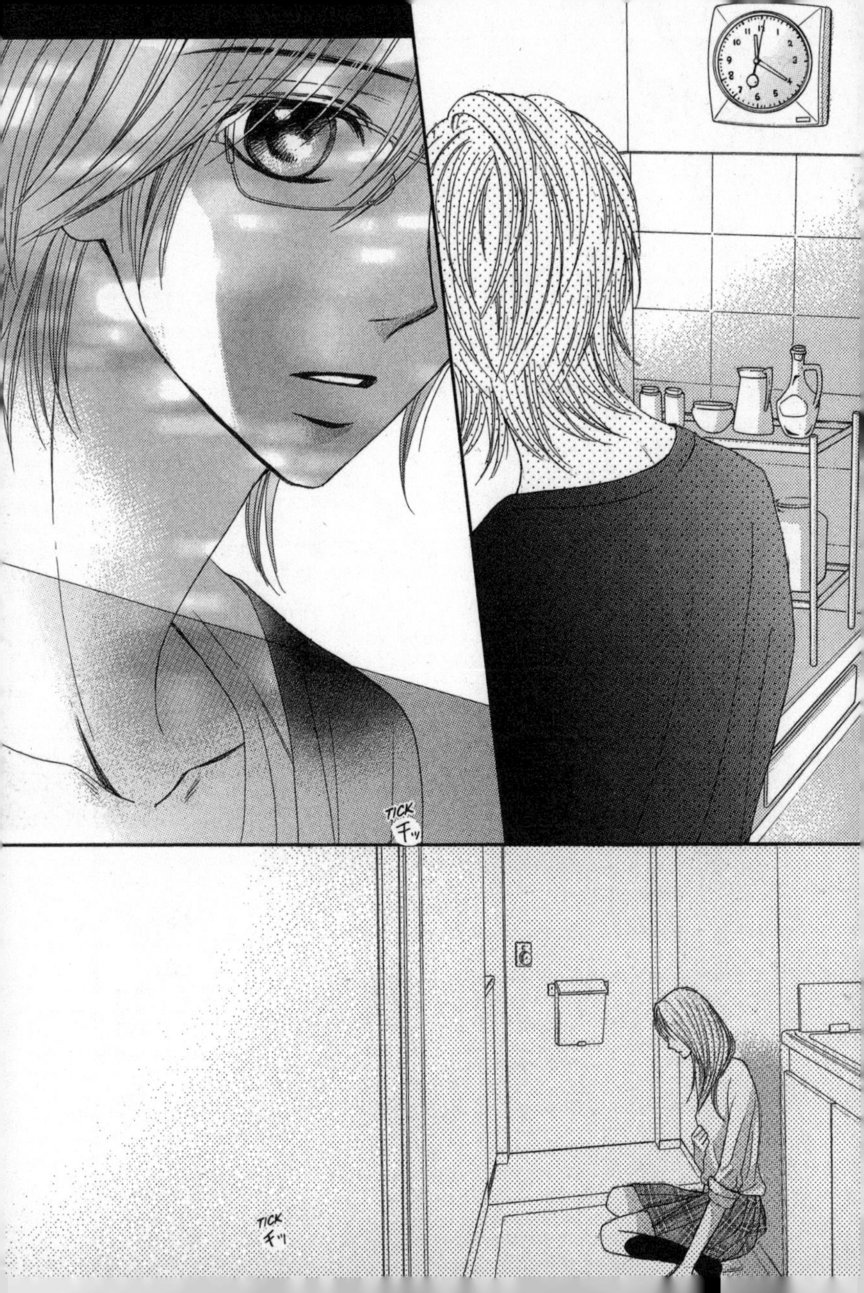
TICK
チッ
TICK
チッ

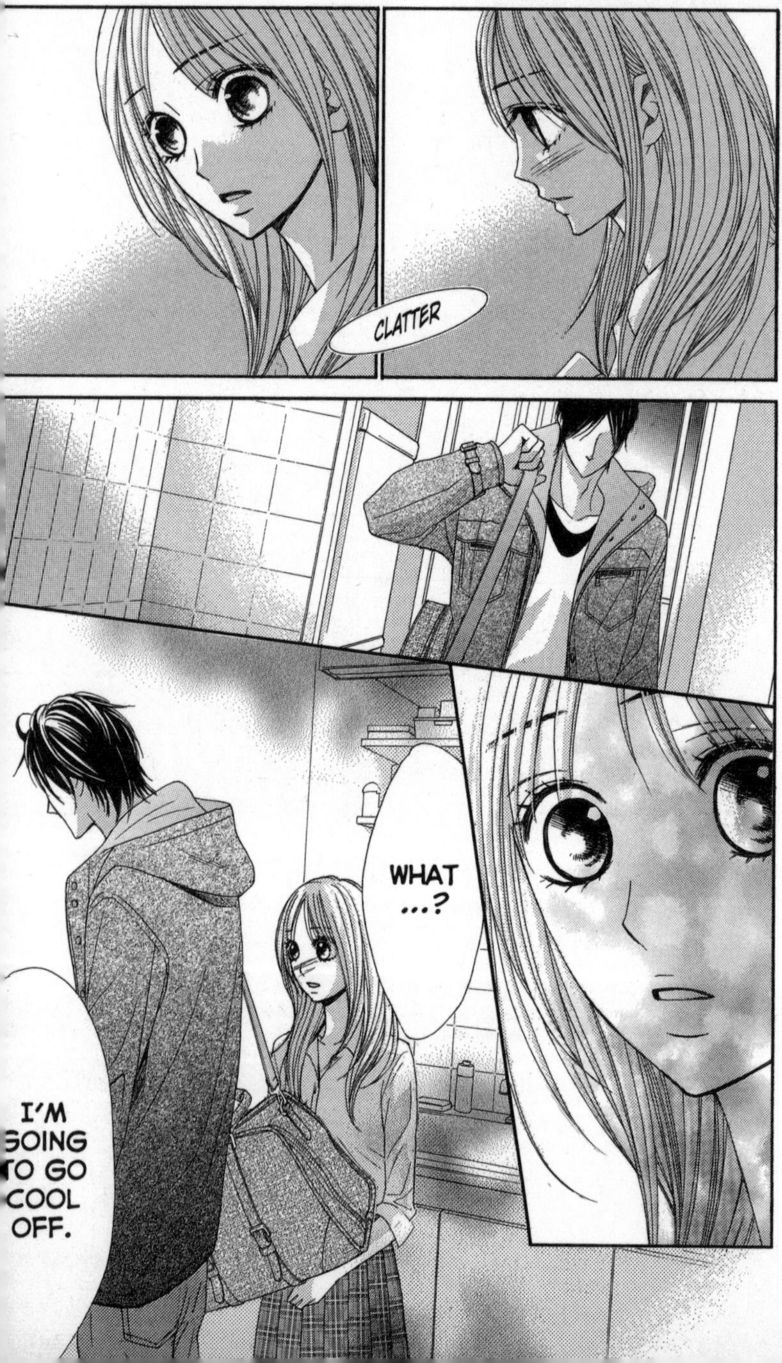
CLATTER
WHAT ...?
I'M GOING TO GO COOL OFF.

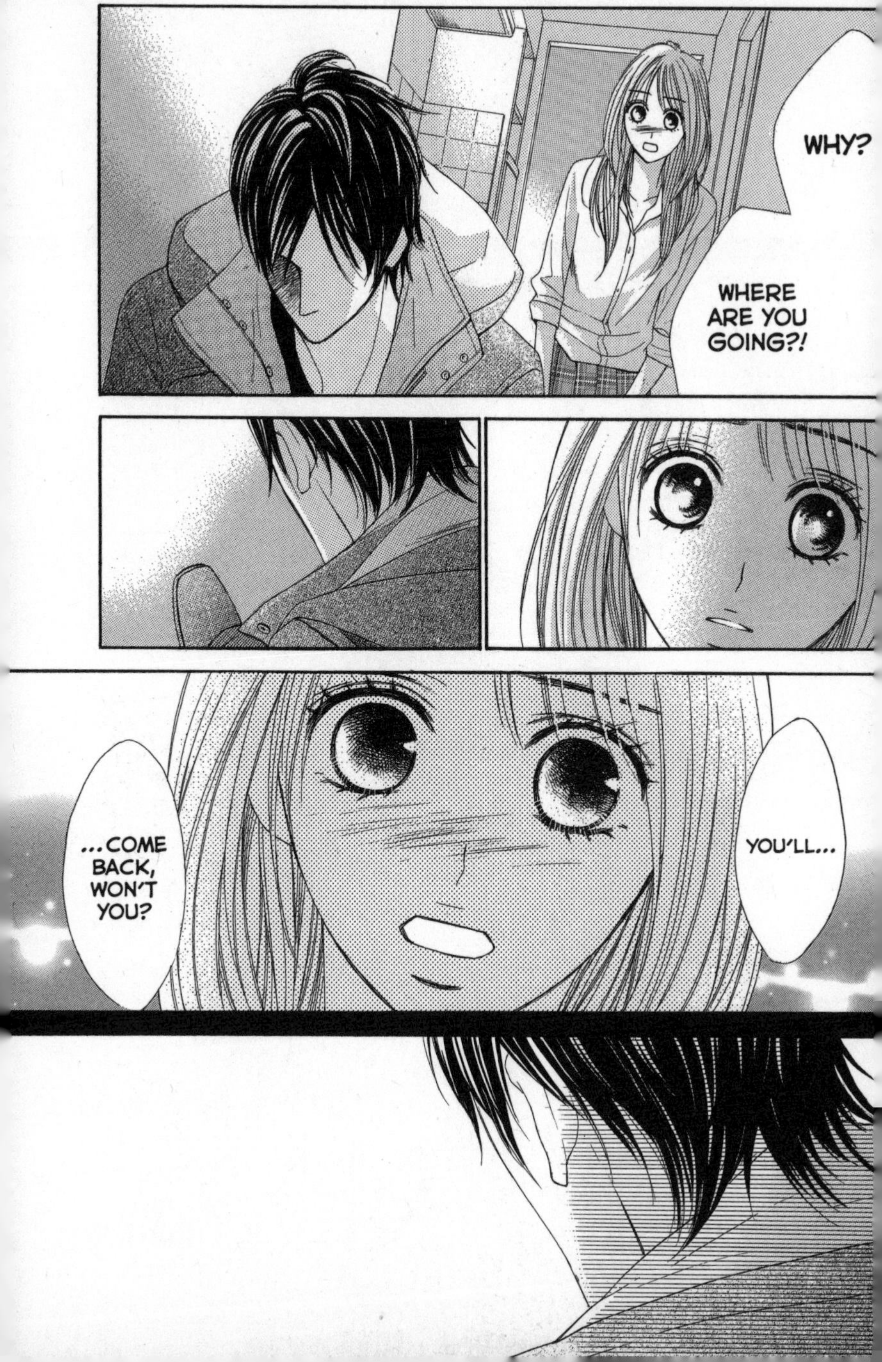
WHY?
WHERE ARE YOU GOING?!
YOU'LL...
...COME BACK, WON'T YOU?

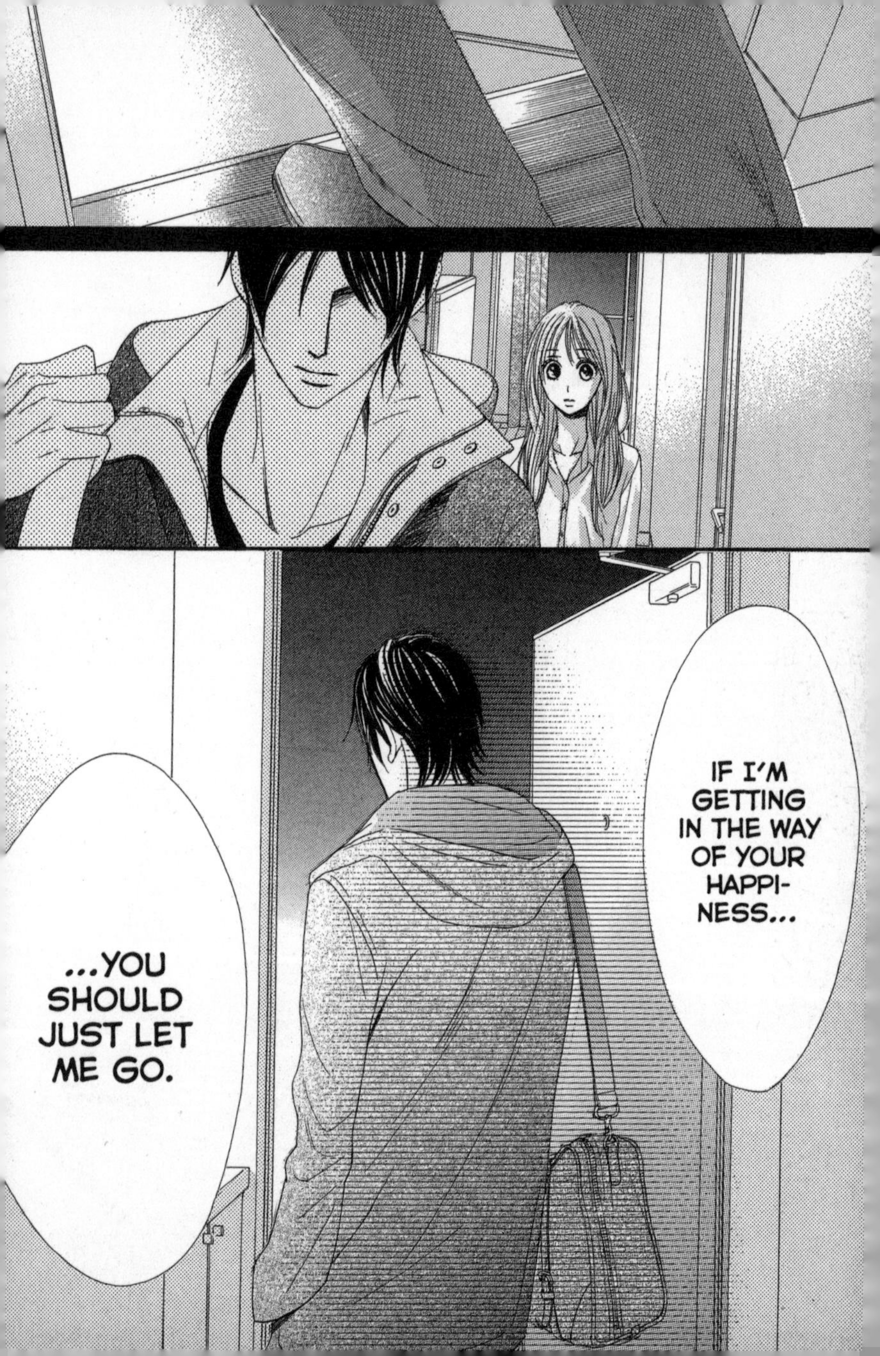
IF I'M GETTING IN THE WAY OF YOUR HAPPI- NESS...
...YOU SHOULD JUST LET ME GO.

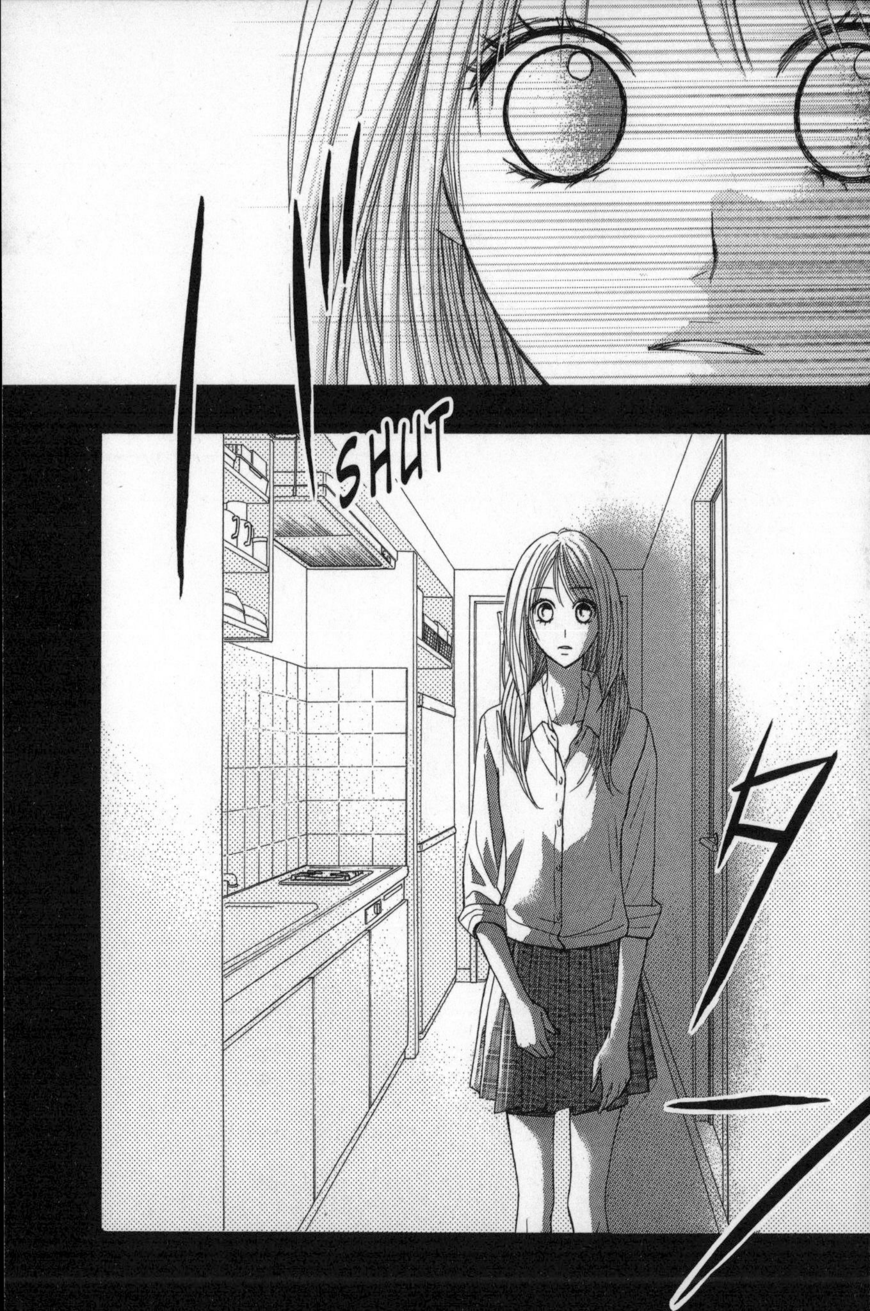
SHUT

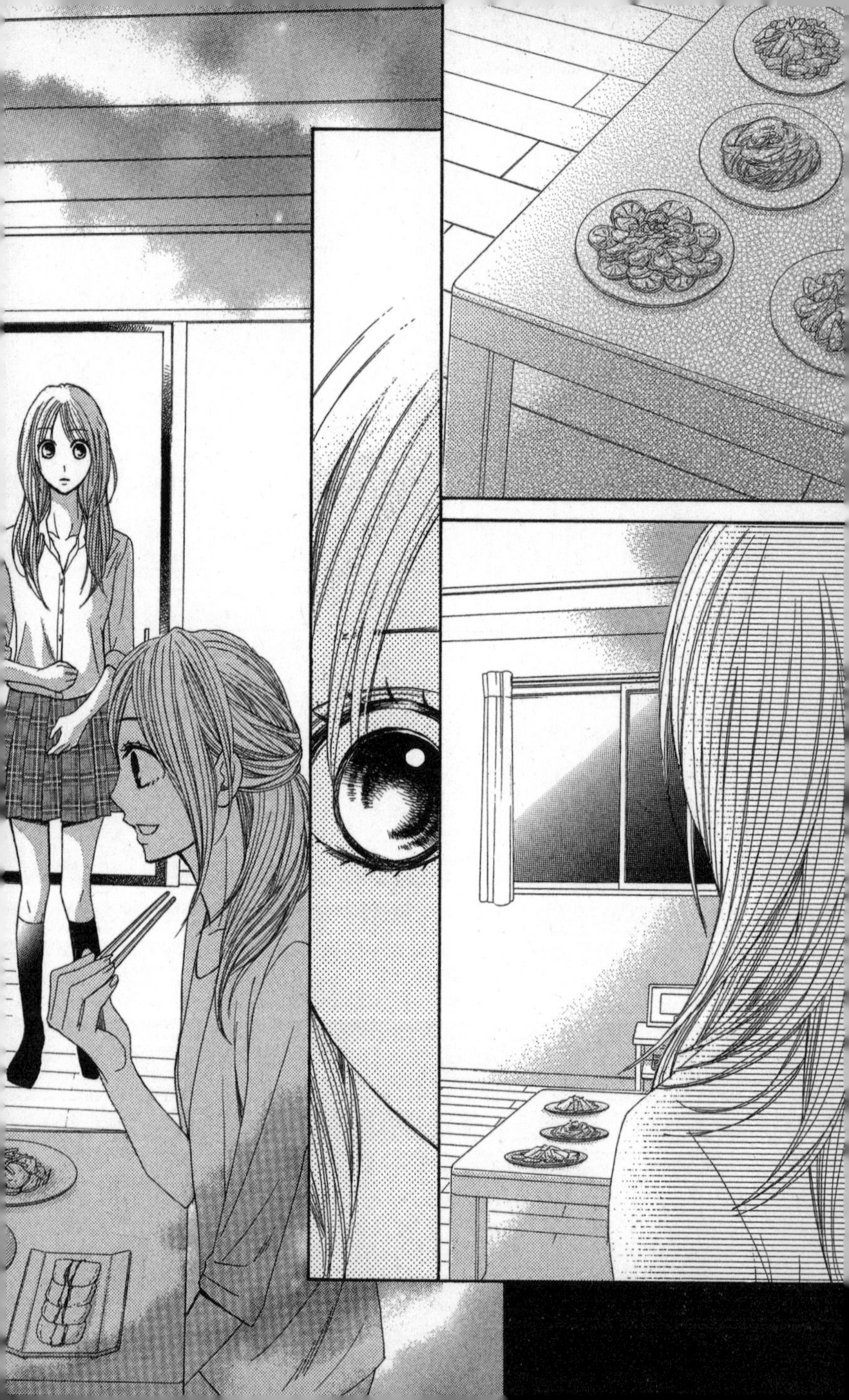

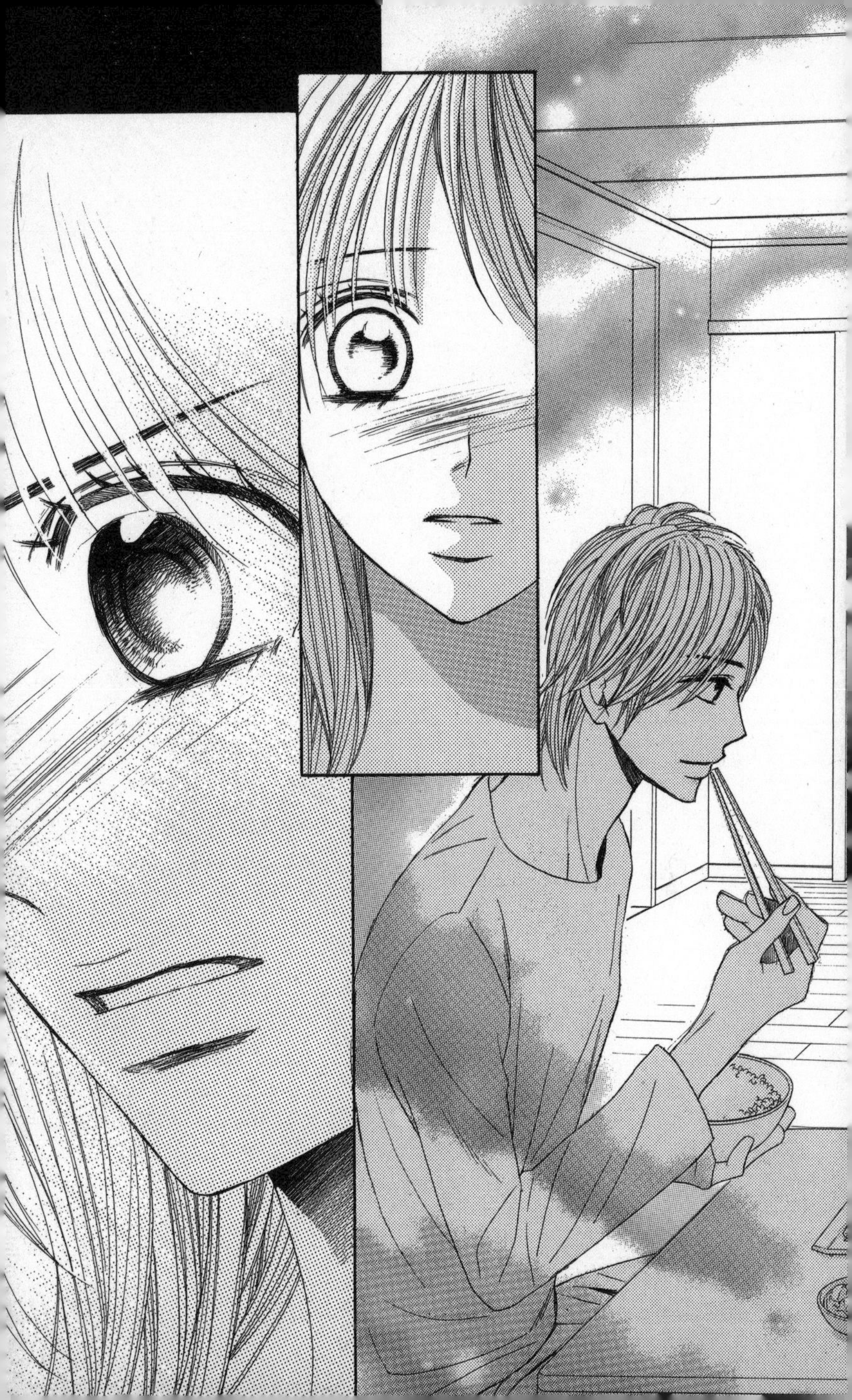

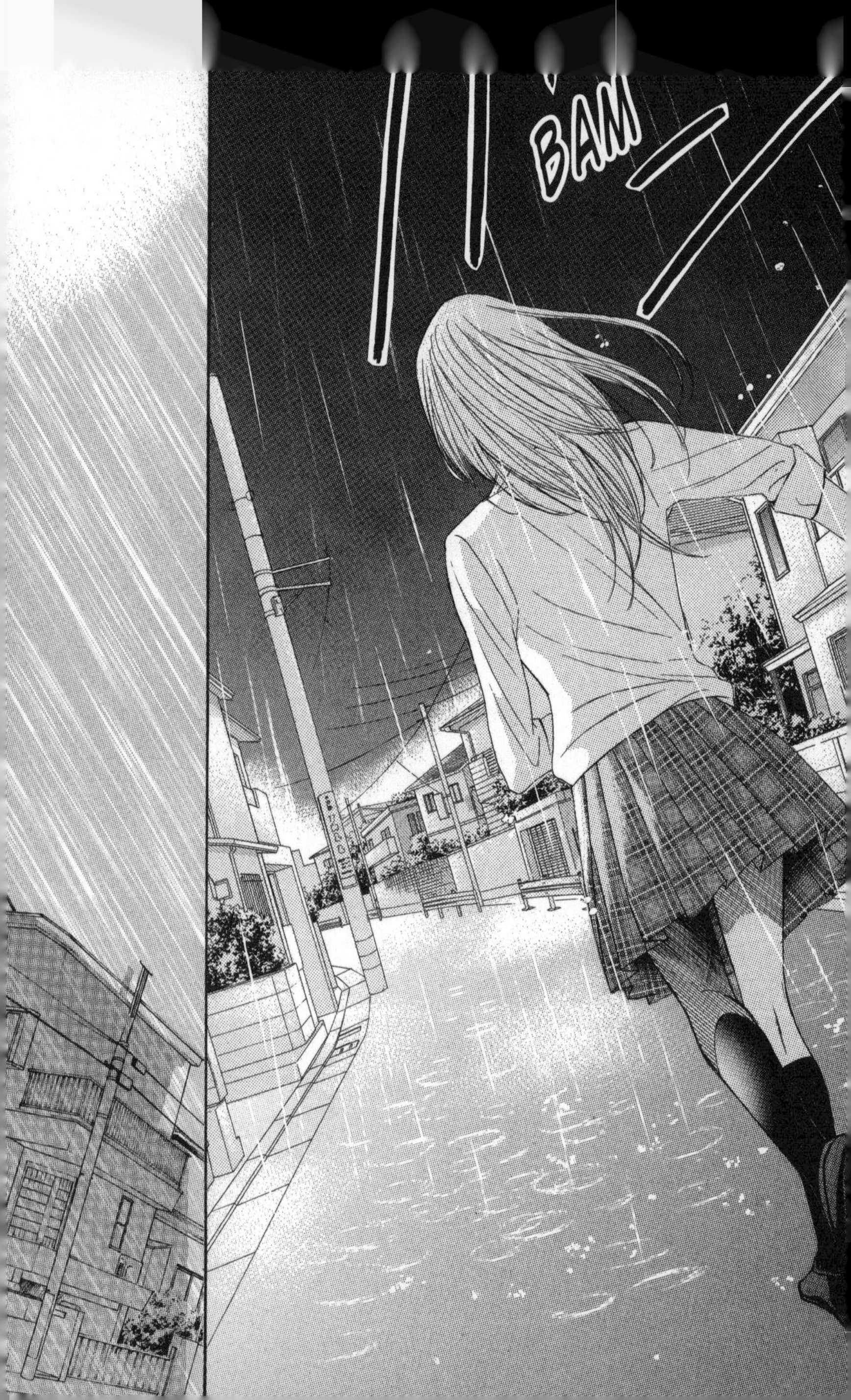
BAM

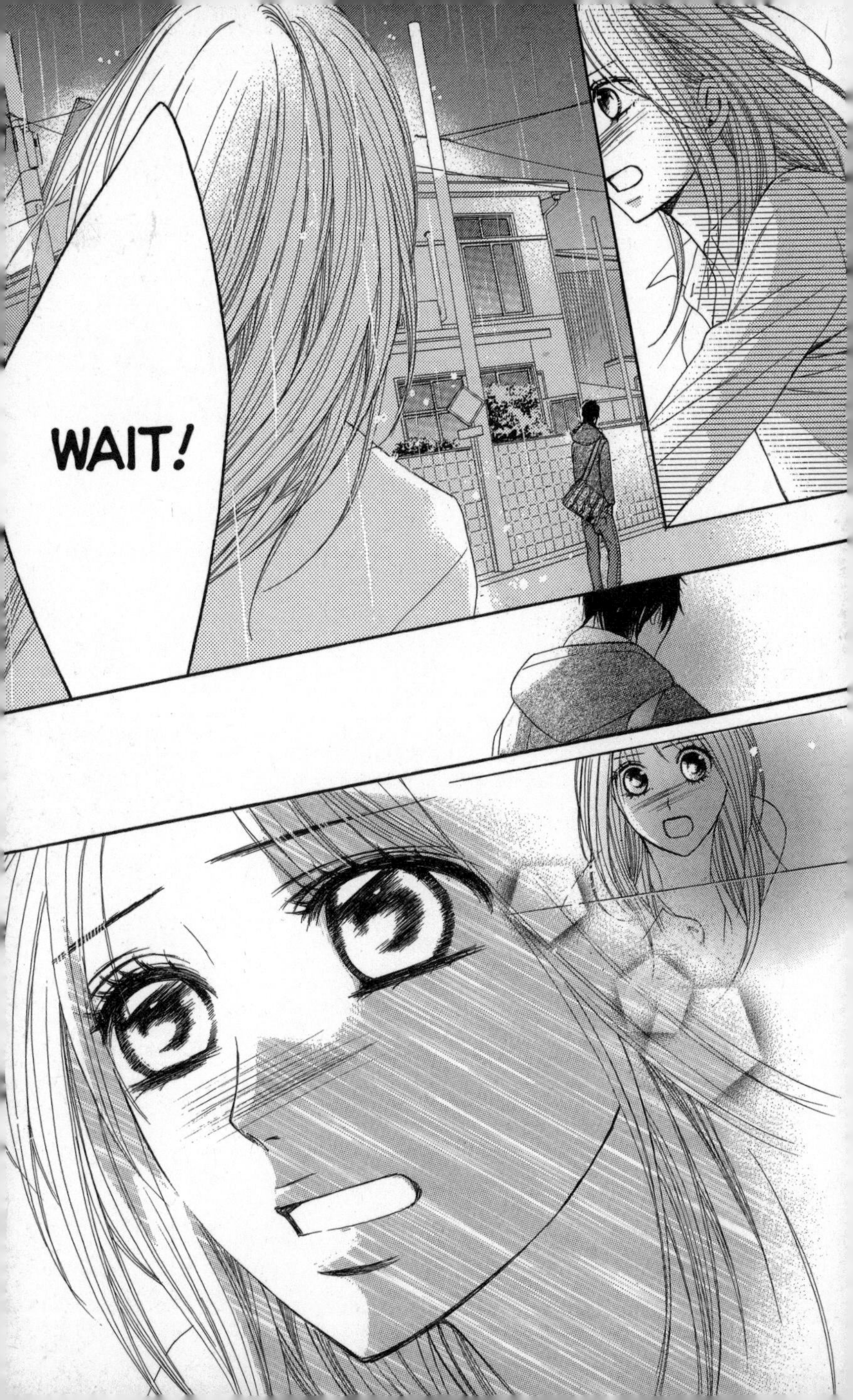
WAIT!

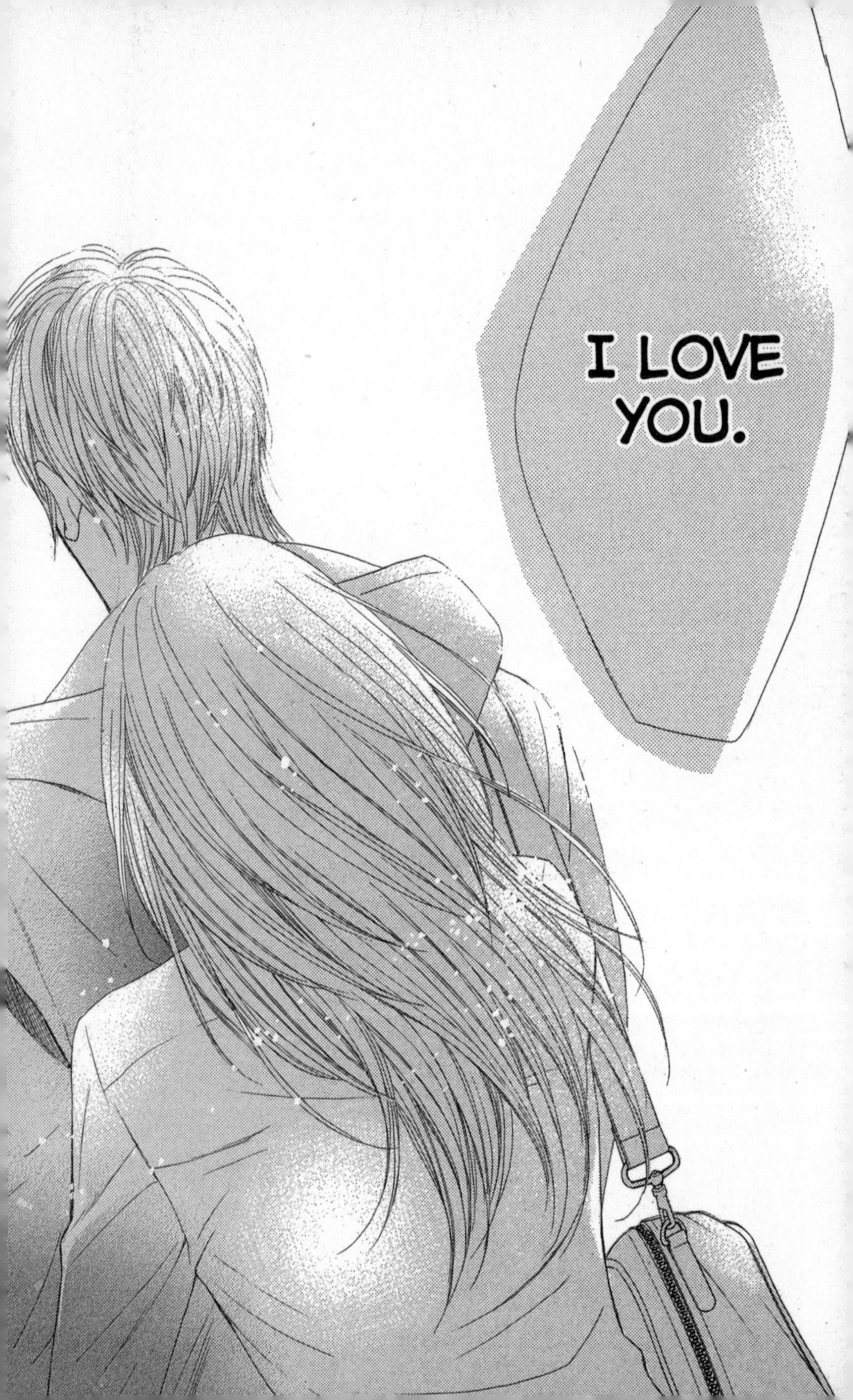
I LOVE YOU.

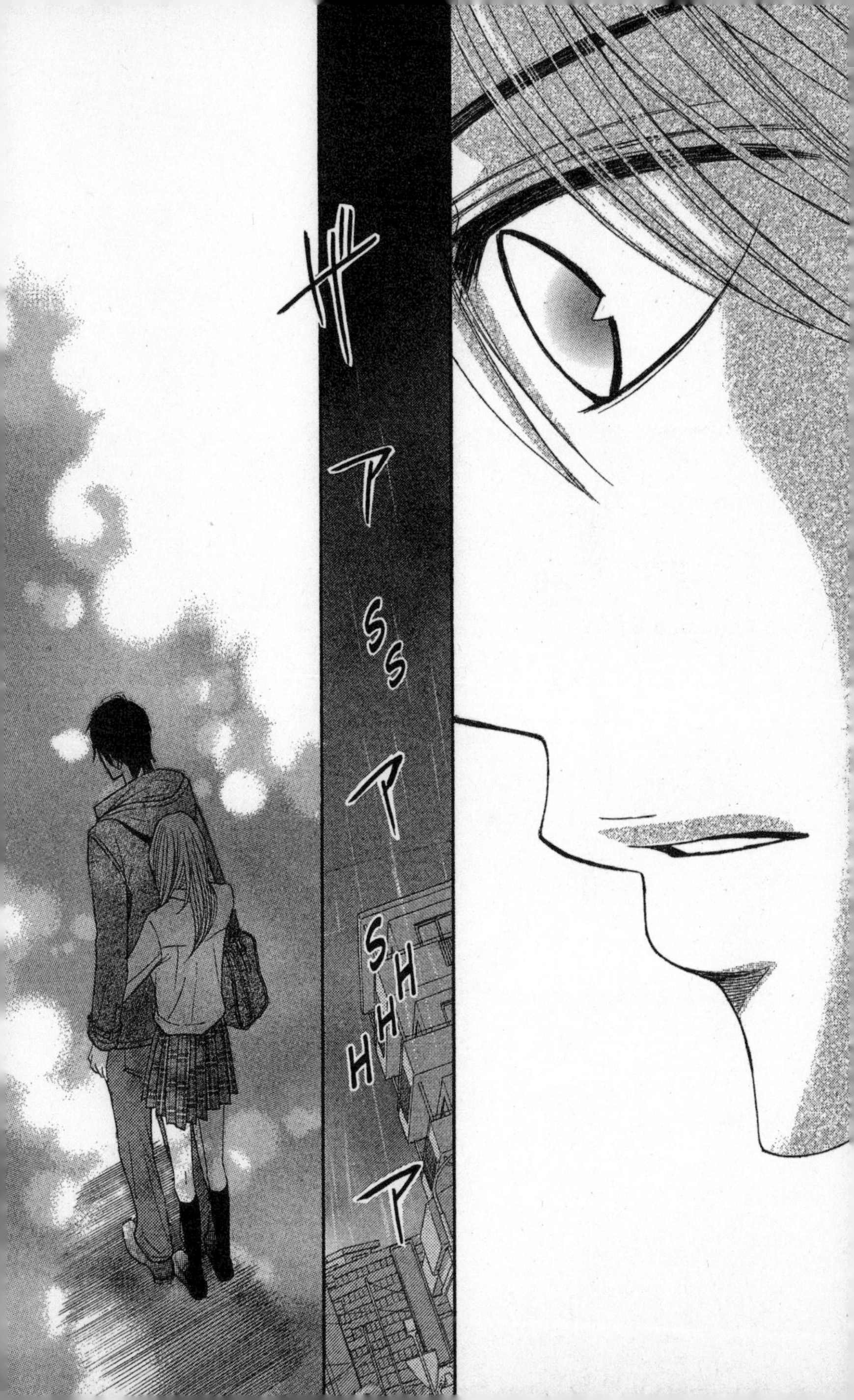
SS
SHHH

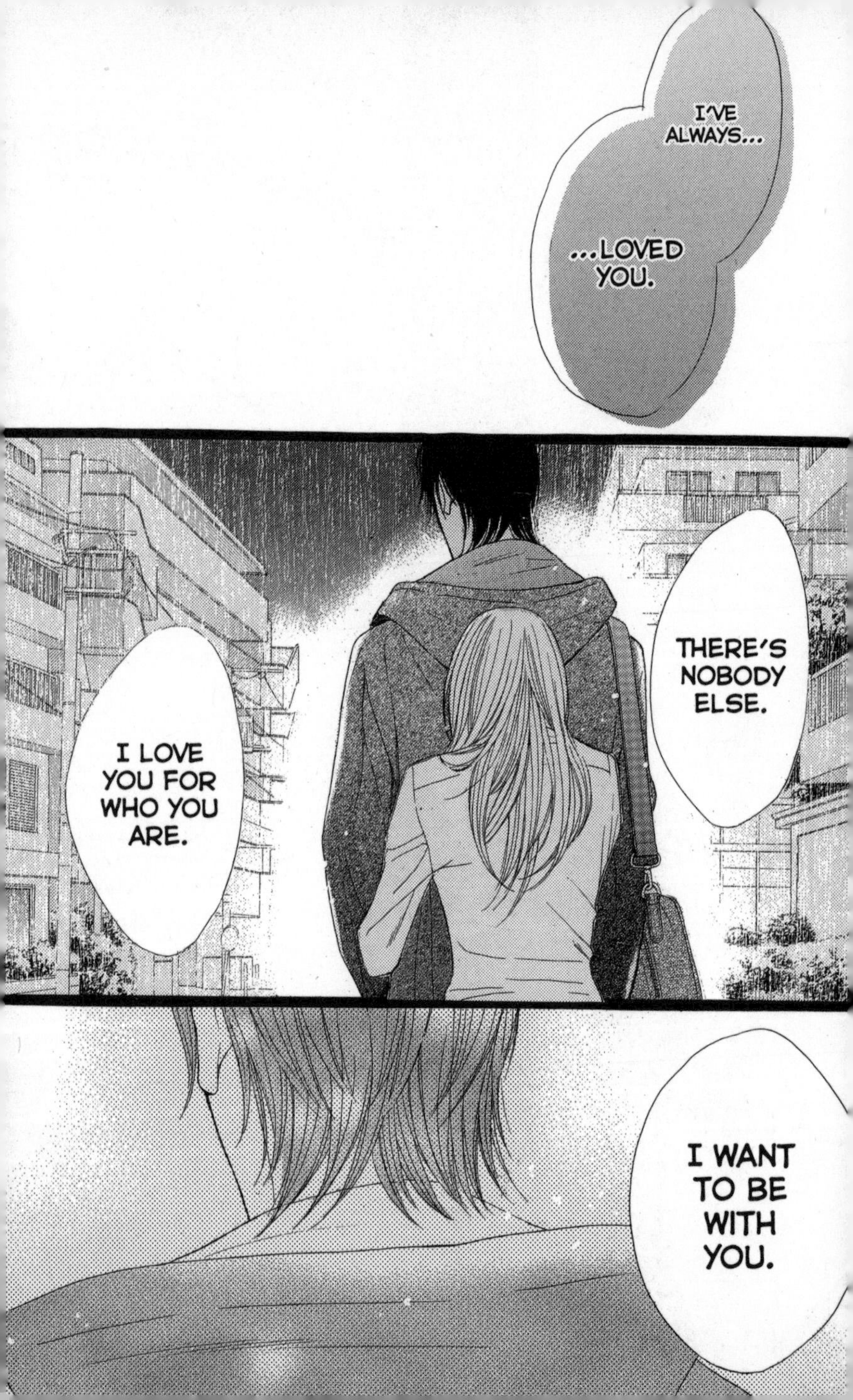
I'VE ALWAYS...
...LOVED YOU.
THERE'S NOBODY ELSE.
I LOVE YOU FOR WHO YOU ARE.
I WANT TO BE WITH YOU.

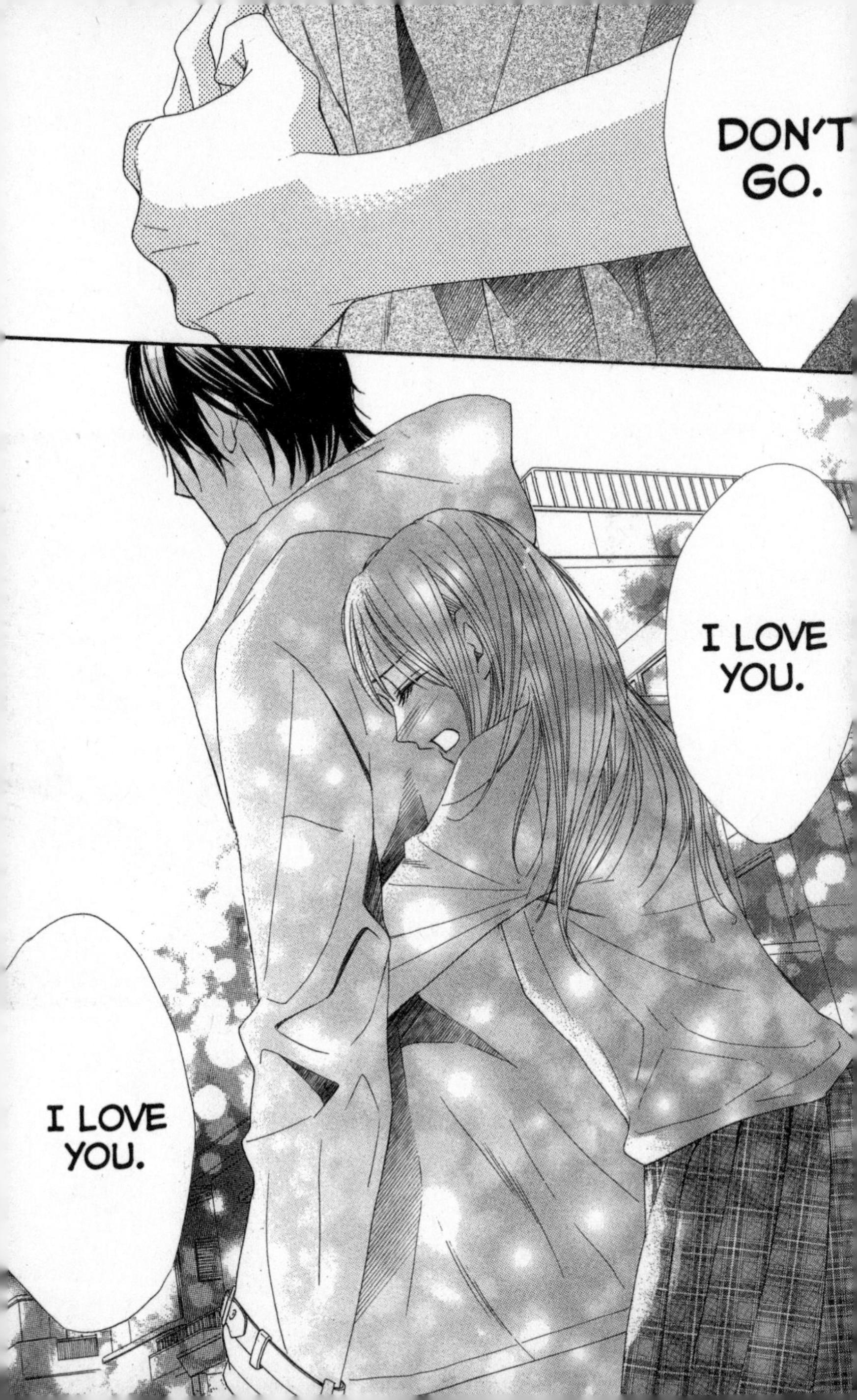
DON'T GO.
I LOVE YOU.
I LOVE YOU.

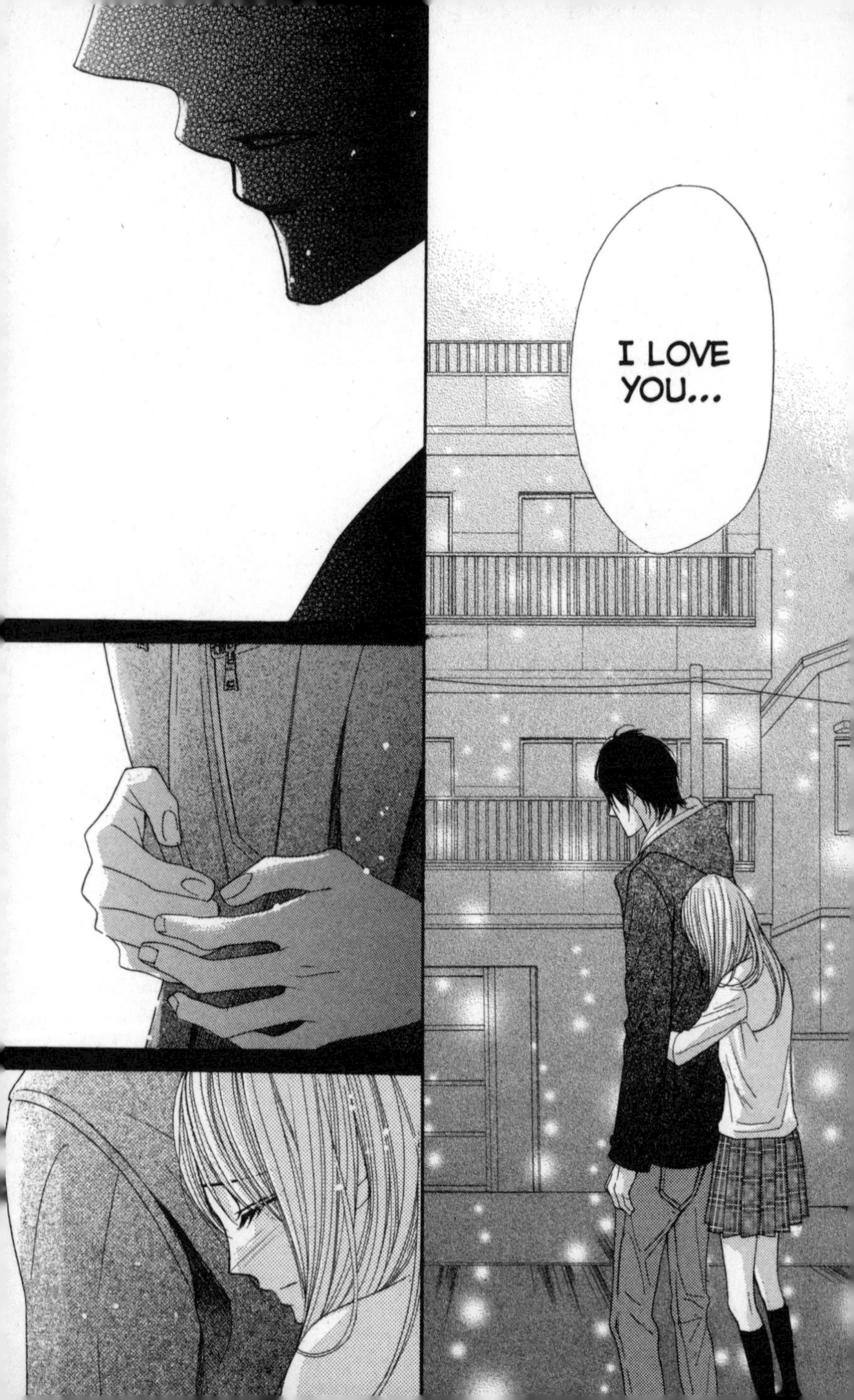
I LOVE YOU...

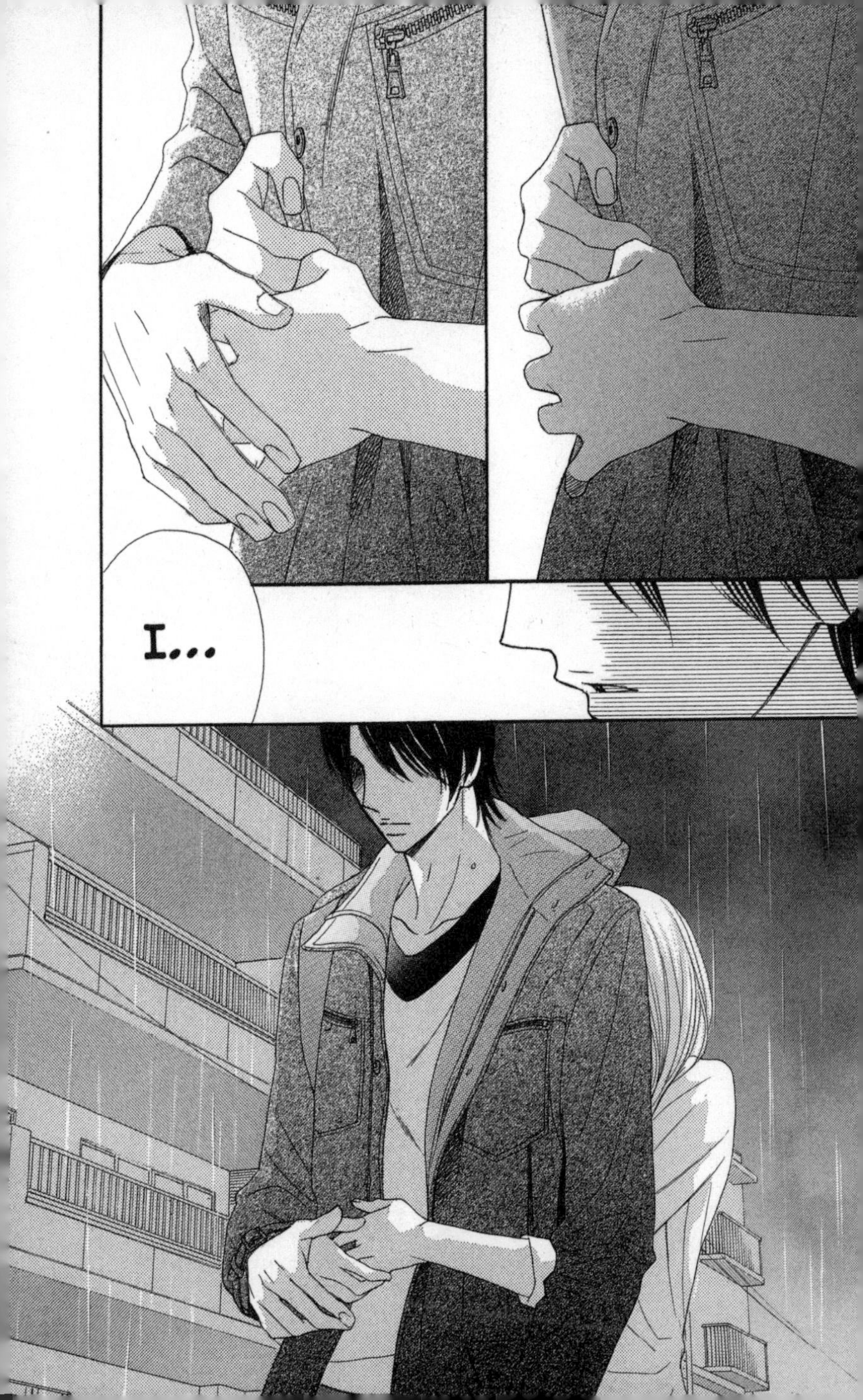
I...

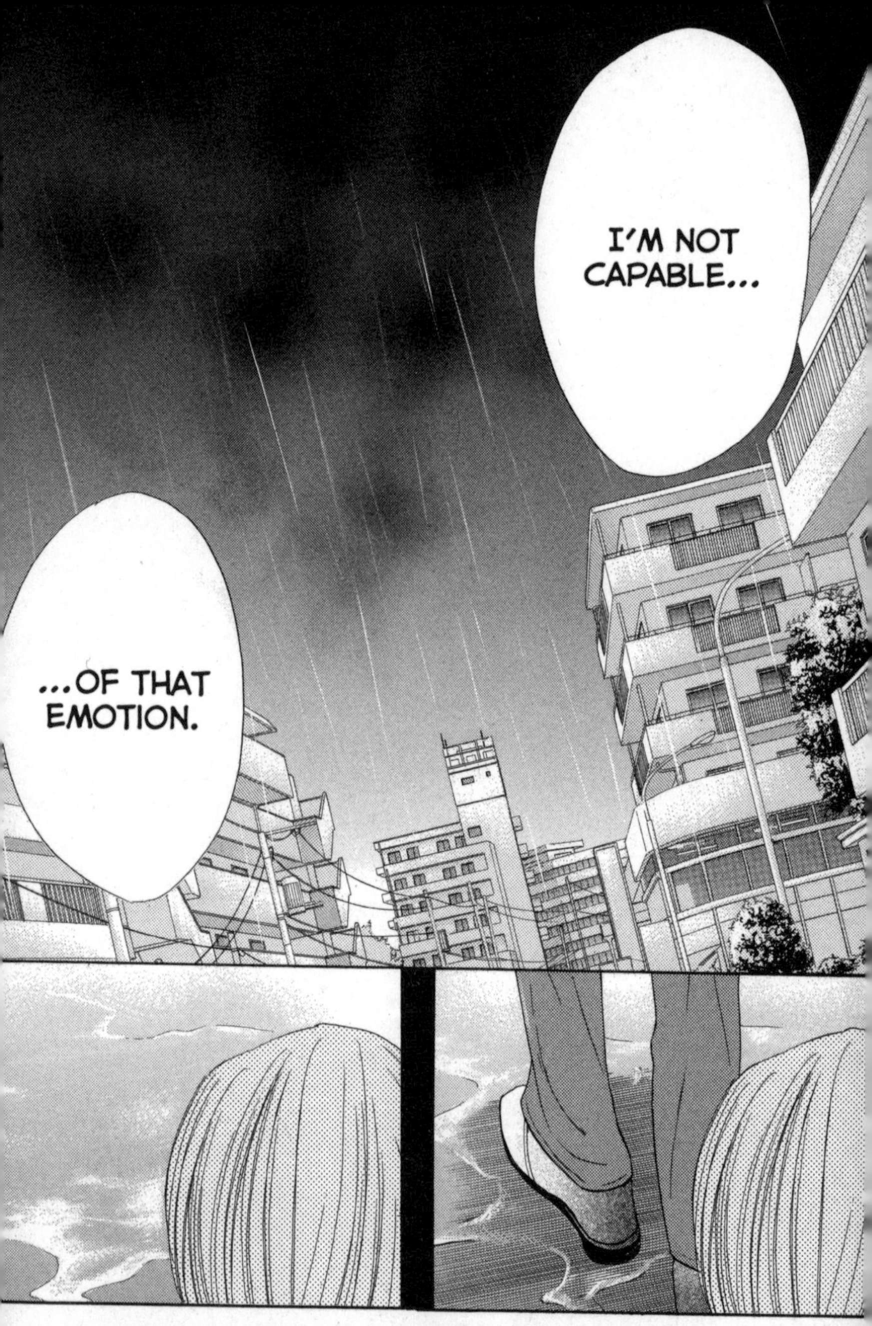
I'M NOT CAPABLE...
...OF THAT EMOTION.

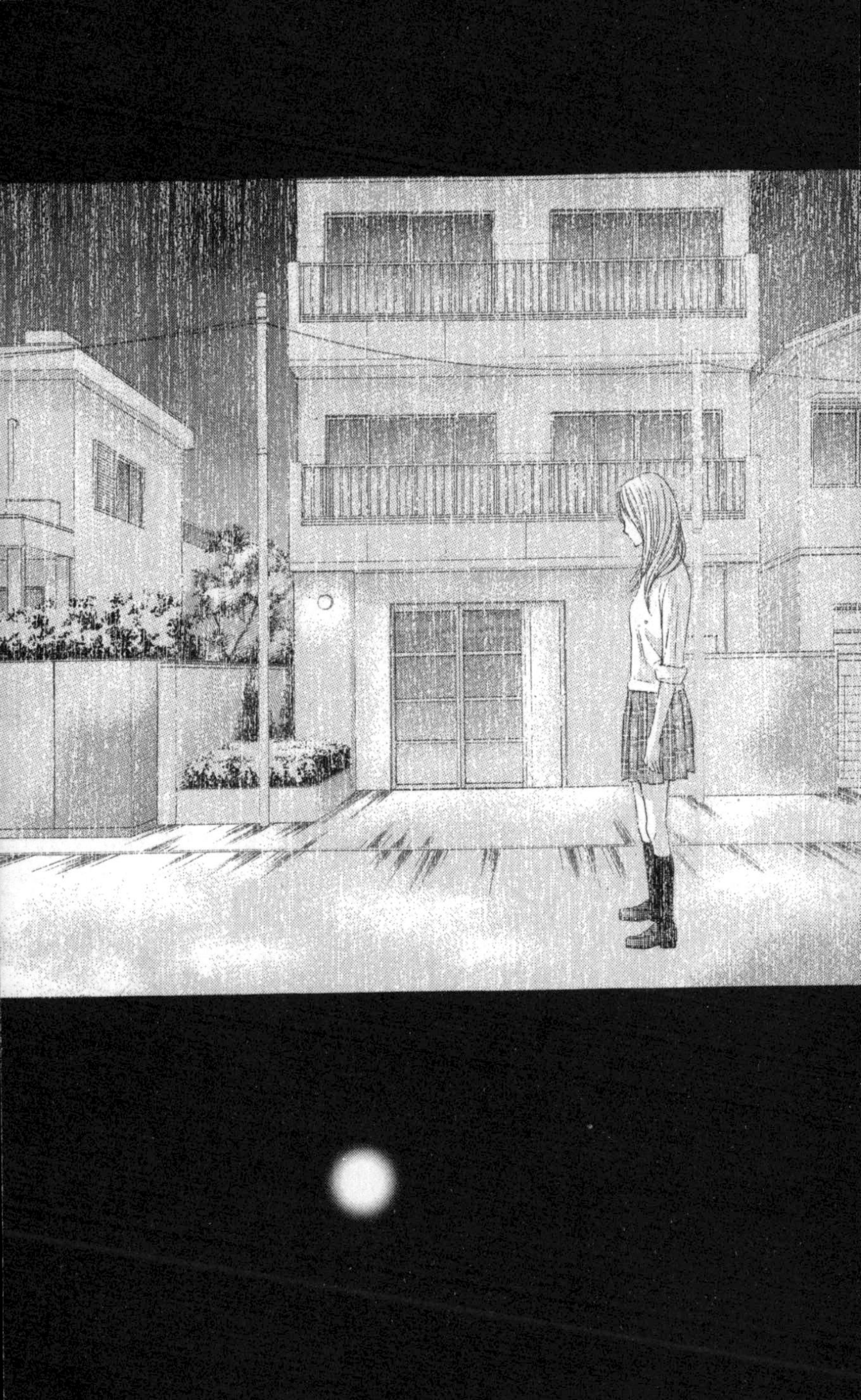

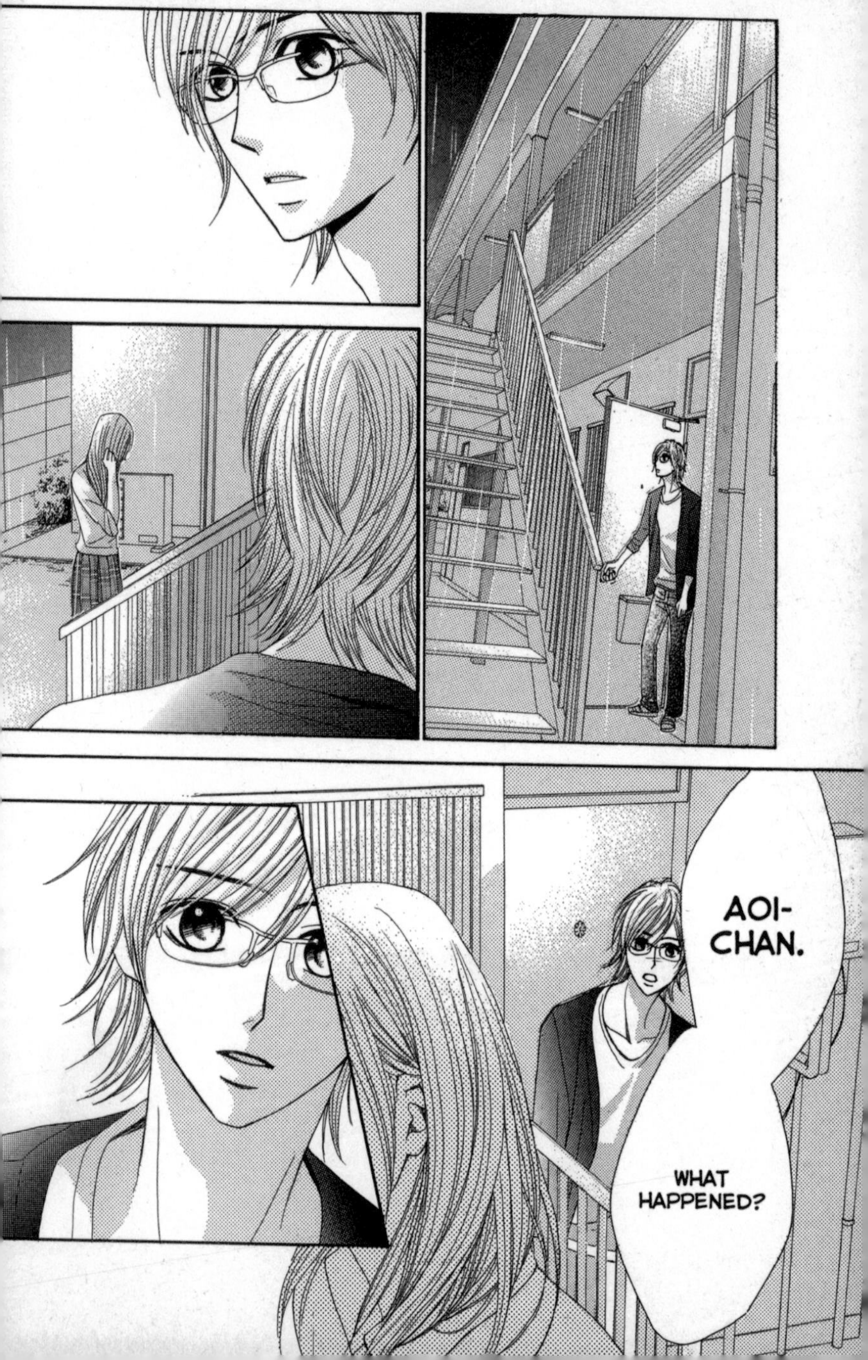
AOI-CHAN.
WHAT HAPPENED?

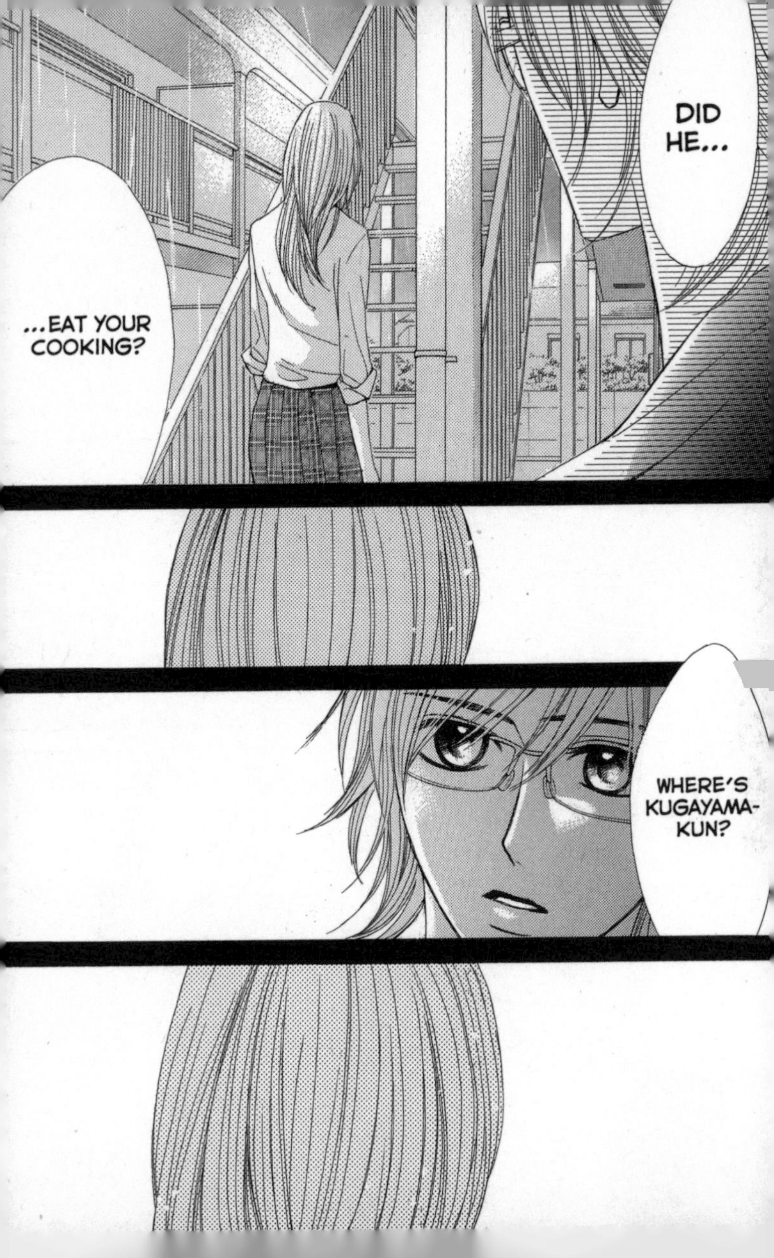
DID HE...
...EAT YOUR COOKING?
WHERE'S KUGAYAMA-KUN?

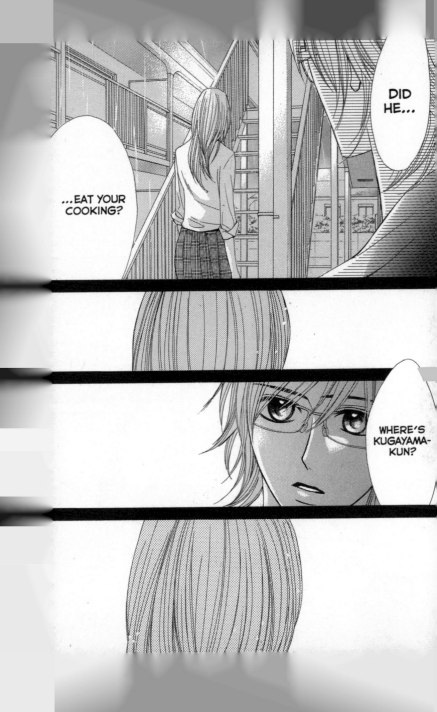

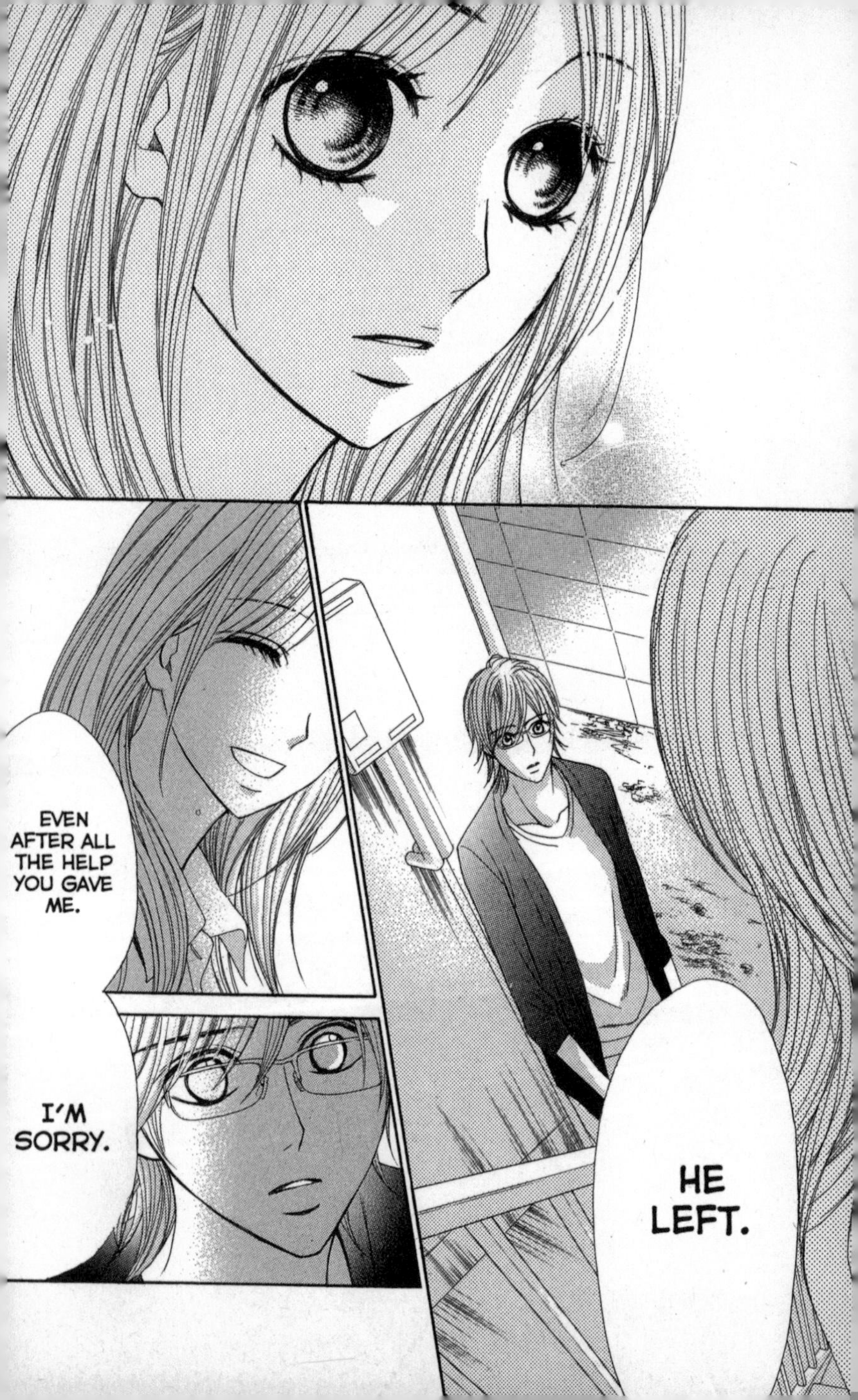
EVEN AFTER ALL THE HELP YOU GAVE ME.
I'M SORRY.
HE LEFT.

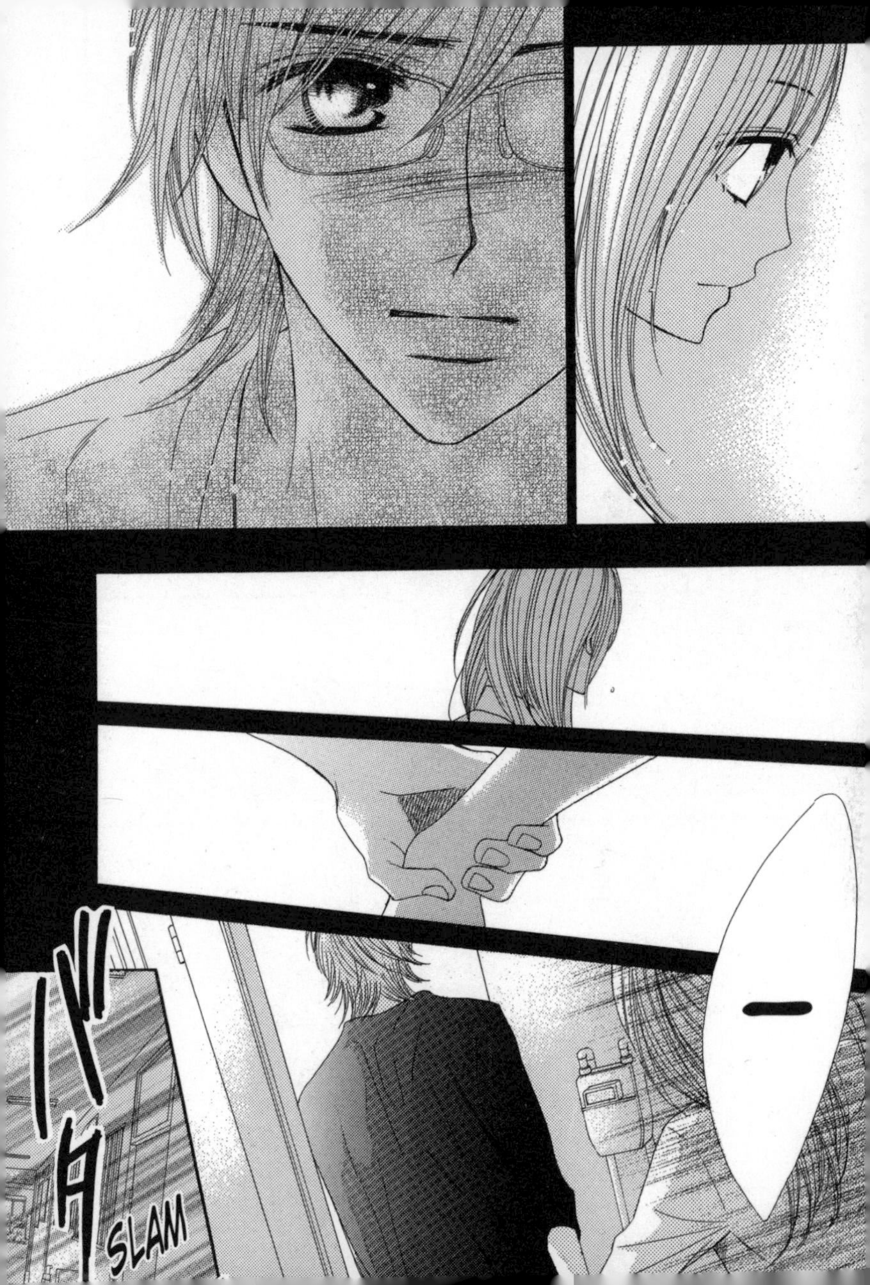
—
SLAM

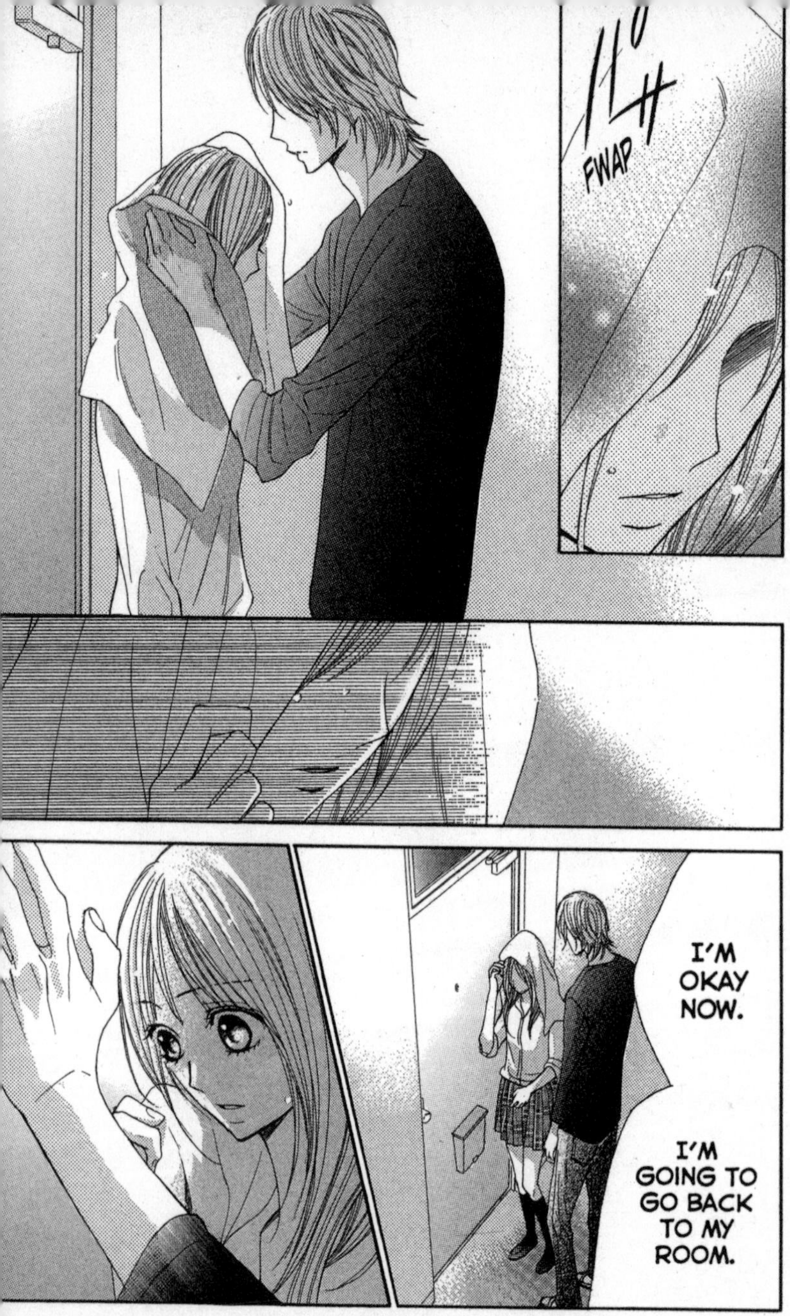
FWAP
I'M OKAY NOW.
I'M GOING TO GO BACK TO MY ROOM.

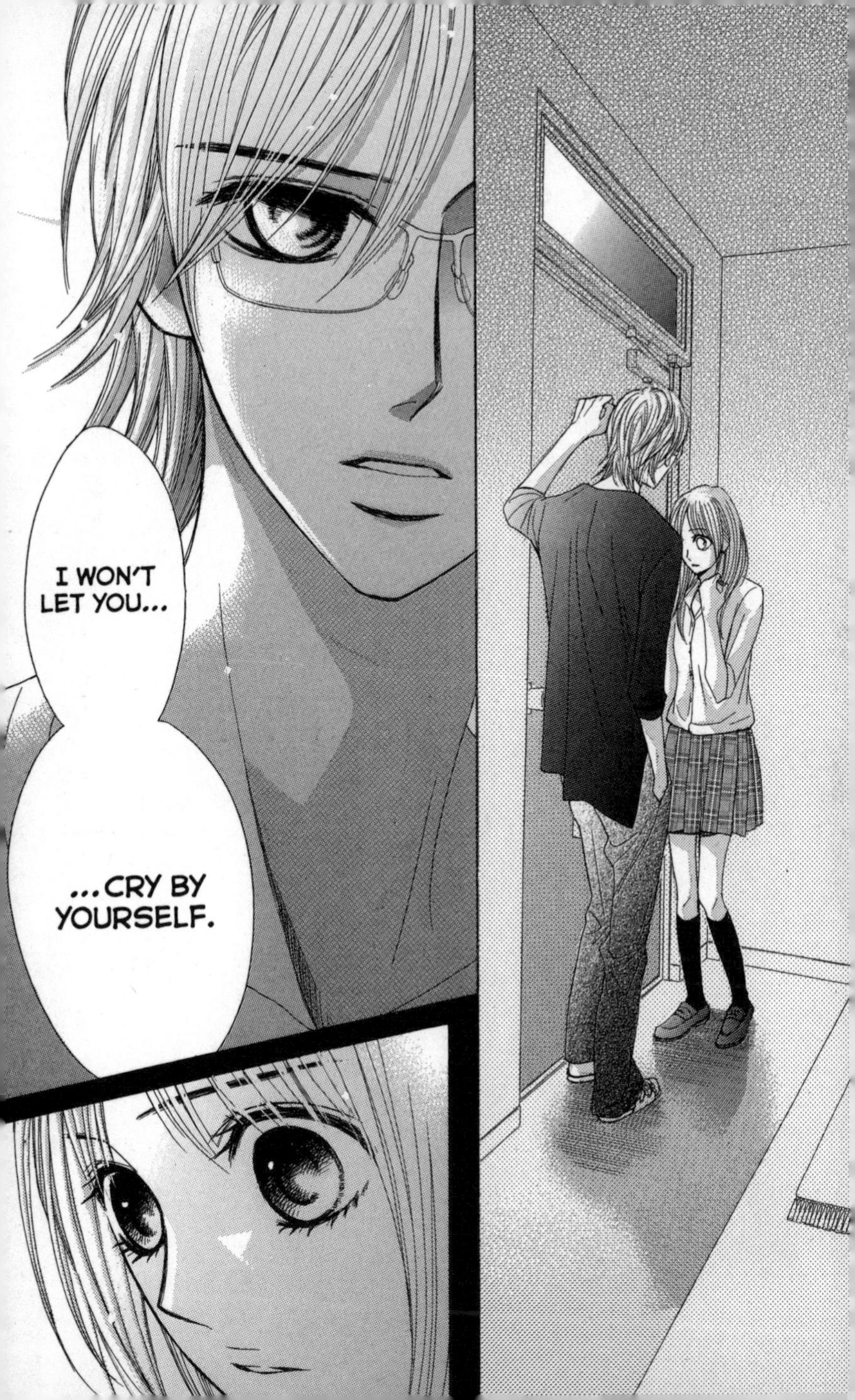
I WON'T LET YOU...
...CRY BY YOURSELF.

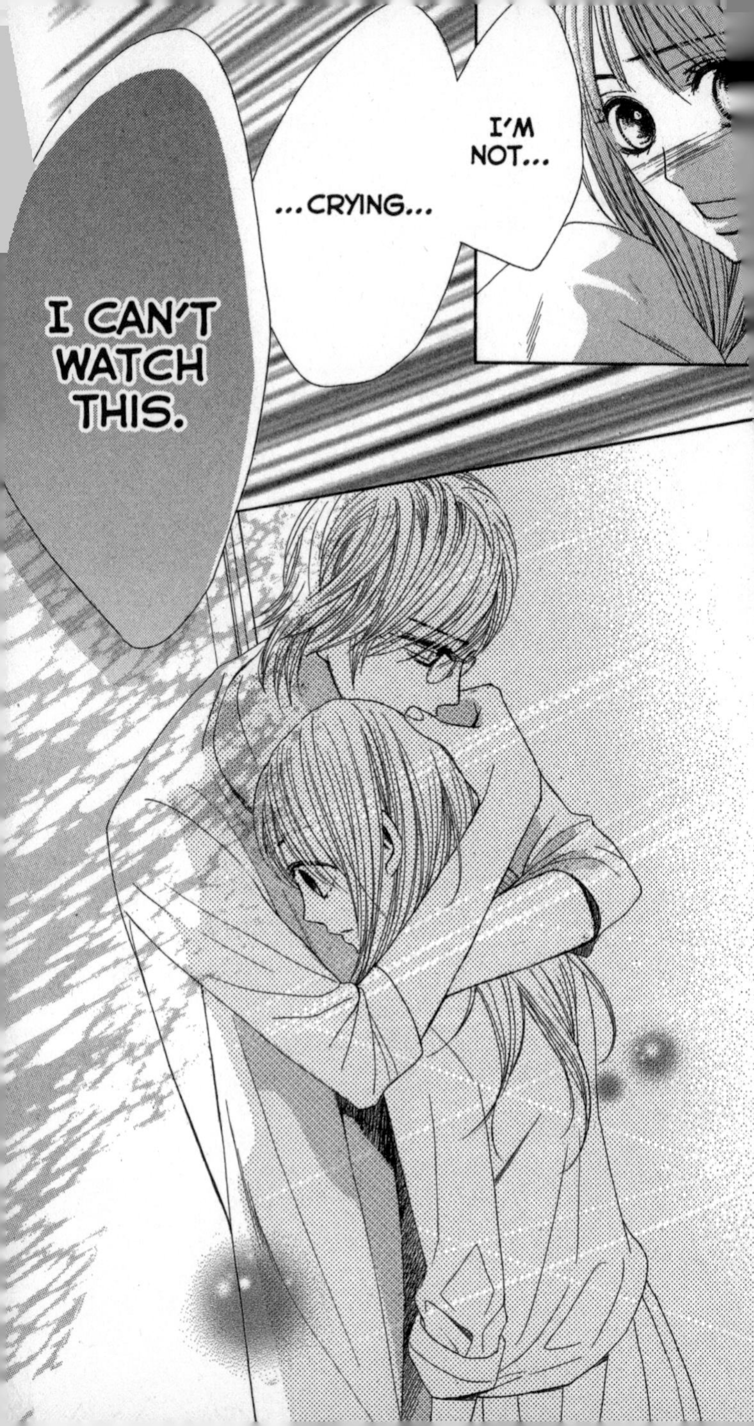
I'M NOT...
...CRYING...
I CAN'T WATCH THIS.

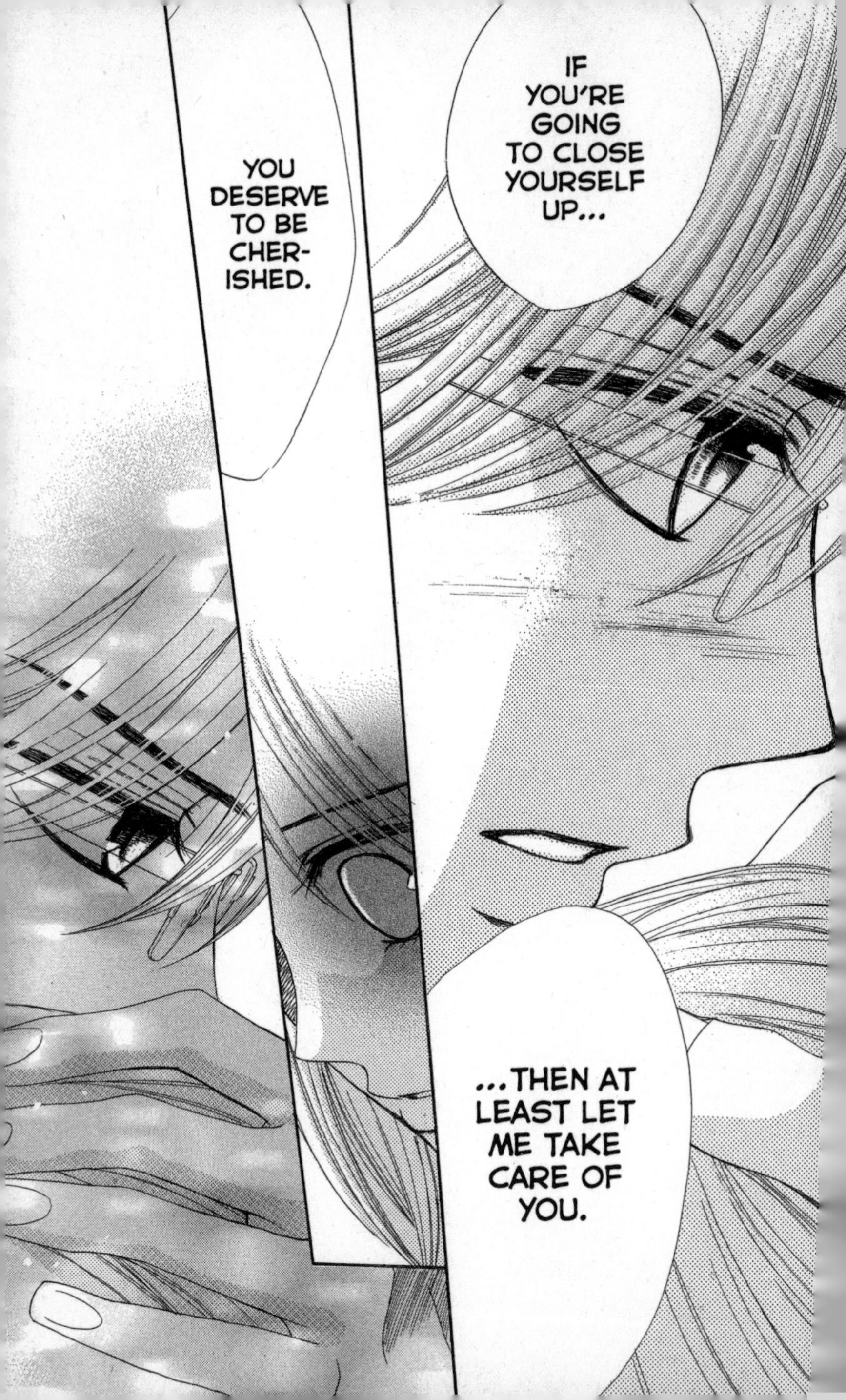
IF YOU'RE GOING TO CLOSE YOURSELF UP...
...THEN AT LEAST LET ME TAKE CARE OF YOU.
YOU DESERVE TO BE CHER-ISHED.

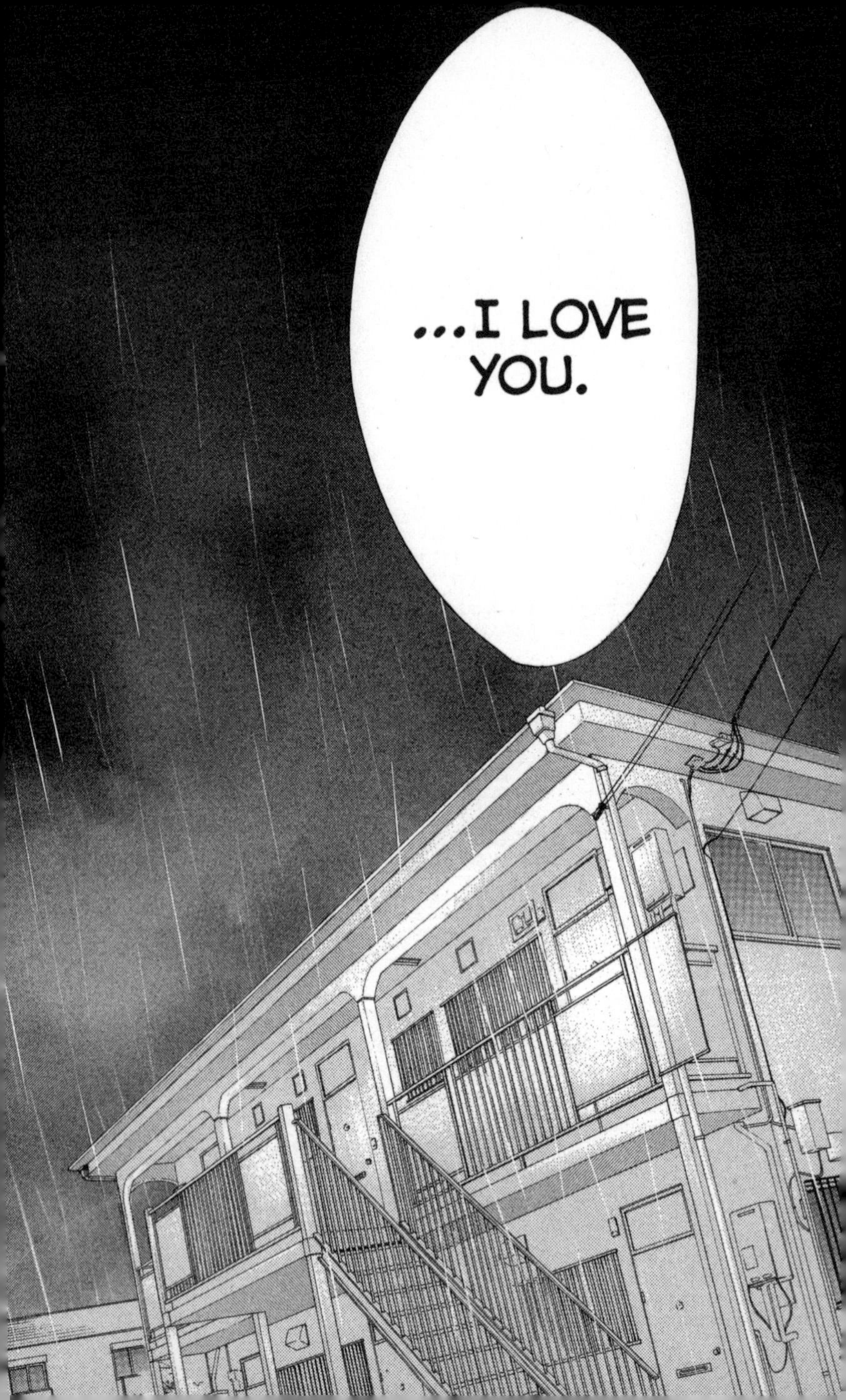
...I LOVE YOU.

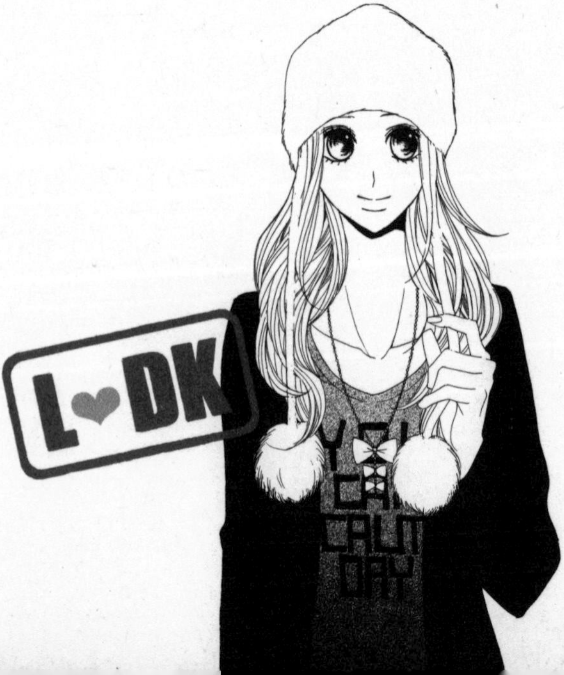
L♥DK

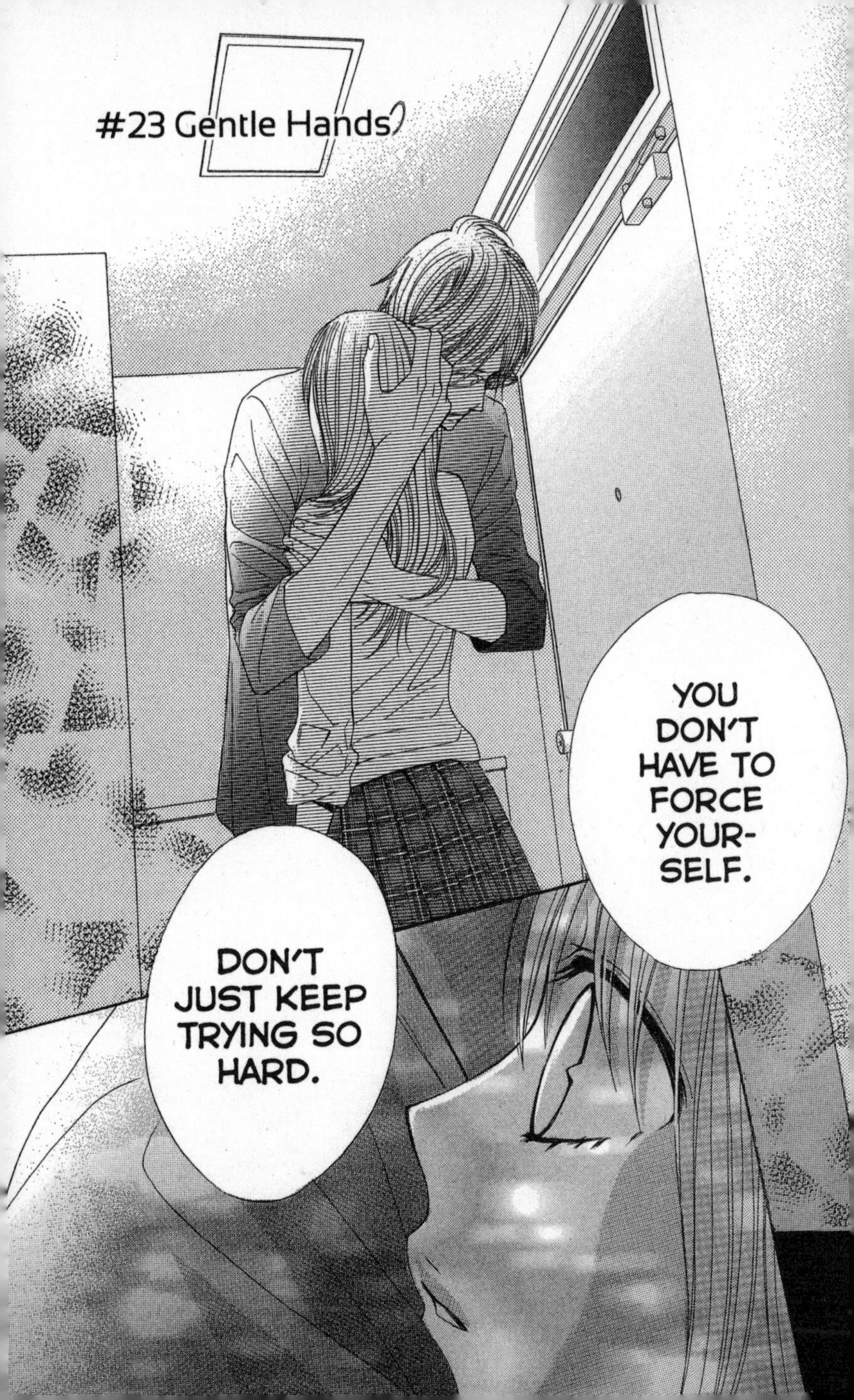
#23 Gentle Hands
YOU DON'T HAVE TO FORCE YOURSELF.
DON'T JUST KEEP TRYING SO HARD.

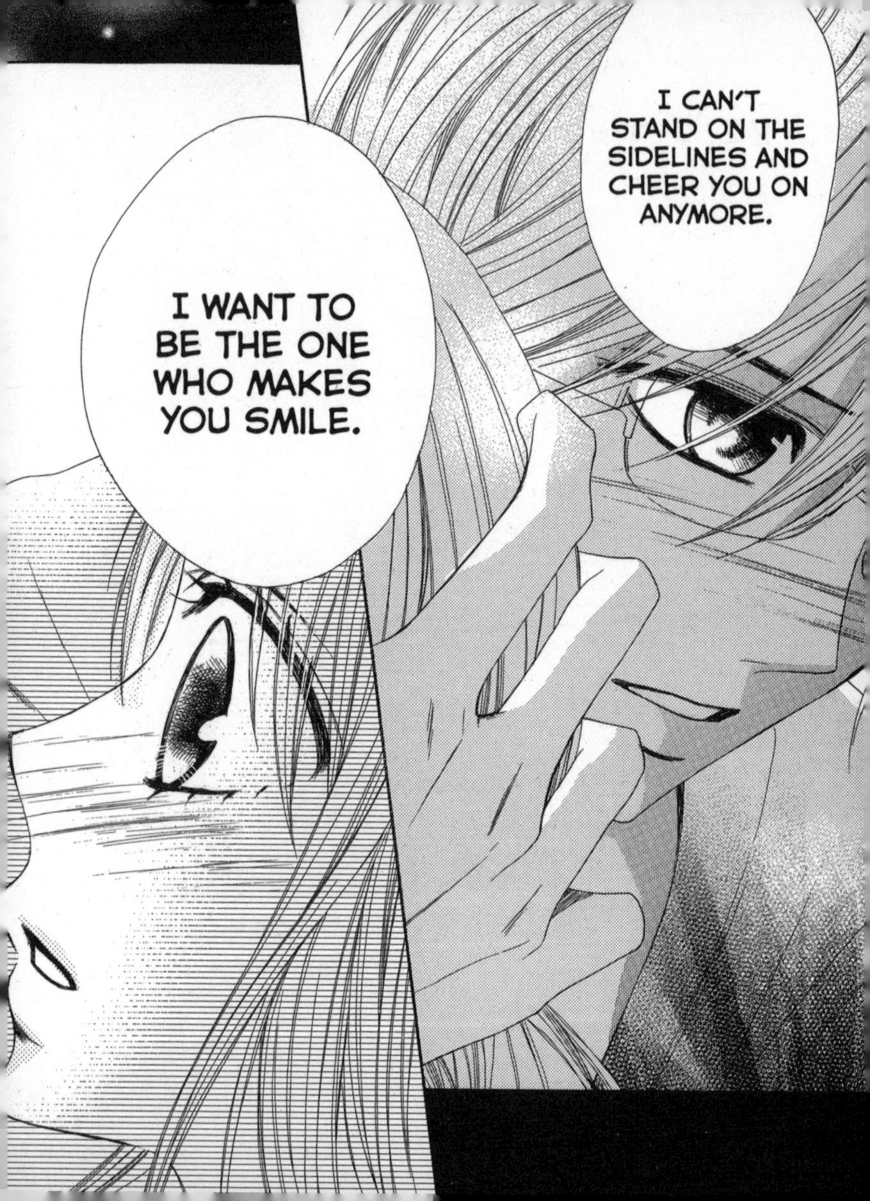
I CAN'T STAND ON THE SIDELINES AND CHEER YOU ON ANYMORE.
I WANT TO BE THE ONE WHO MAKES YOU SMILE.

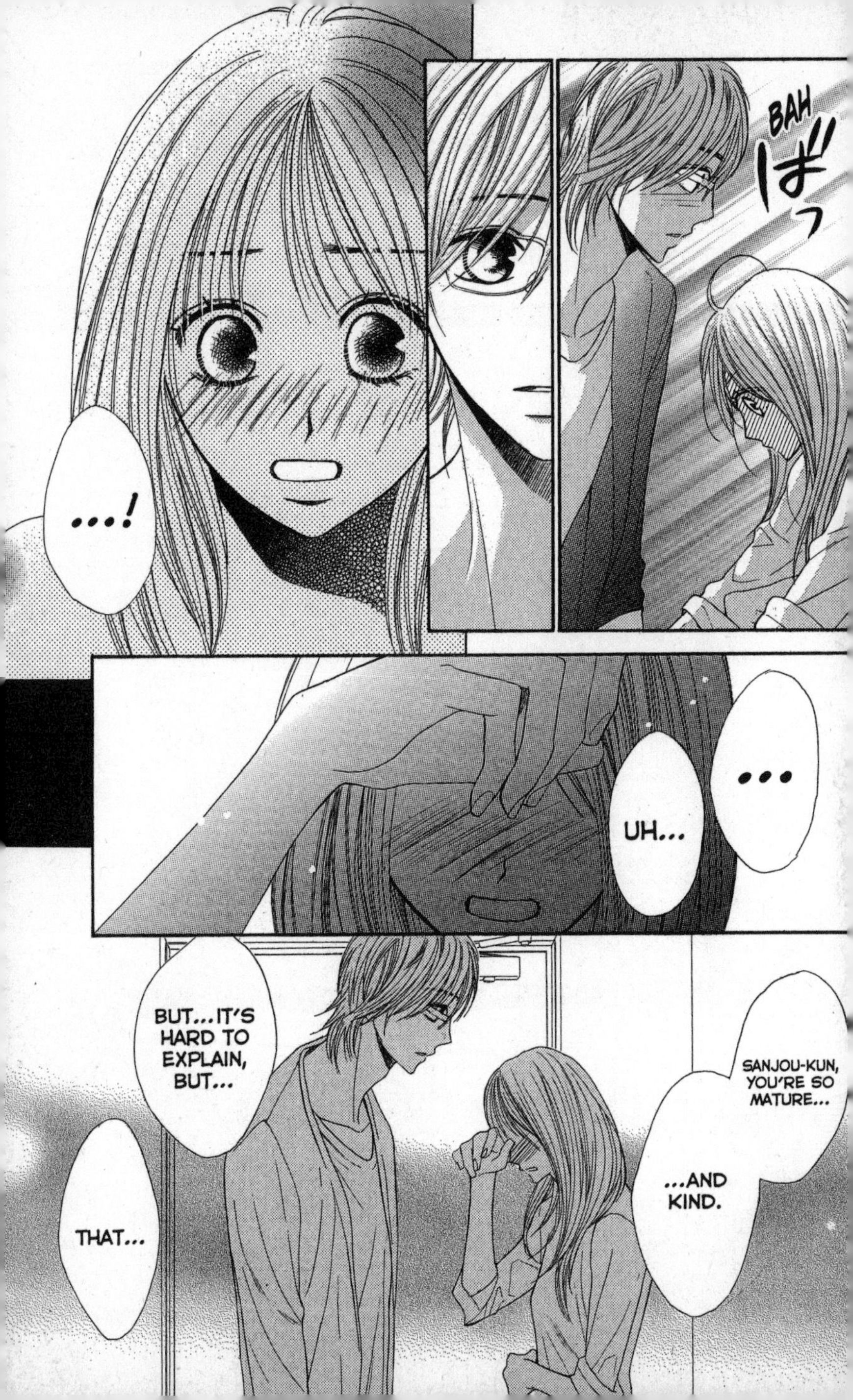
BAH
ぼっ
...!
...
UH...
SANJOU-KUN, YOU'RE SO MATURE...
...AND KIND.
BUT...IT'S HARD TO EXPLAIN, BUT...
THAT...

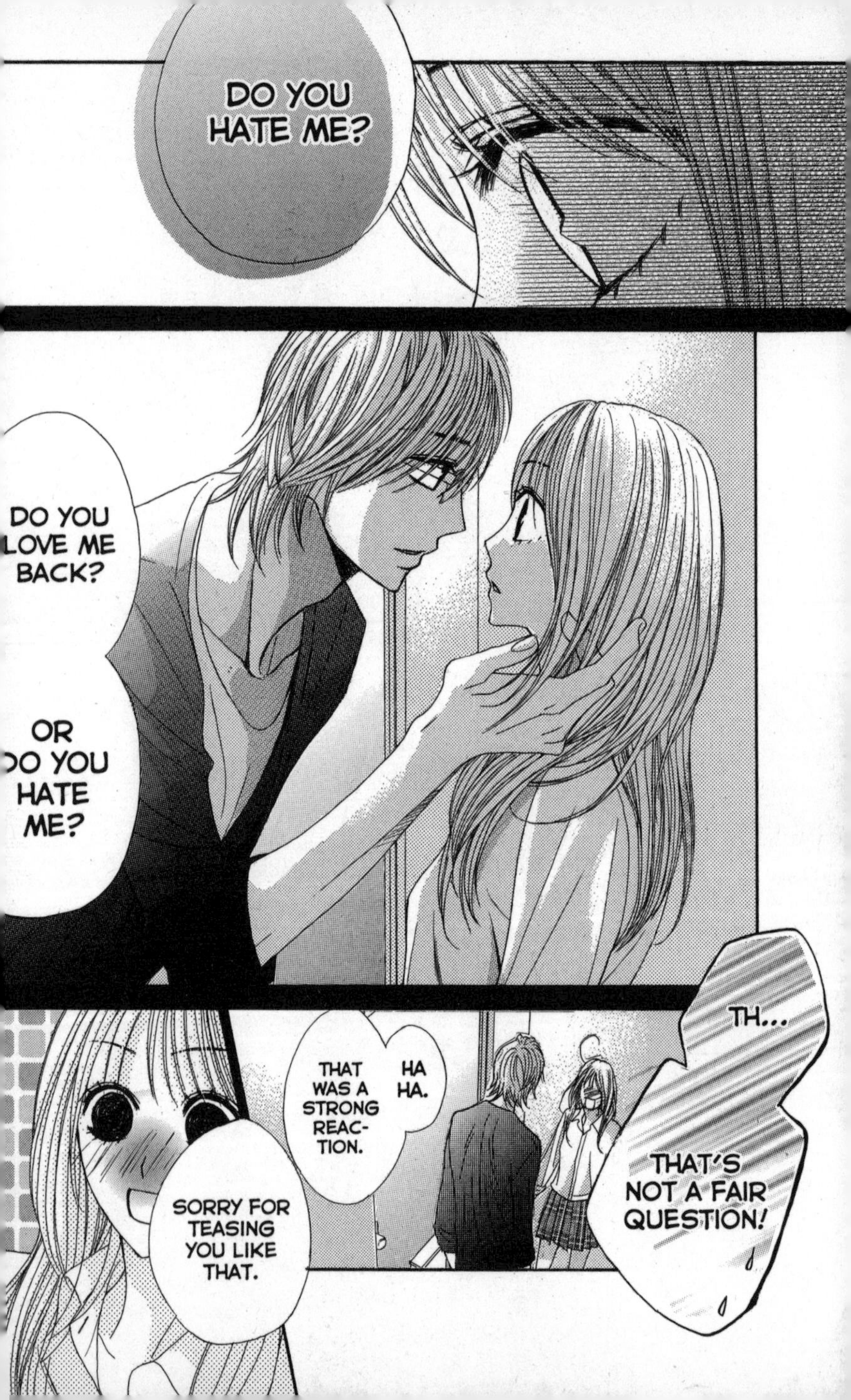
DO YOU HATE ME?
DO YOU LOVE ME BACK?
OR DO YOU HATE ME?
TH...
THAT'S NOT A FAIR QUESTION!
HA HA.
THAT WAS A STRONG REAC-TION.
SORRY FOR TEASING YOU LIKE THAT.

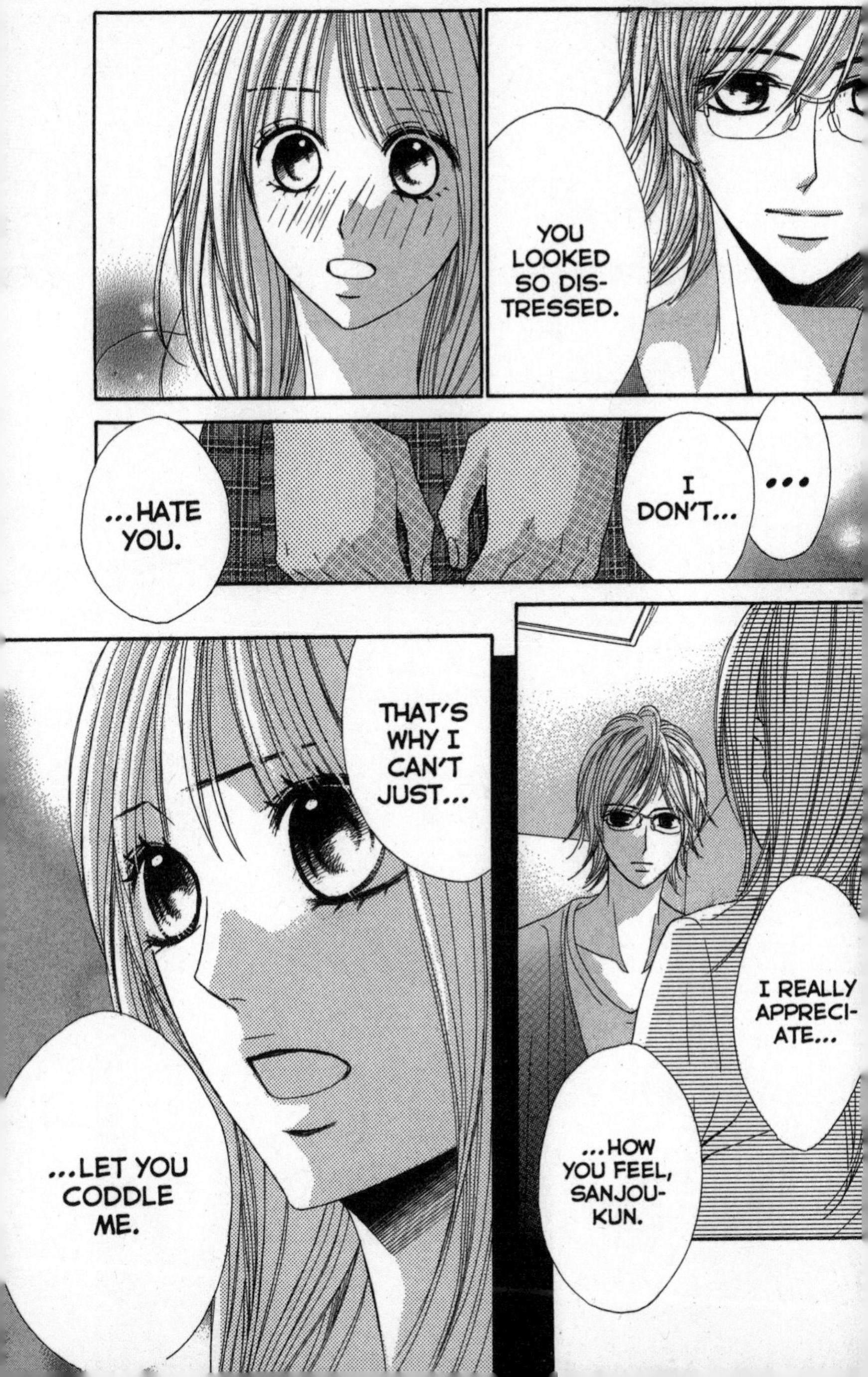
YOU LOOKED SO DIS-TRESSED.
...
I DON'T...
...HATE YOU.
I REALLY APPRECI-ATE...
...HOW YOU FEEL, SANJOU-KUN.
THAT'S WHY I CAN'T JUST...
...LET YOU CODDLE ME.

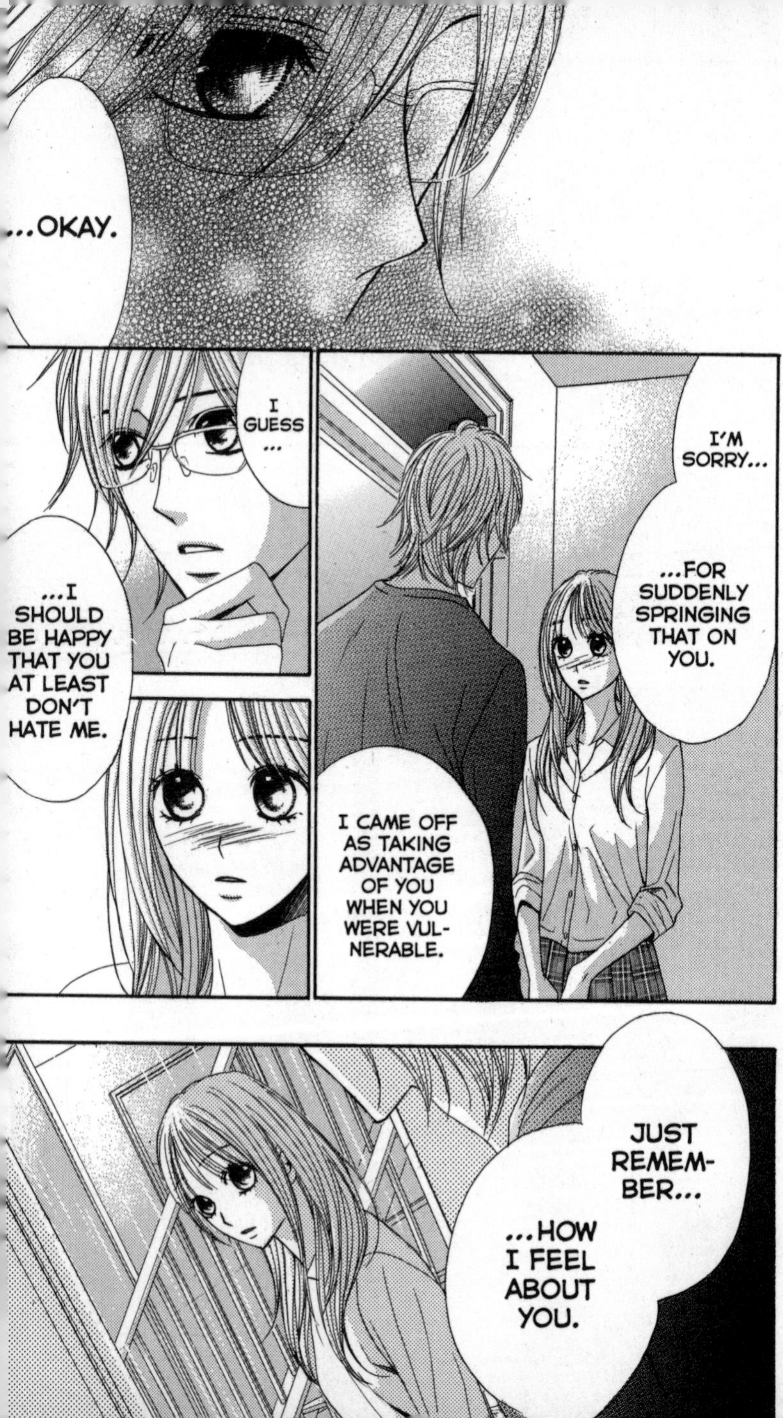
...OKAY.
I'M SORRY...
...FOR SUDDENLY SPRINGING THAT ON YOU.
I CAME OFF AS TAKING ADVANTAGE OF YOU WHEN YOU WERE VUL-NERABLE.
I GUESS ...
...I SHOULD BE HAPPY THAT YOU AT LEAST DON'T HATE ME.
JUST REMEM-BER...
...HOW I FEEL ABOUT YOU.

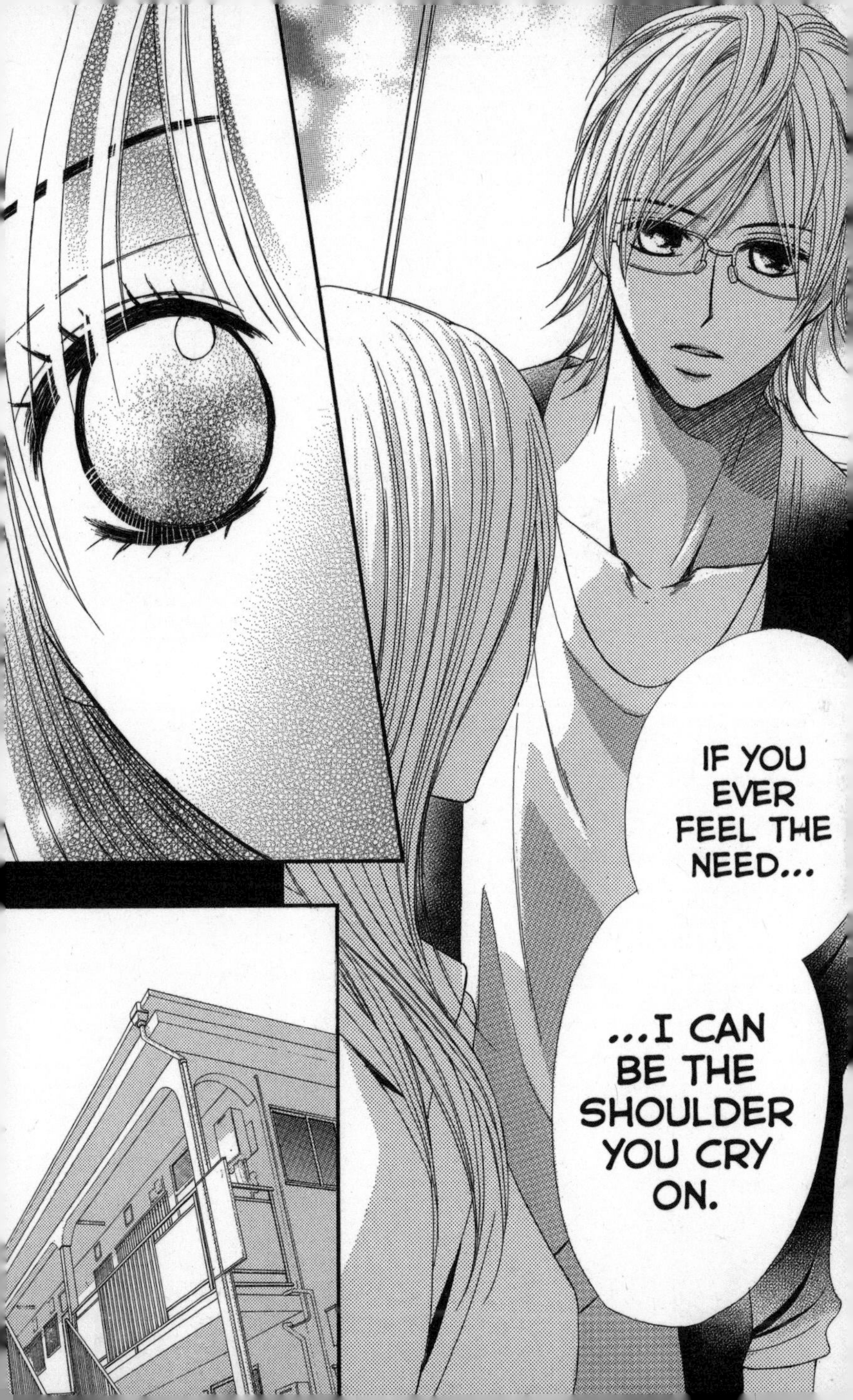
IF YOU EVER FEEL THE NEED...
...I CAN BE THE SHOULDER YOU CRY ON.

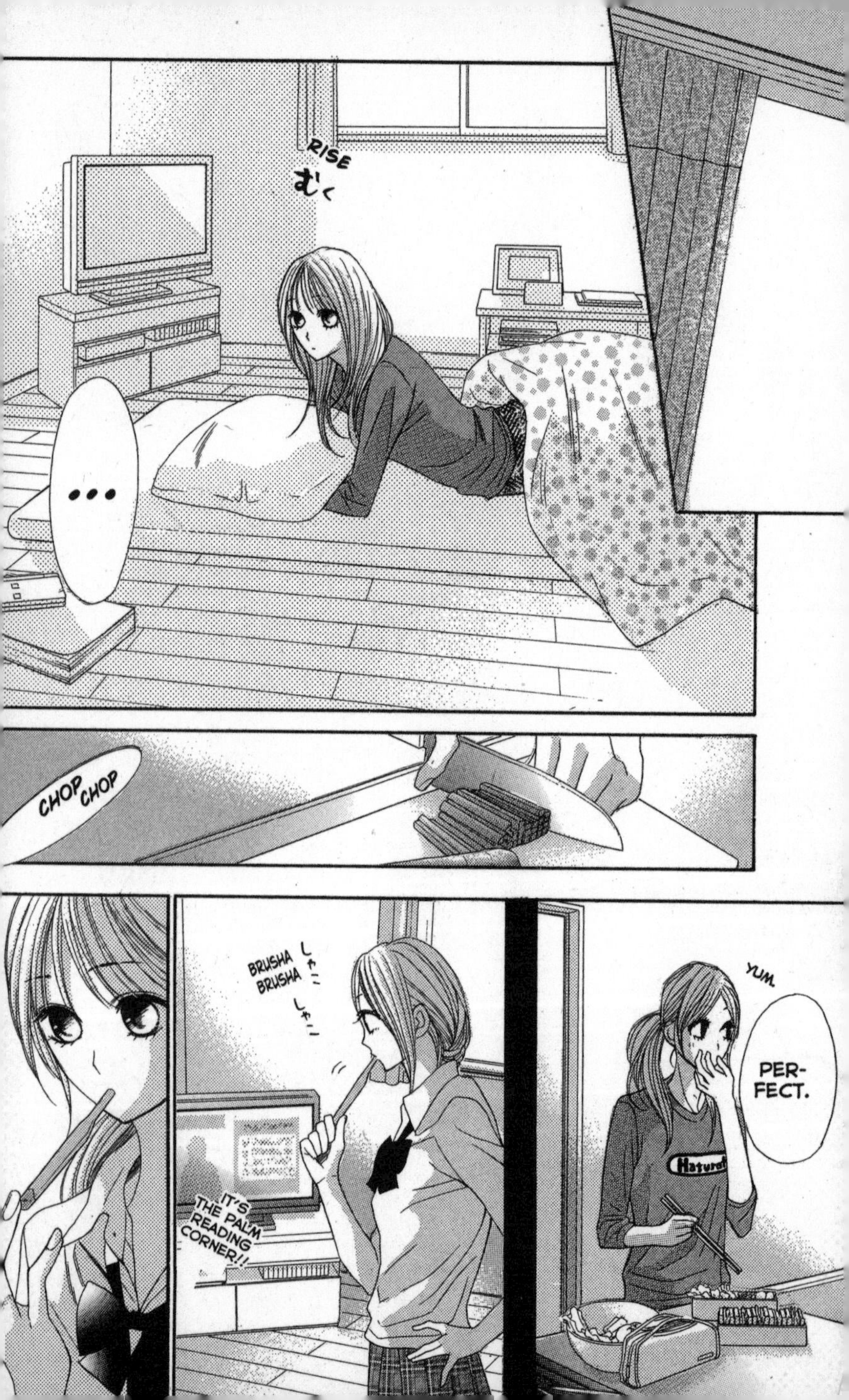
RISE
むく
...
CHOP CHOP
YUM.
PER-FECT.
BRUSHA BRUSHA
しゃこ しゃこ
IT'S THE PALM READING CORNER!!

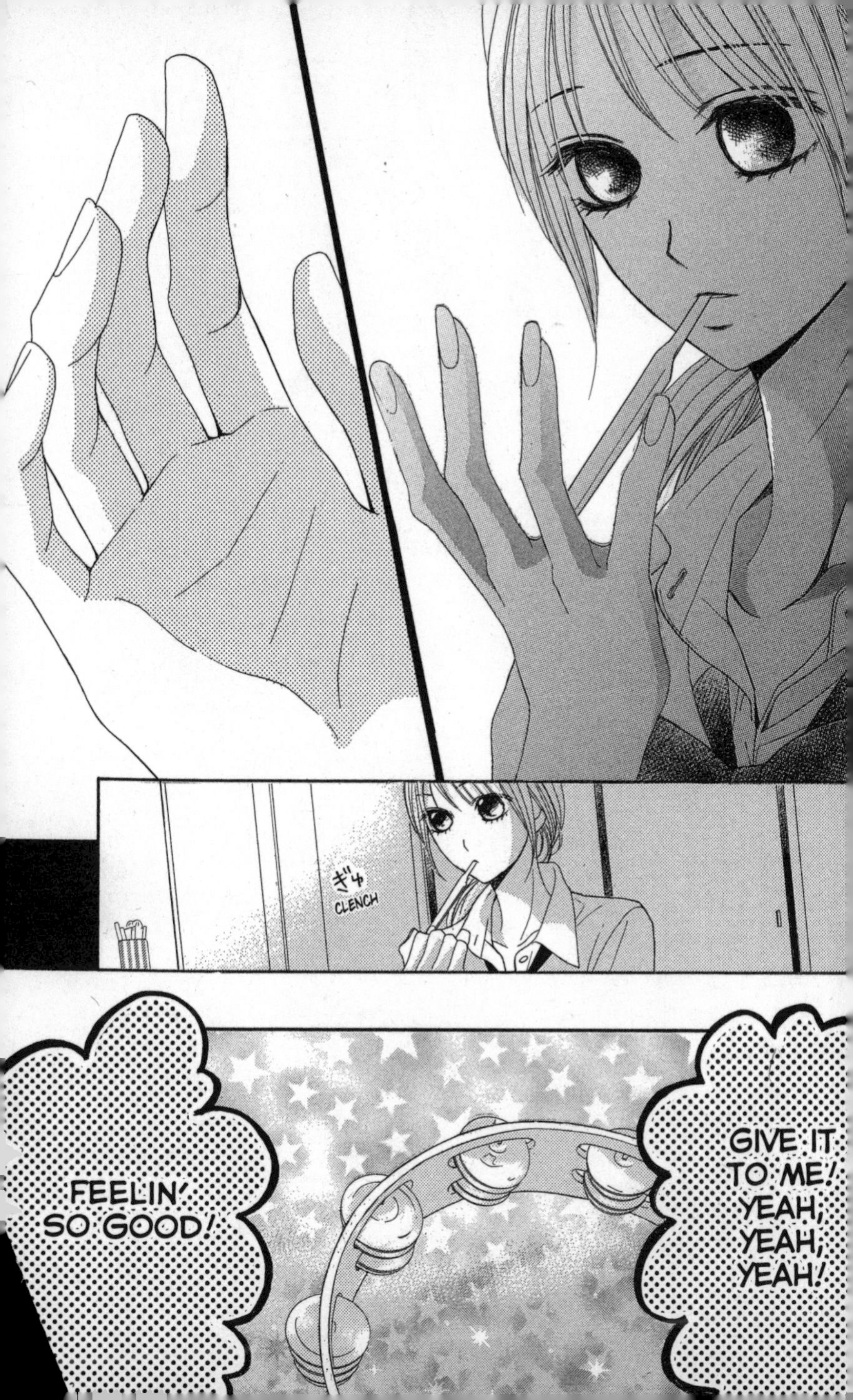
ぎゅ
CLENCH
GIVE IT TO ME! YEAH, YEAH, YEAH!
FEELIN' SO GOOD!

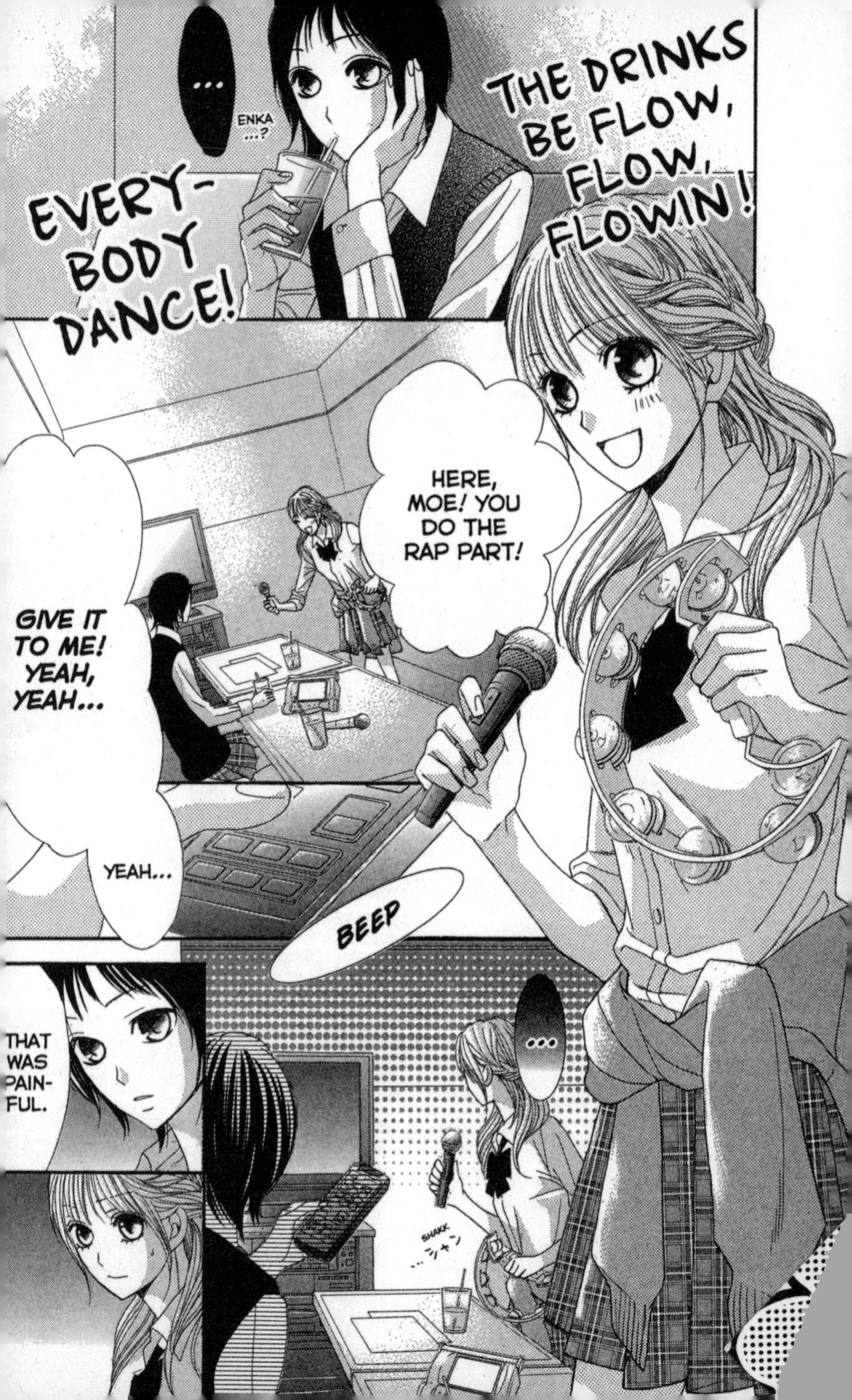
THE DRINKS BE FLOW, FLOW, FLOWIN!
...
ENKA ...?
EVERY-BODY DANCE!
HERE, MOE! YOU DO THE RAP PART!
GIVE IT TO ME! YEAH, YEAH...
YEAH...
BEEP
...
SHAKK
...シャン
THAT WAS PAIN-FUL.

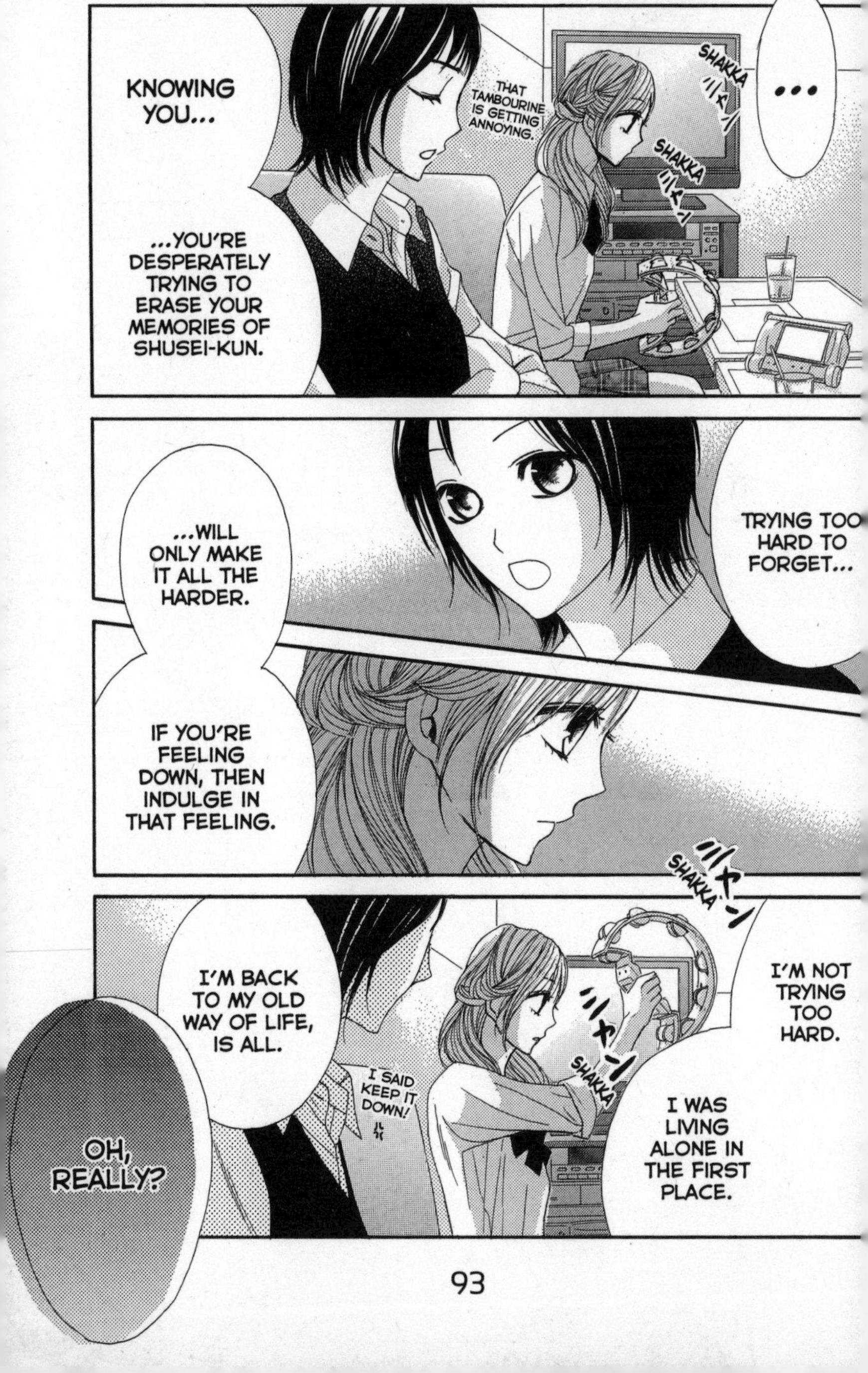
...
SHAKKA
SHAKKA
THAT TAMBOURINE IS GETTING ANNOYING.
KNOWING YOU...
...YOU'RE DESPERATELY TRYING TO ERASE YOUR MEMORIES OF SHUSEI-KUN.
TRYING TOO HARD TO FORGET...
...WILL ONLY MAKE IT ALL THE HARDER.
IF YOU'RE FEELING DOWN, THEN INDULGE IN THAT FEELING.
SHAKKA
I'M NOT TRYING TOO HARD.
I WAS LIVING ALONE IN THE FIRST PLACE.
SHAKKA
I SAID KEEP IT DOWN!
I'M BACK TO MY OLD WAY OF LIFE, IS ALL.
OH, REALLY?

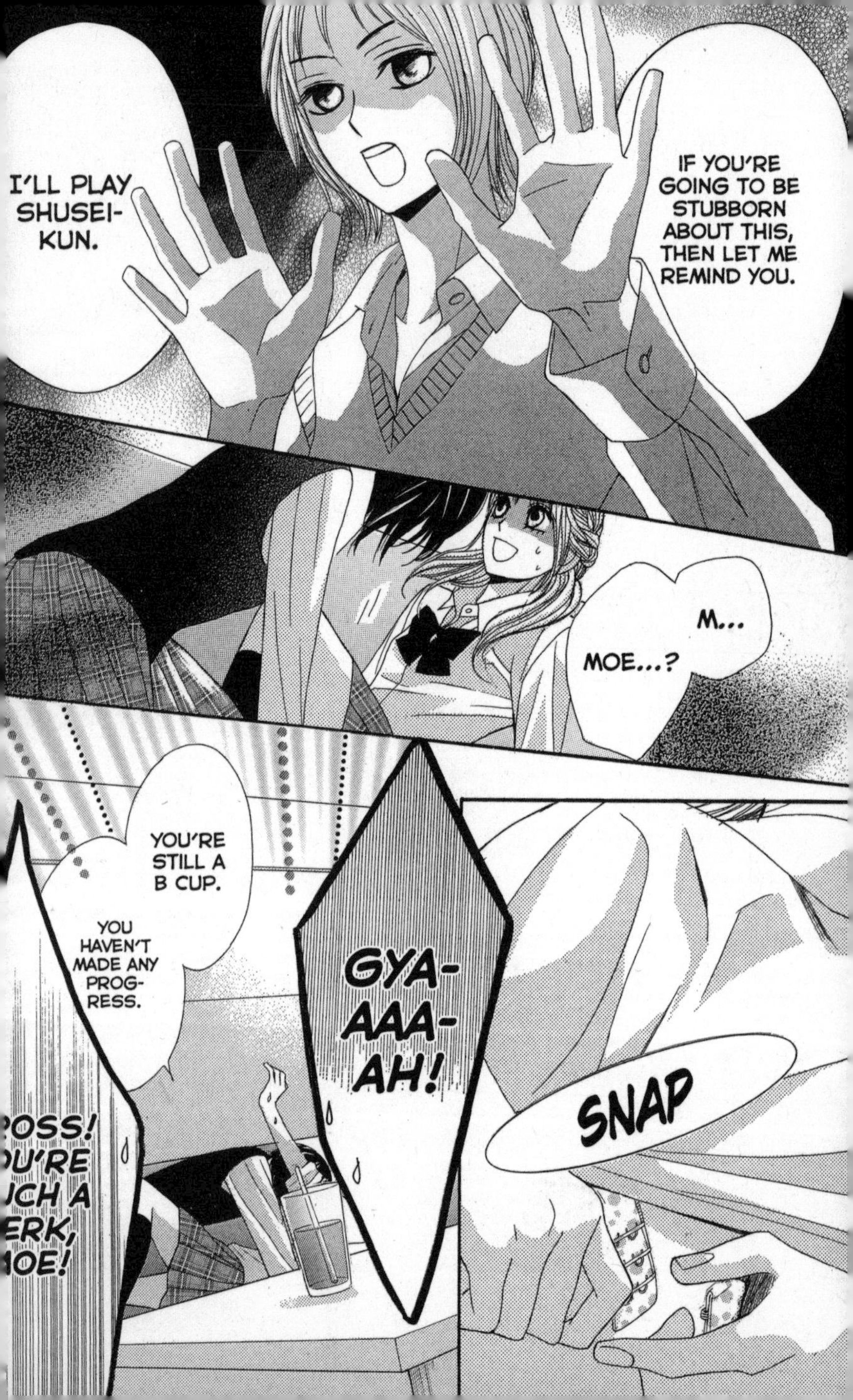
IF YOU'RE GOING TO BE STUBBORN ABOUT THIS, THEN LET ME REMIND YOU.
I'LL PLAY SHUSEI-KUN.
M... MOE...?
SNAP
YOU'RE STILL A B CUP.
YOU HAVEN'T MADE ANY PROG-RESS.
GYA-AAA-AH!

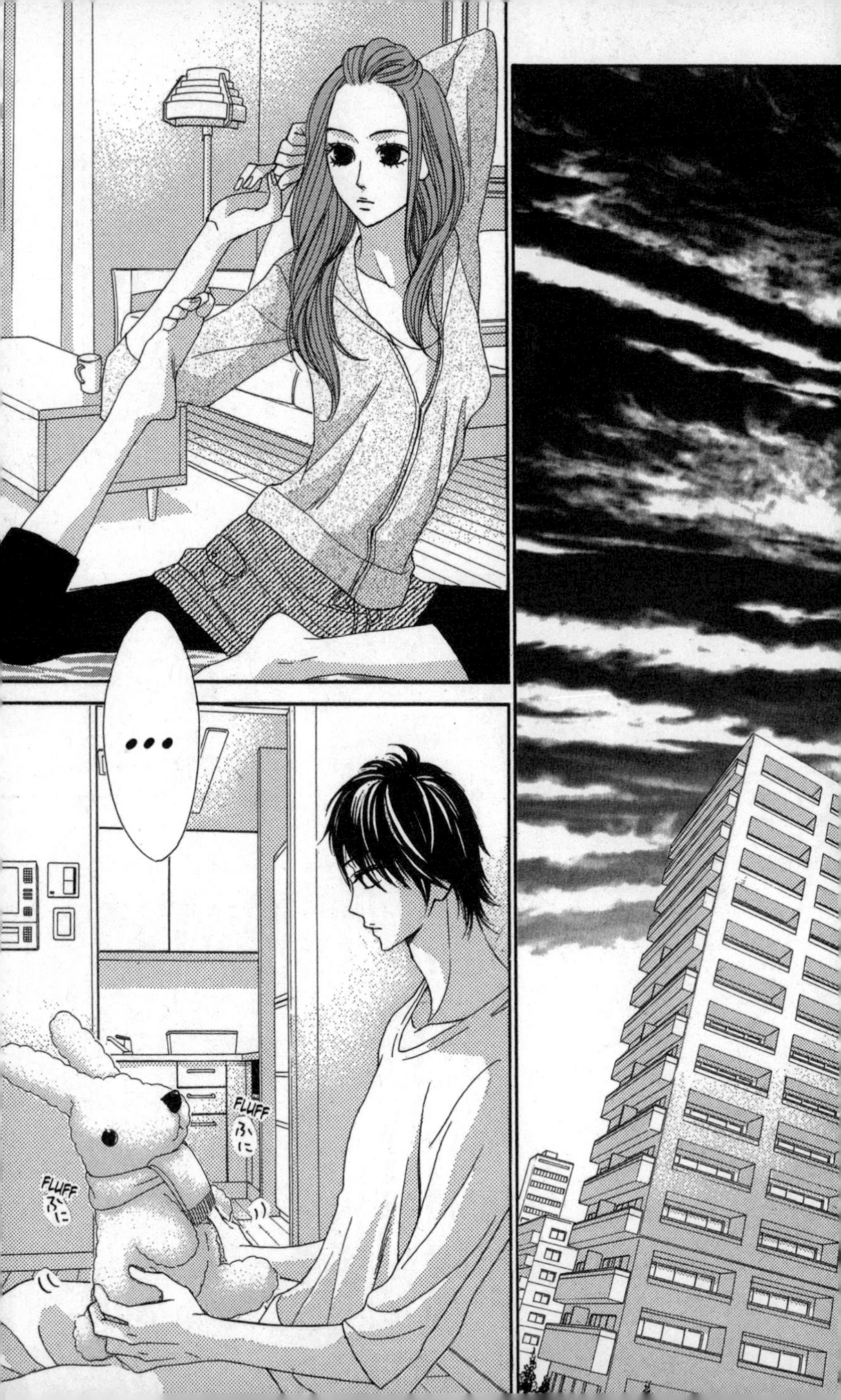
...
FLUFF ふに
FLUFF ふに

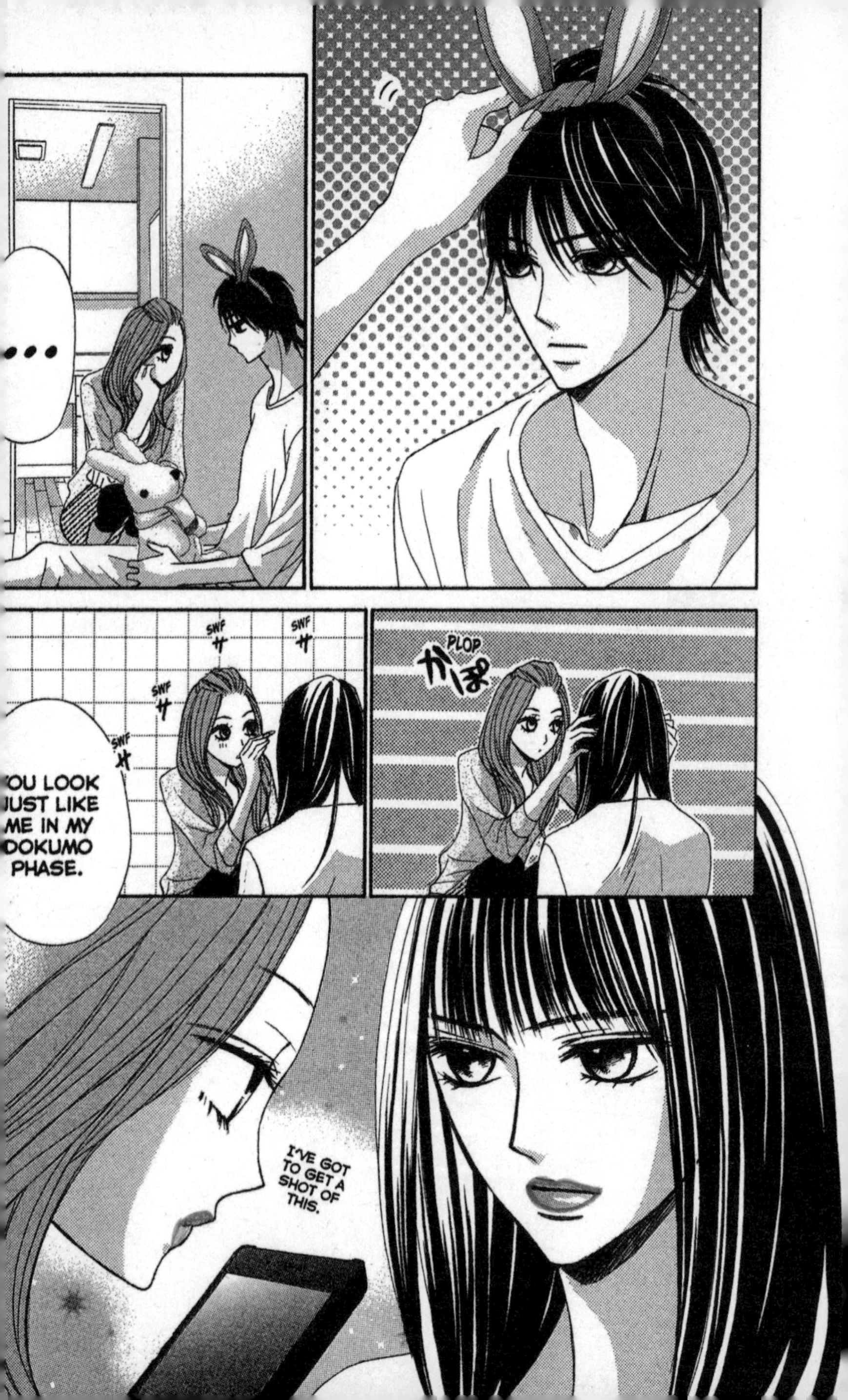
...
PLOP
かぽ
SWF
SWF
SWF
SWF
YOU LOOK JUST LIKE ME IN MY DOKUMO PHASE.
I'VE GOT TO GET A SHOT OF THIS.

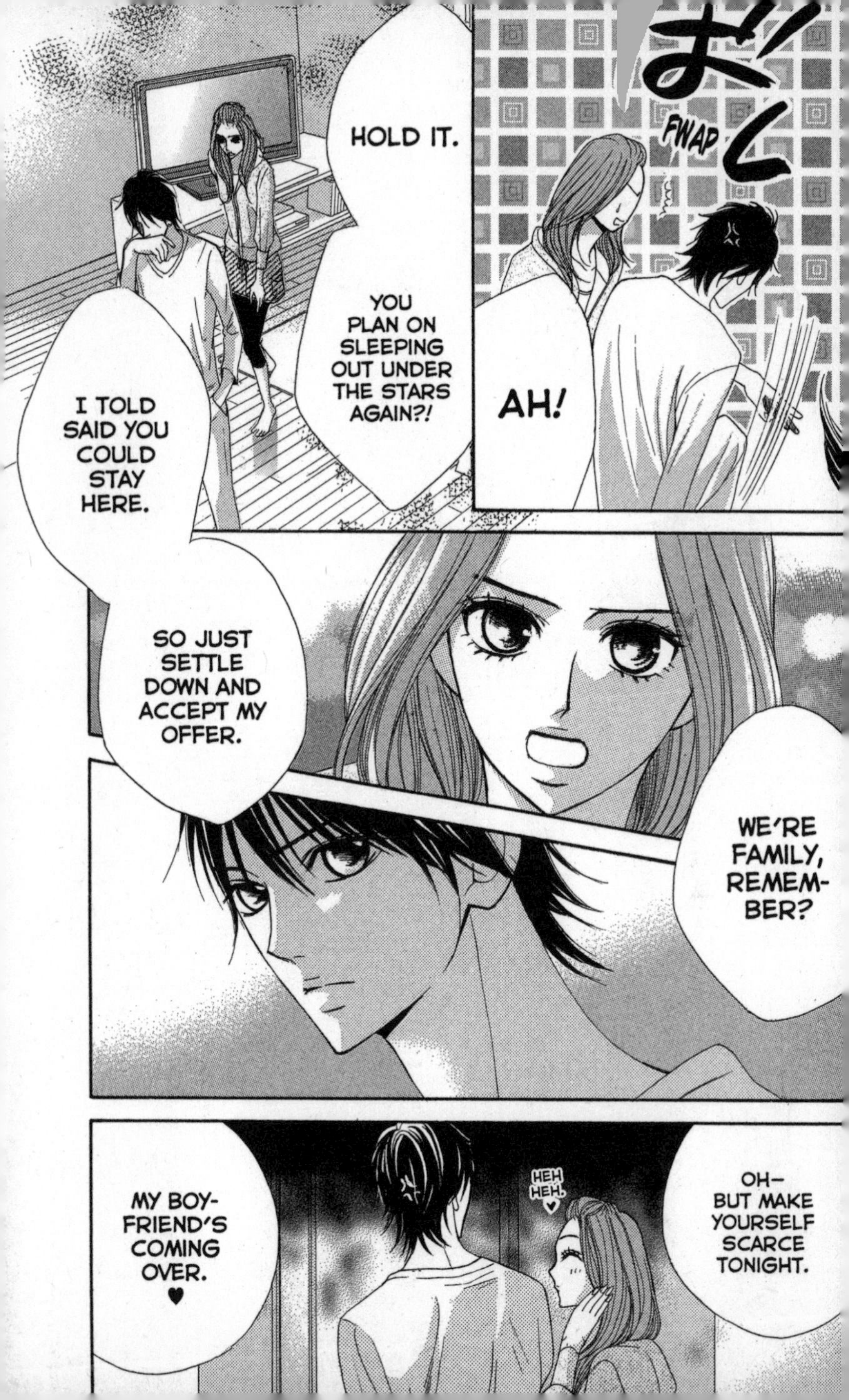
FWAP
AH!
HOLD IT.
YOU PLAN ON SLEEPING OUT UNDER THE STARS AGAIN?!
I TOLD SAID YOU COULD STAY HERE.
SO JUST SETTLE DOWN AND ACCEPT MY OFFER.
WE'RE FAMILY, REMEMBER?
OH— BUT MAKE YOURSELF SCARCE TONIGHT.
HEH HEH. ♥
MY BOY-FRIEND'S COMING OVER. ♥

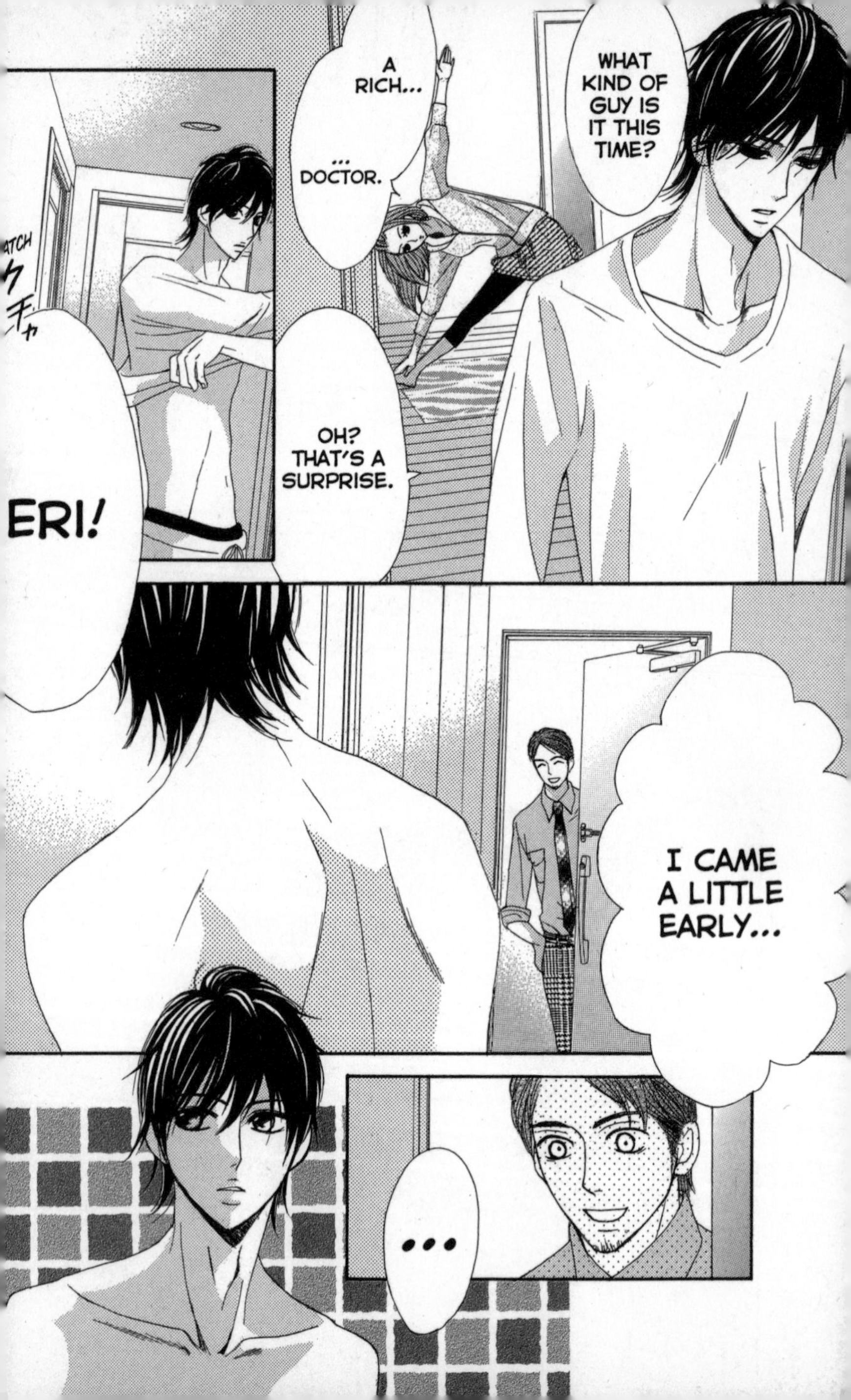
WHAT KIND OF GUY IS IT THIS TIME?
A RICH... ... DOCTOR.
OH? THAT'S A SURPRISE.
ATCH
カチャ
ERI!
I CAME A LITTLE EARLY...
...

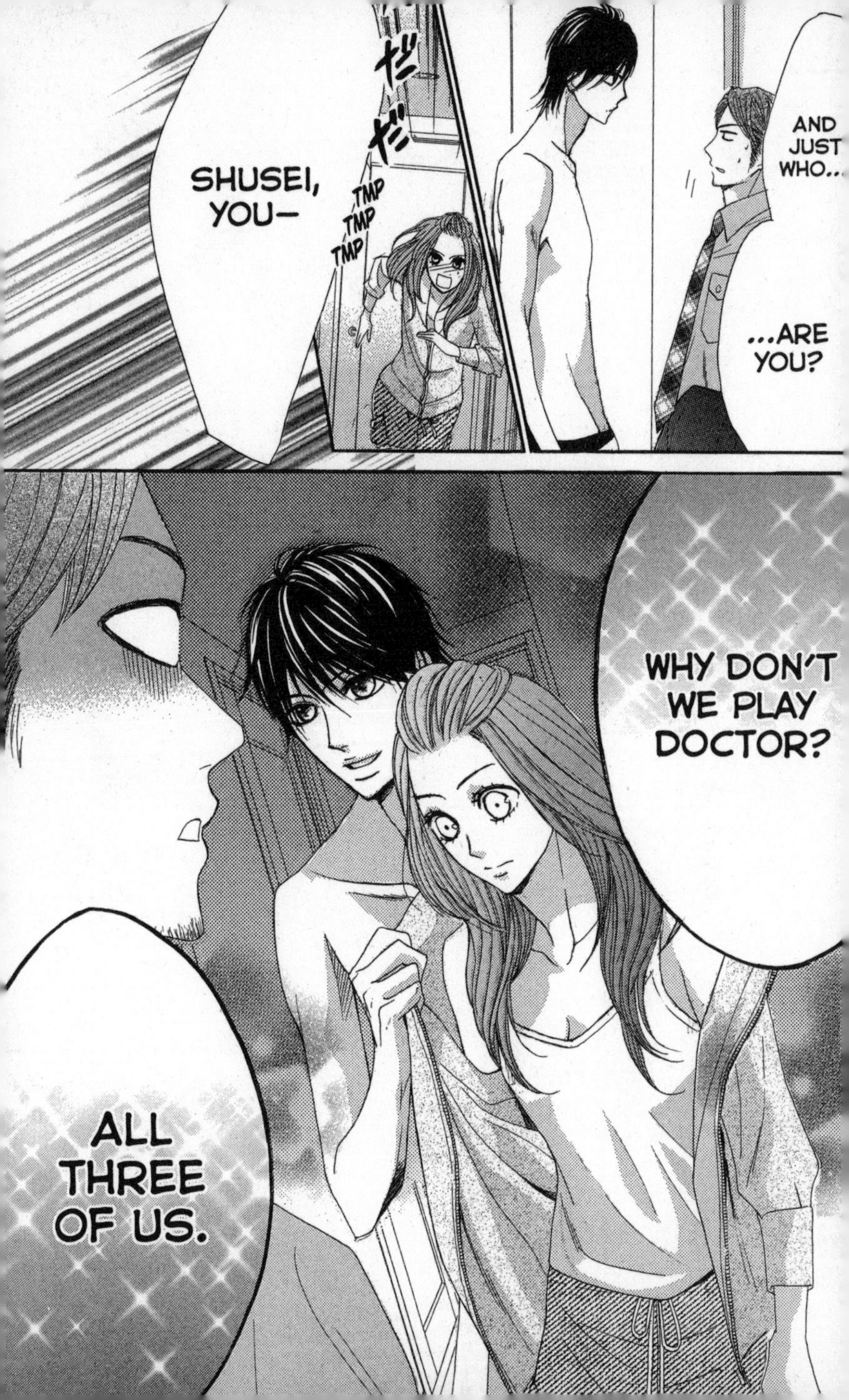
AND JUST WHO...
...ARE YOU?
SHUSEI, YOU—
TMP TMP TMP
WHY DON'T WE PLAY DOCTOR?
ALL THREE OF US.

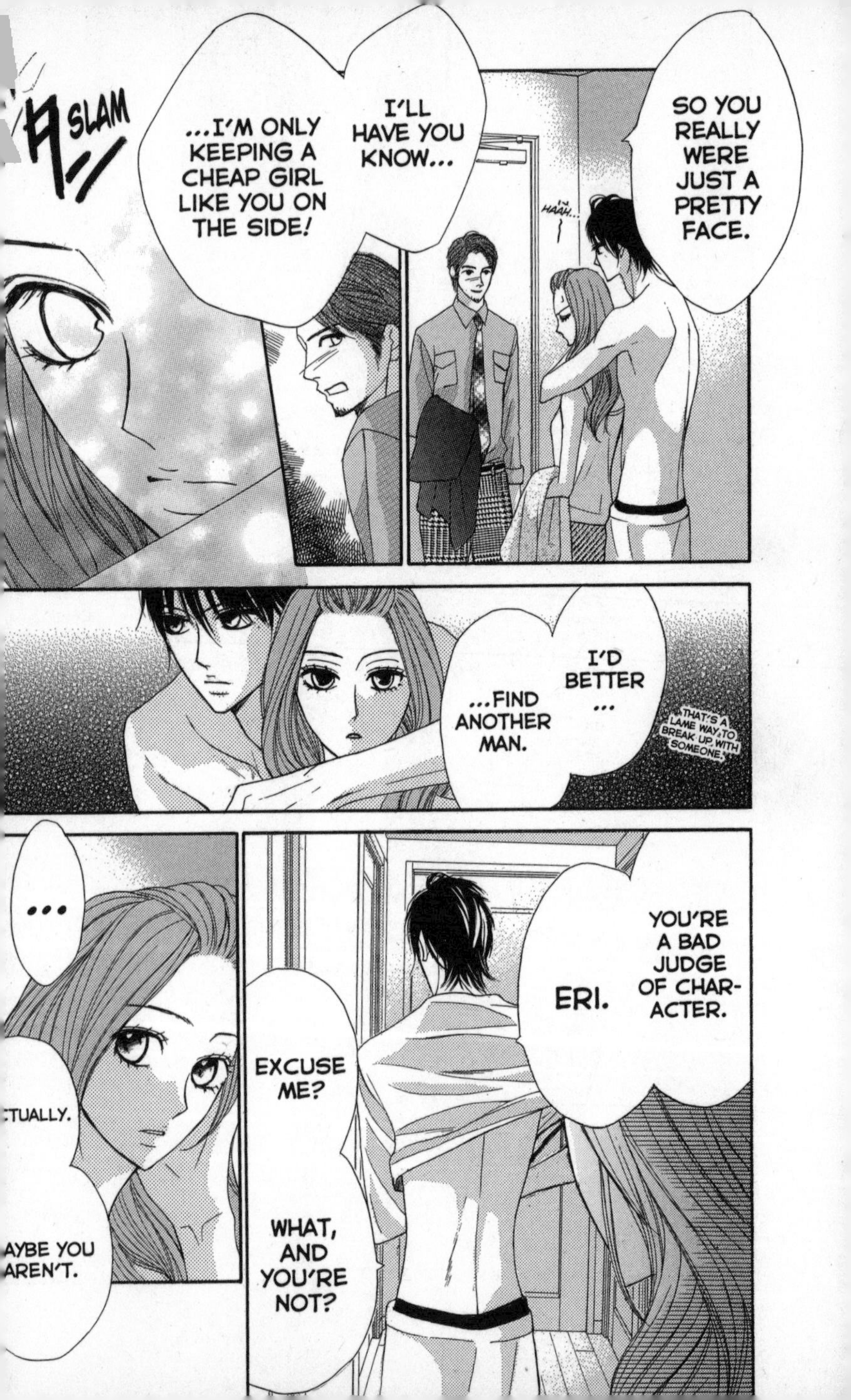
SO YOU REALLY WERE JUST A PRETTY FACE.
HAAH...
I'LL HAVE YOU KNOW...
...I'M ONLY KEEPING A CHEAP GIRL LIKE YOU ON THE SIDE!
SLAM
THAT'S A LAME WAY TO BREAK UP WITH SOMEONE.
I'D BETTER...
...FIND ANOTHER MAN.
YOU'RE A BAD JUDGE OF CHARACTER.
ERI.
EXCUSE ME?
WHAT, AND YOU'RE NOT?
...
CTUALLY.
AYBE YOU AREN'T.

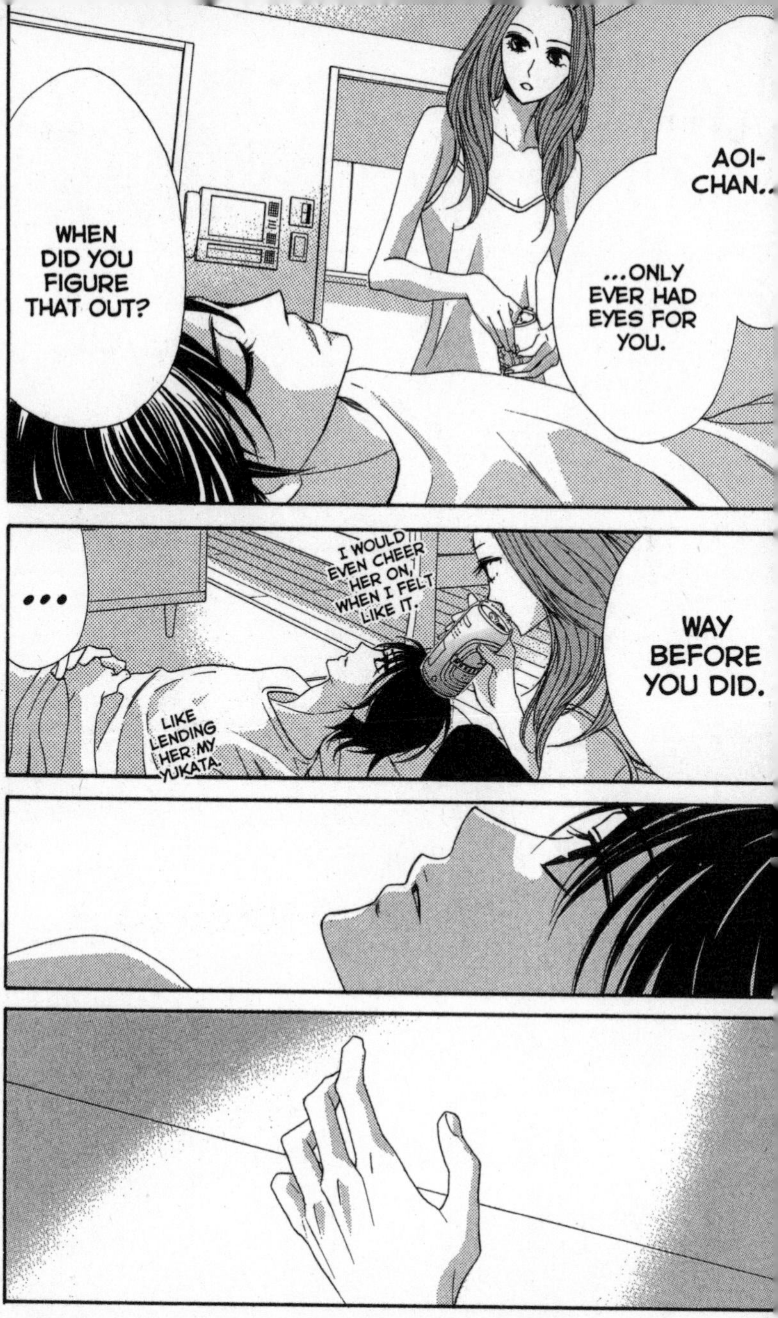
AOI-CHAN...
...ONLY EVER HAD EYES FOR YOU.
WHEN DID YOU FIGURE THAT OUT?
WAY BEFORE YOU DID.
I WOULD EVEN CHEER HER ON, WHEN I FELT LIKE IT.
LIKE LENDING HER MY YUKATA.
...

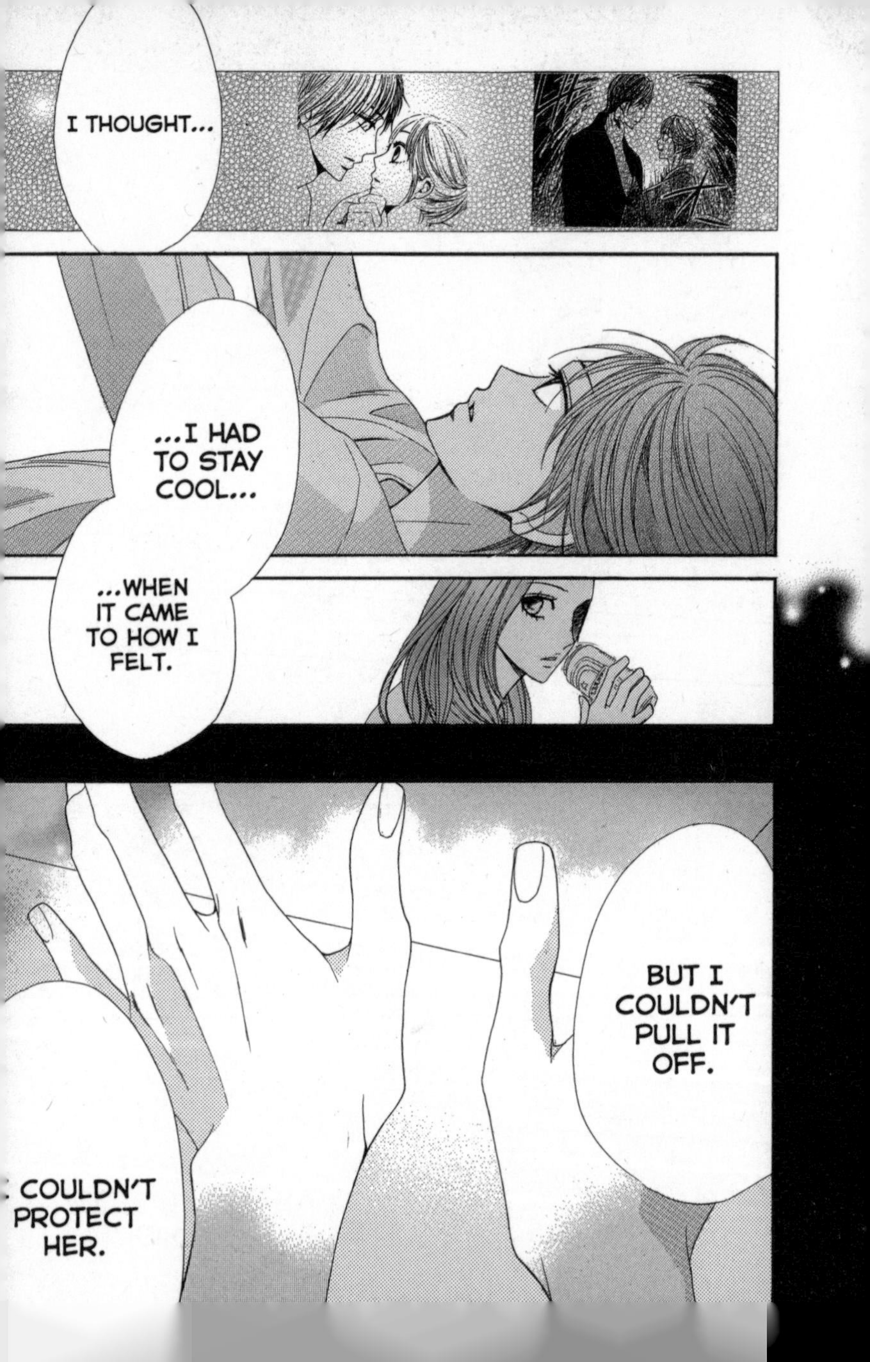
I THOUGHT...
...I HAD TO STAY COOL...
...WHEN IT CAME TO HOW I FELT.
BUT I COULDN'T PULL IT OFF.
COULDN'T PROTECT HER.

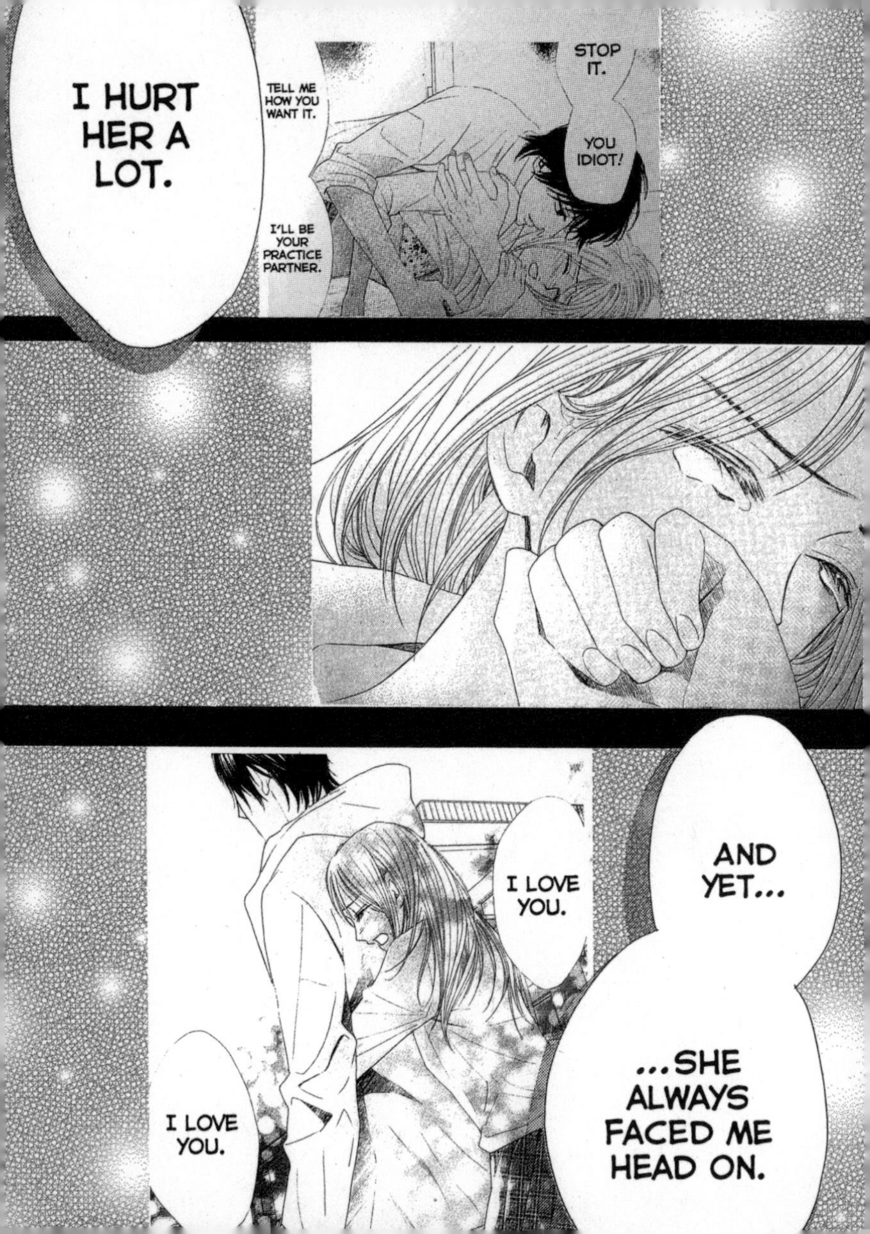
STOP IT.
YOU IDIOT!
TELL ME HOW YOU WANT IT.
I'LL BE YOUR PRACTICE PARTNER.
I HURT HER A LOT.
AND YET...
I LOVE YOU.
...SHE ALWAYS FACED ME HEAD ON.
I LOVE YOU.

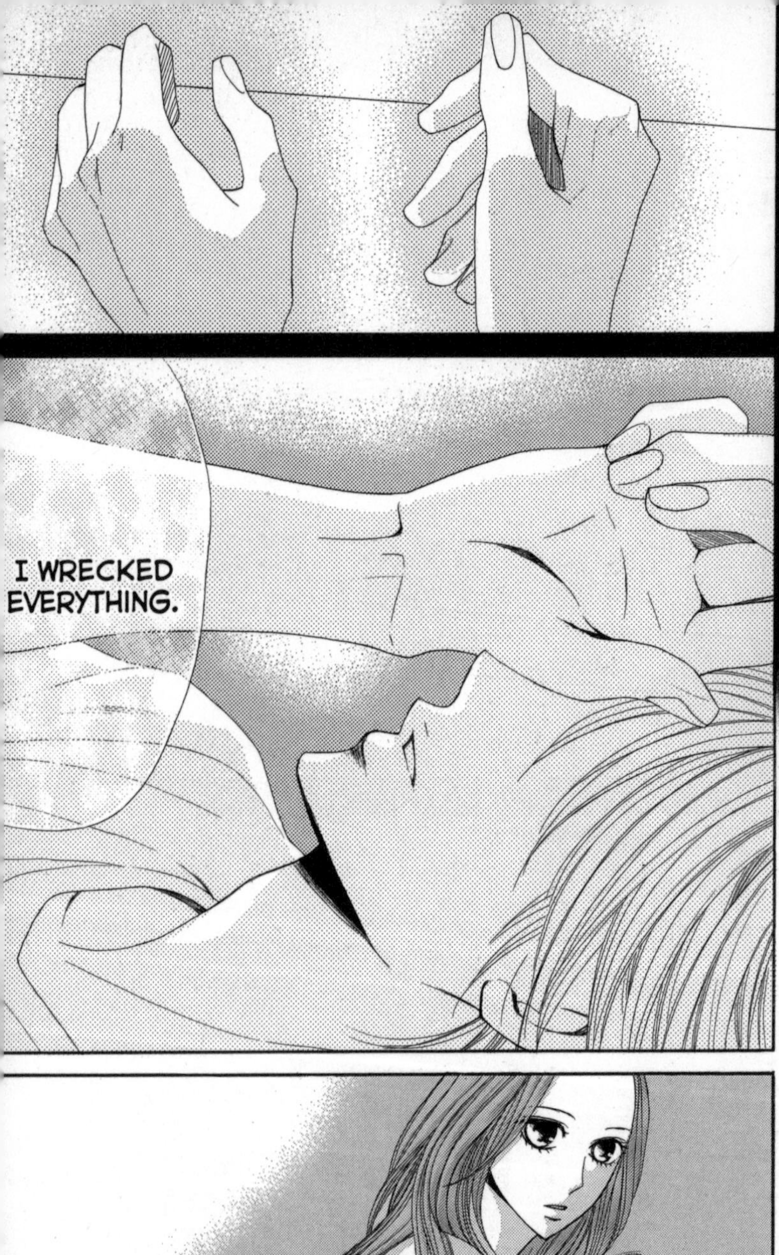
I WRECKED EVERYTHING.

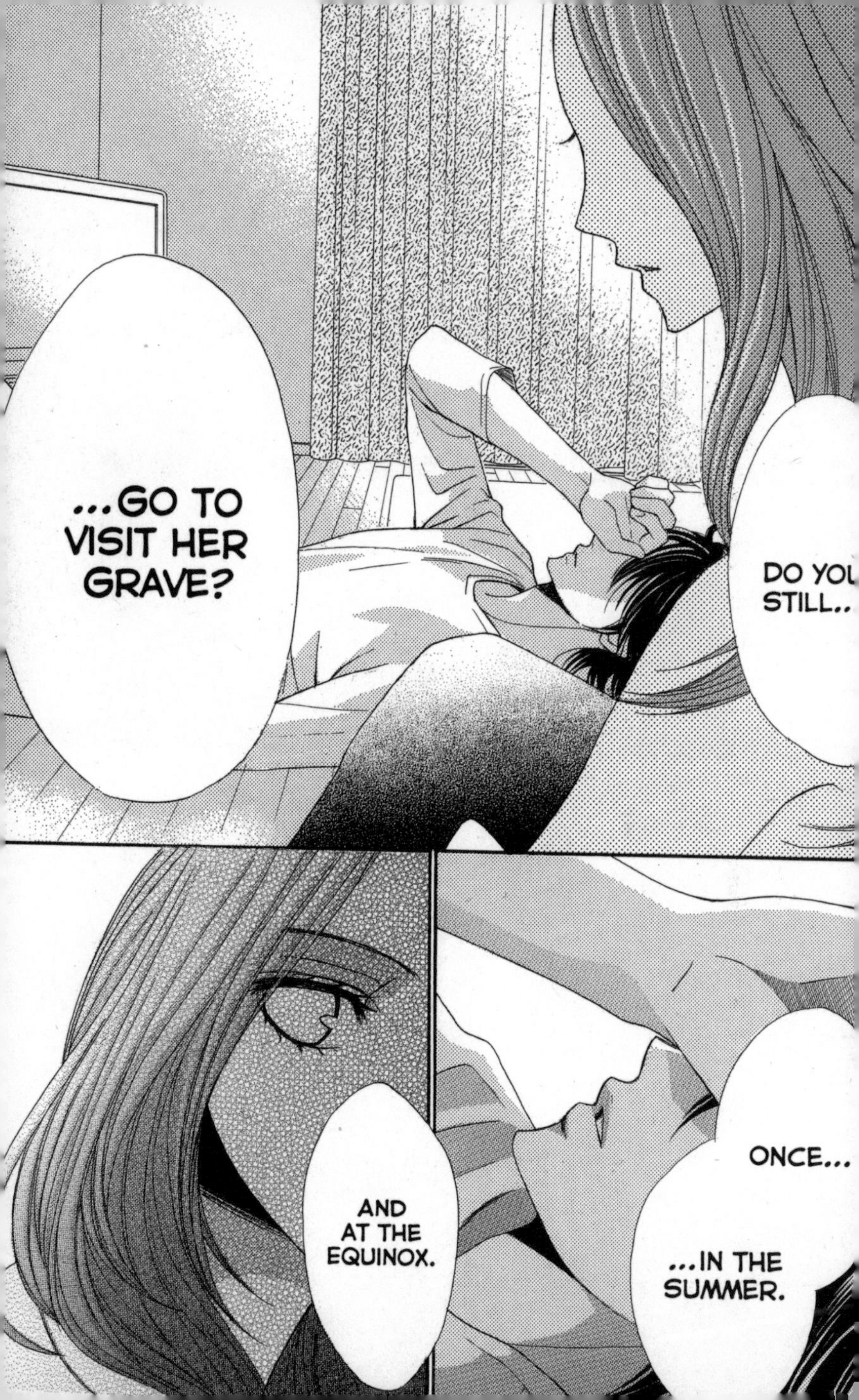
DO YOU STILL..
...GO TO VISIT HER GRAVE?
ONCE...
...IN THE SUMMER.
AND AT THE EQUINOX.

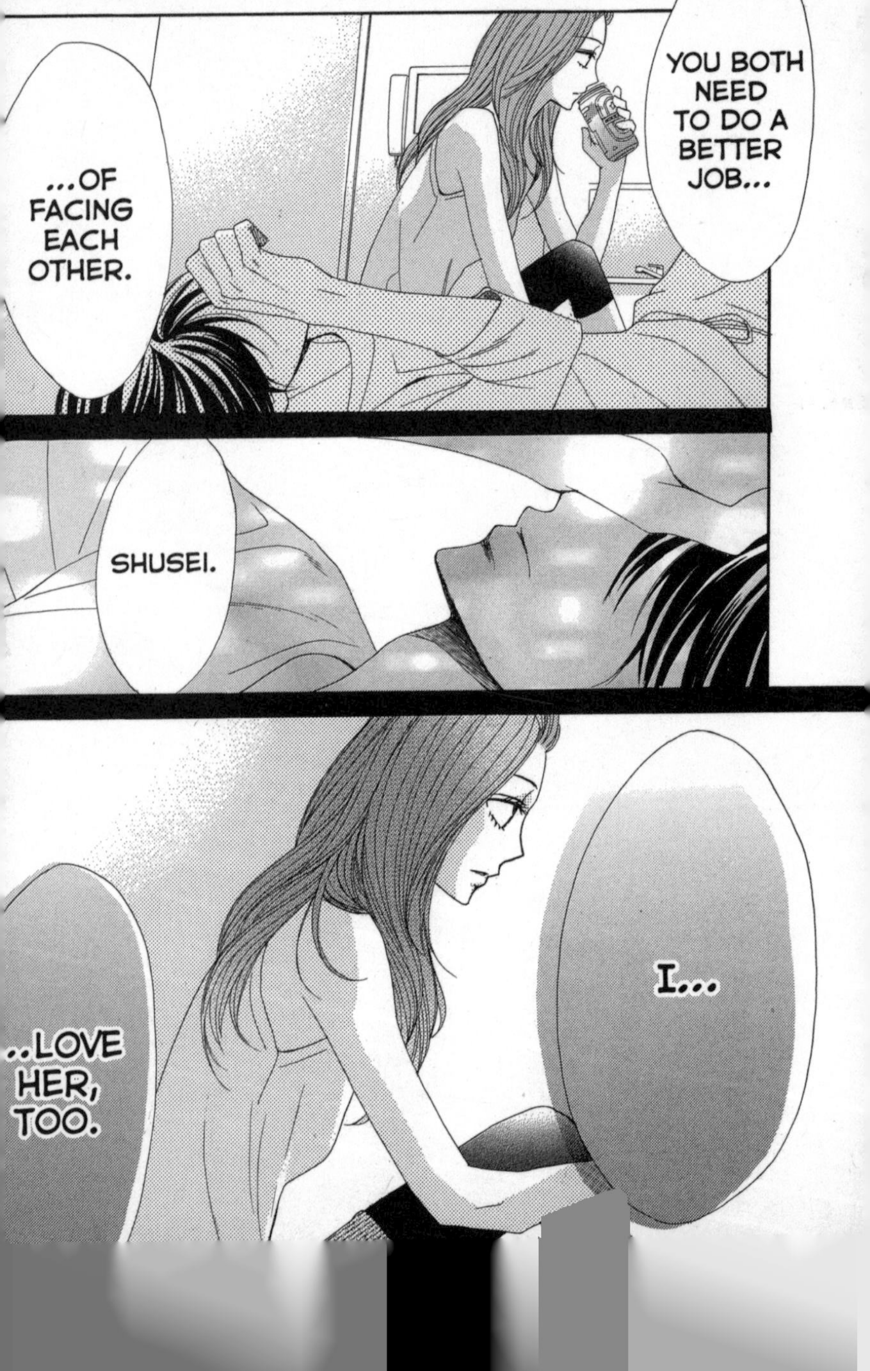
YOU BOTH NEED TO DO A BETTER JOB...
...OF FACING EACH OTHER.
SHUSEI.
I...
..LOVE HER, TOO.

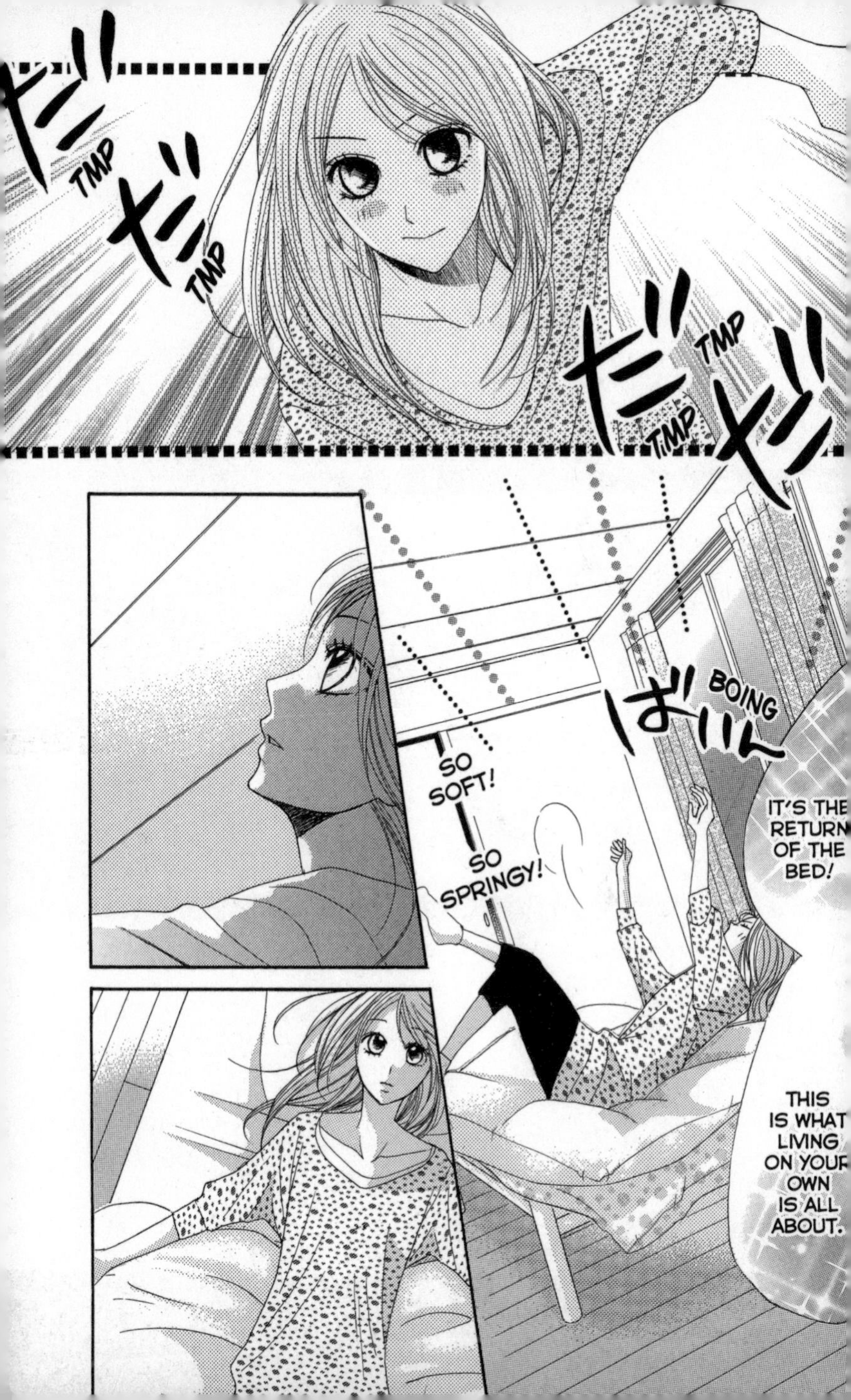
TMP
TMP
TMP
TMP
BOING
IT'S THE RETURN OF THE BED!
SO SOFT!
SO SPRINGY!
THIS IS WHAT LIVING ON YOUR OWN IS ALL ABOUT.

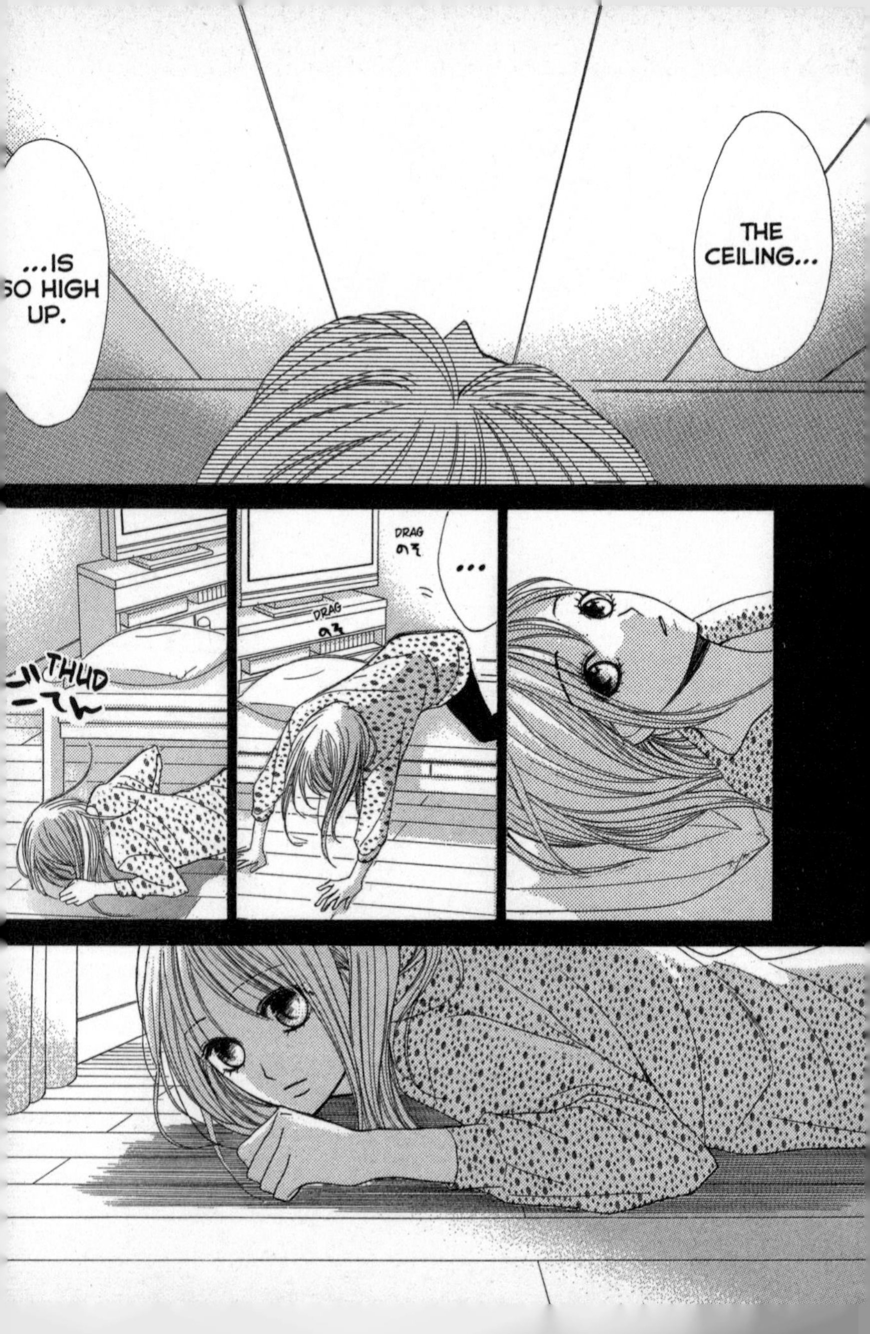
THE CEILING...
...IS SO HIGH UP.
...
DRAG
のそ
DRAG
のそ
THUD

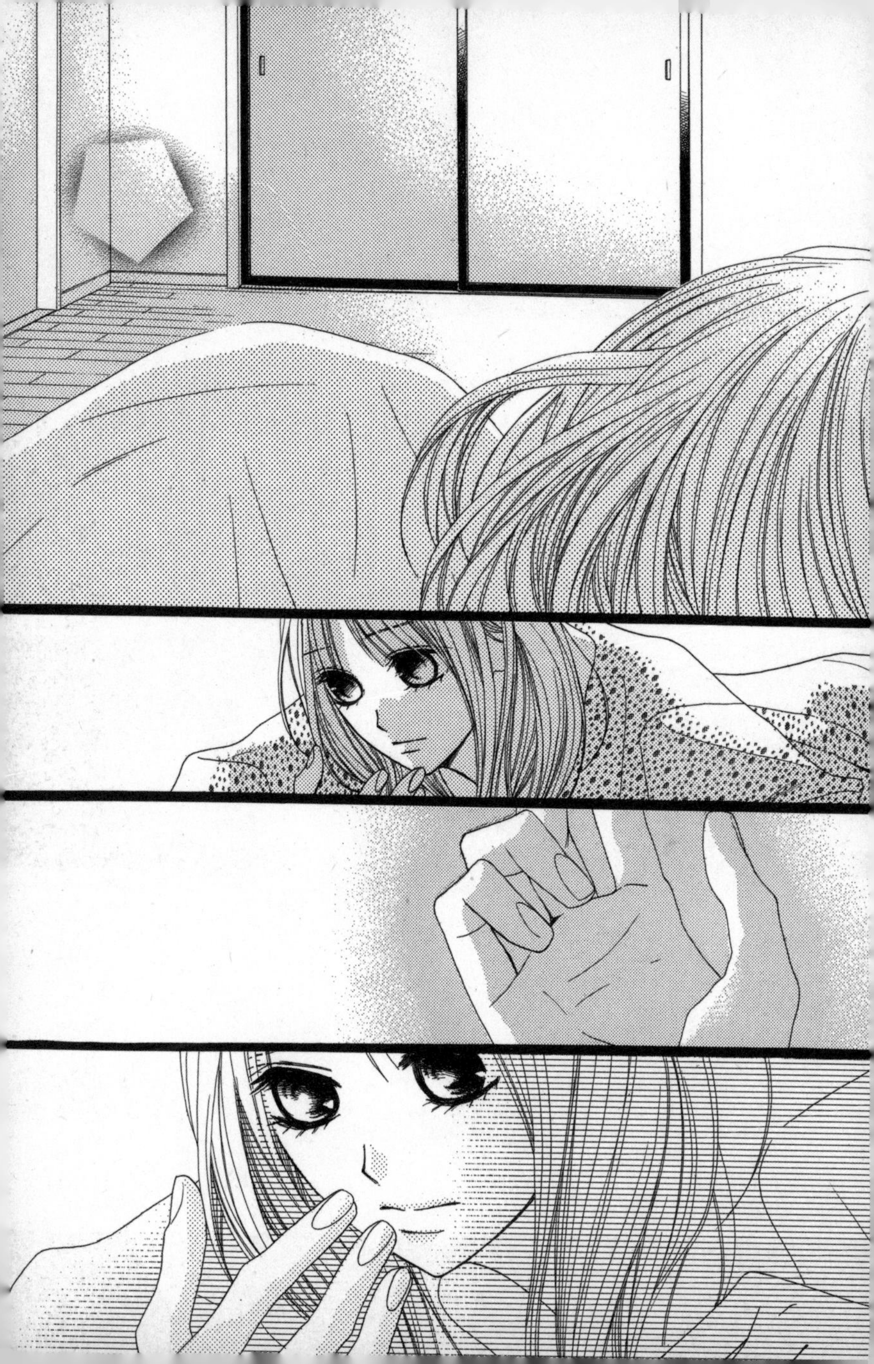

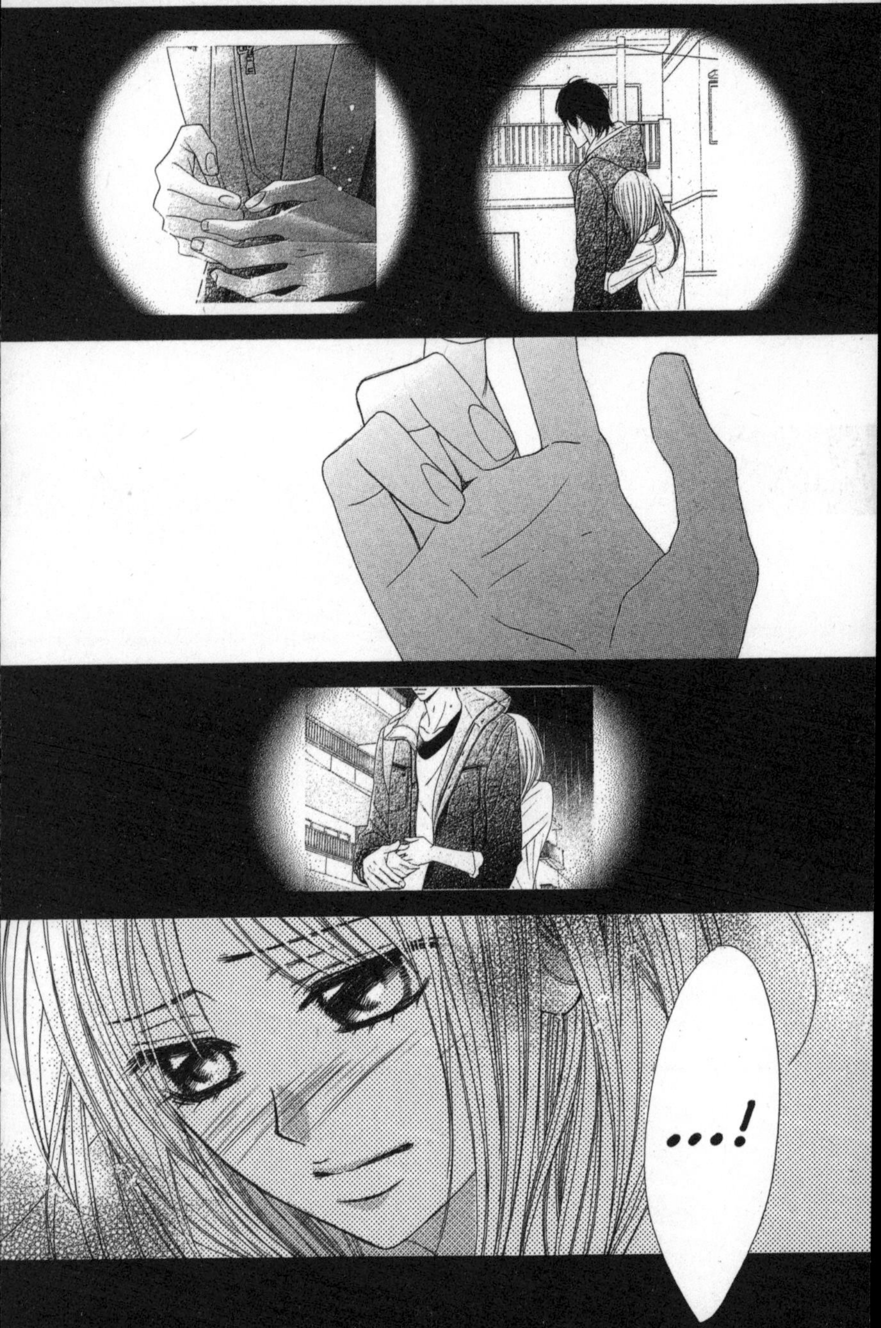
...!

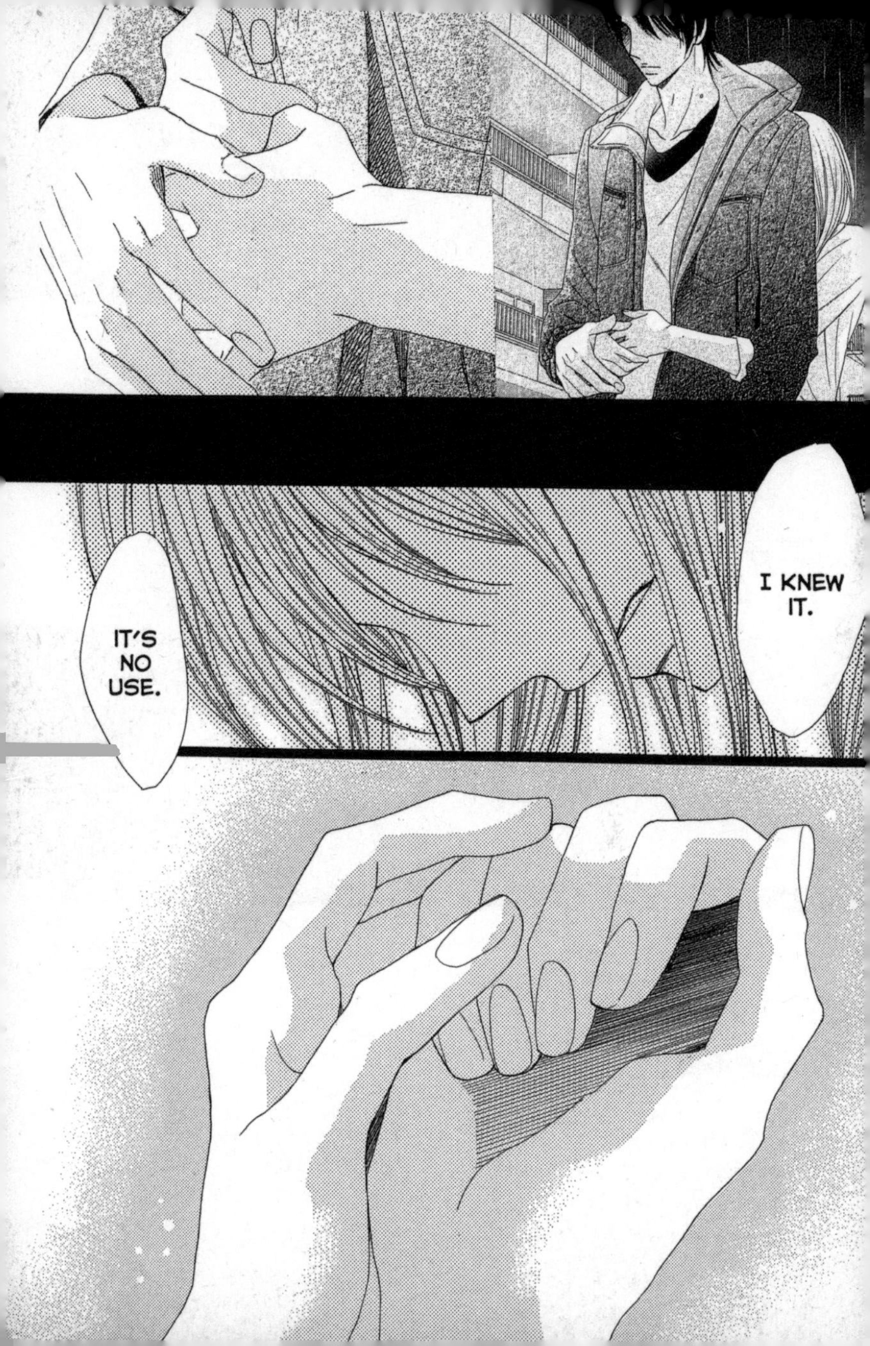
I KNEW IT.
IT'S NO USE.

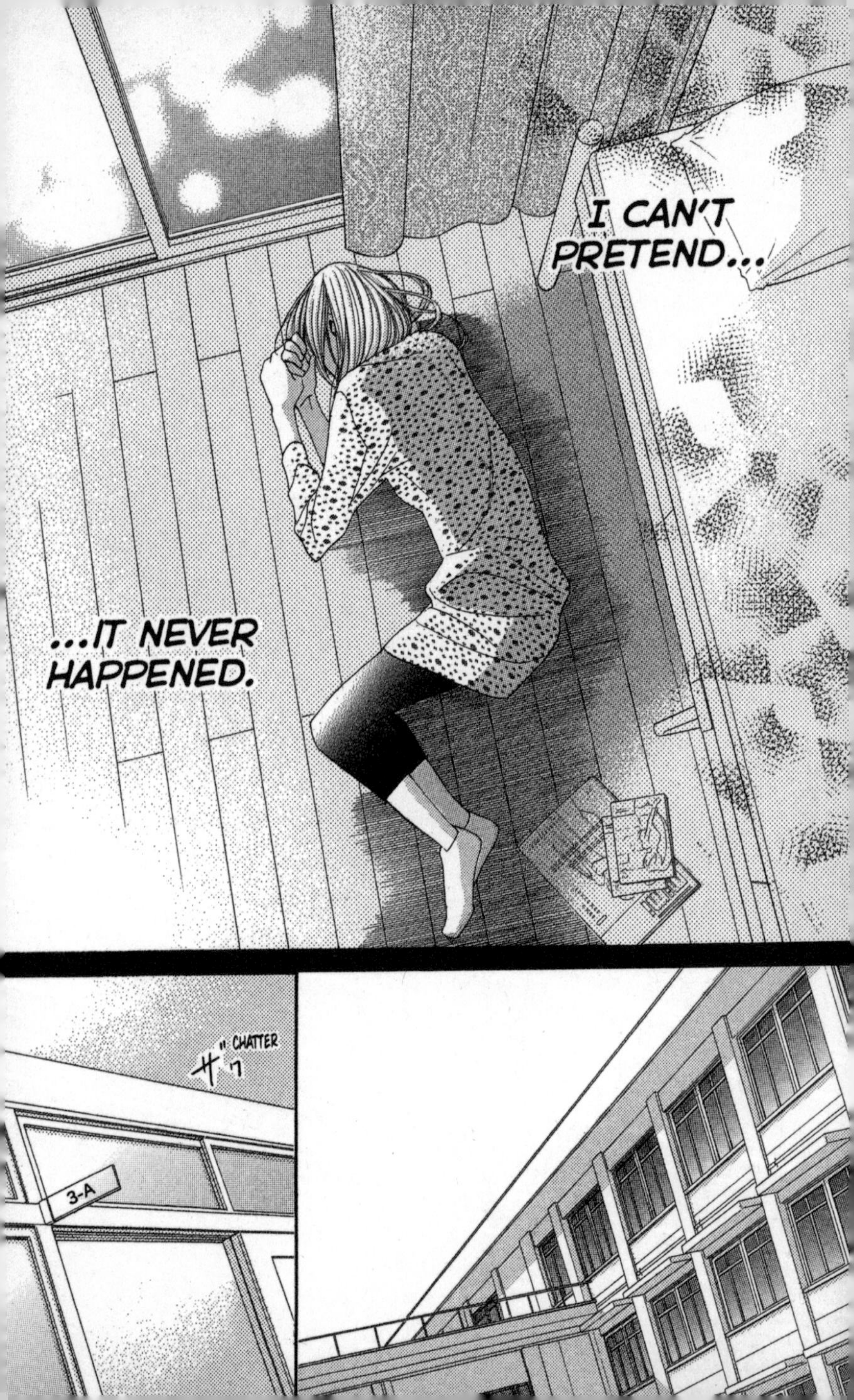
I CAN'T PRETEND...
...IT NEVER HAPPENED.
CHATTER
3-A

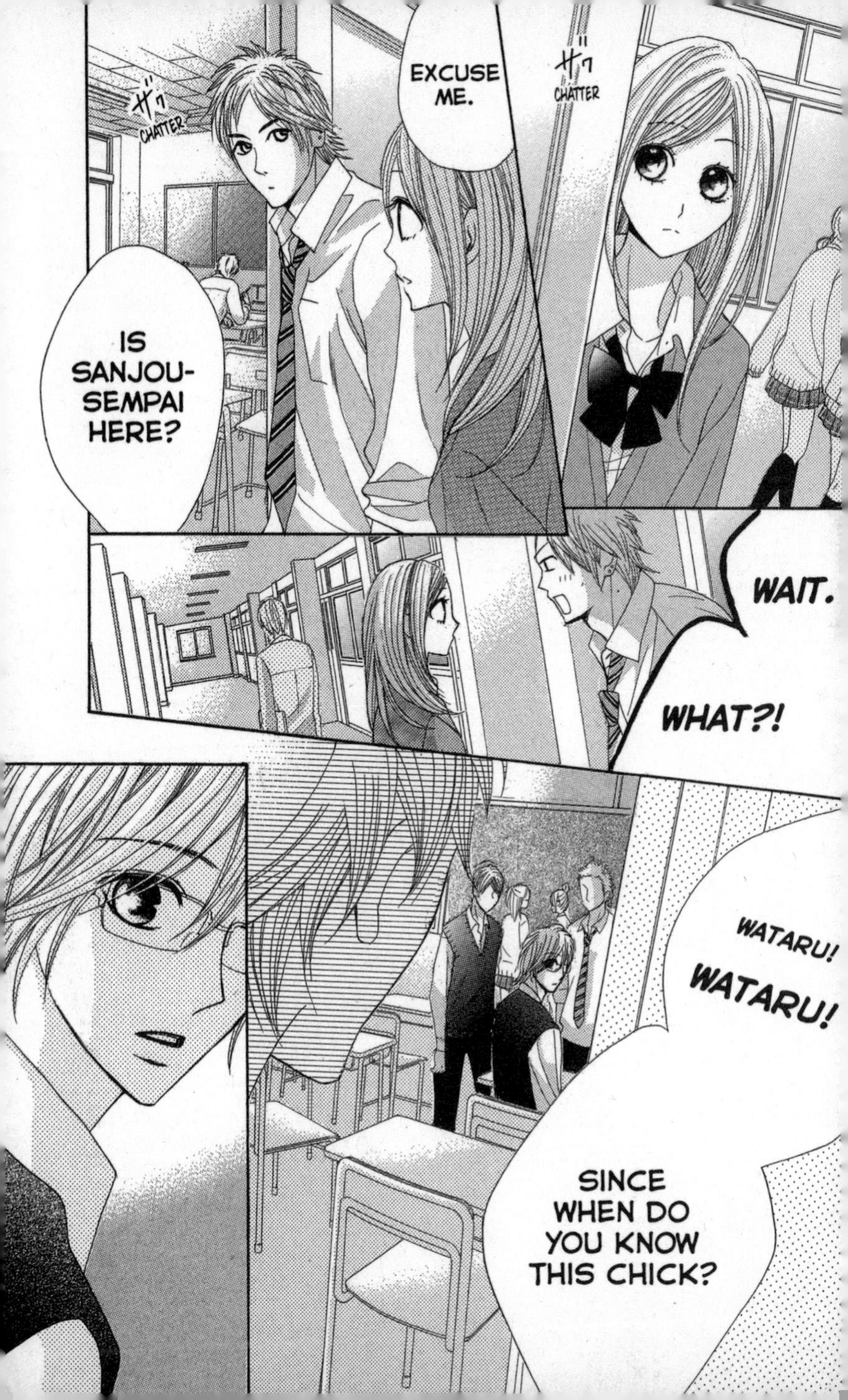
ザワ CHATTER
EXCUSE ME.
ザワ CHATTER
IS SANJOU-SEMPAI HERE?
WAIT.
WHAT?!
WATARU!
WATARU!
SINCE WHEN DO YOU KNOW THIS CHICK?

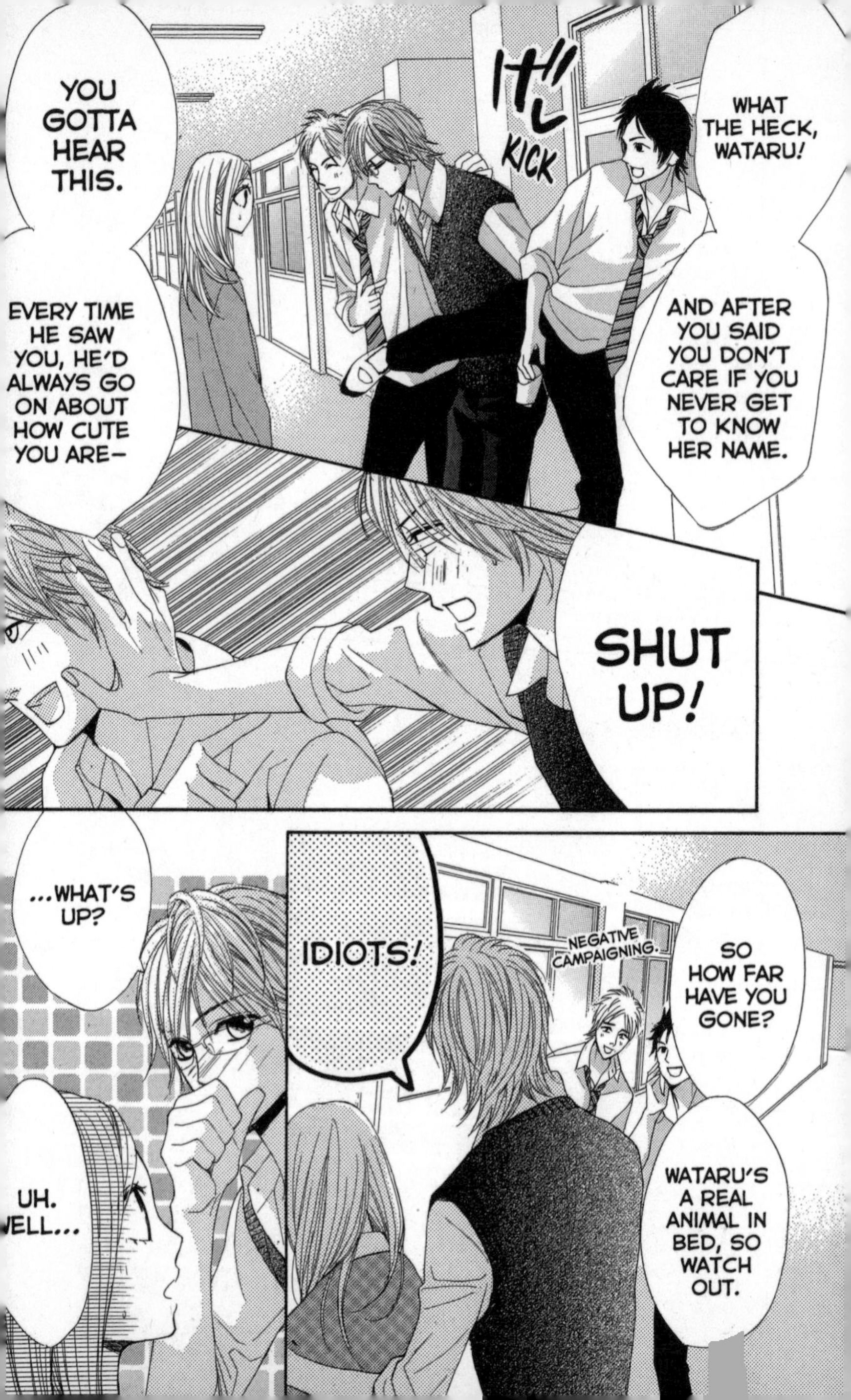
WHAT THE HECK, WATARU!
げし
KICK
YOU GOTTA HEAR THIS.
EVERY TIME HE SAW YOU, HE'D ALWAYS GO ON ABOUT HOW CUTE YOU ARE—
AND AFTER YOU SAID YOU DON'T CARE IF YOU NEVER GET TO KNOW HER NAME.
SHUT UP!
SO HOW FAR HAVE YOU GONE?
NEGATIVE CAMPAIGNING.
WATARU'S A REAL ANIMAL IN BED, SO WATCH OUT.
IDIOTS!
...WHAT'S UP?
UH. WELL...

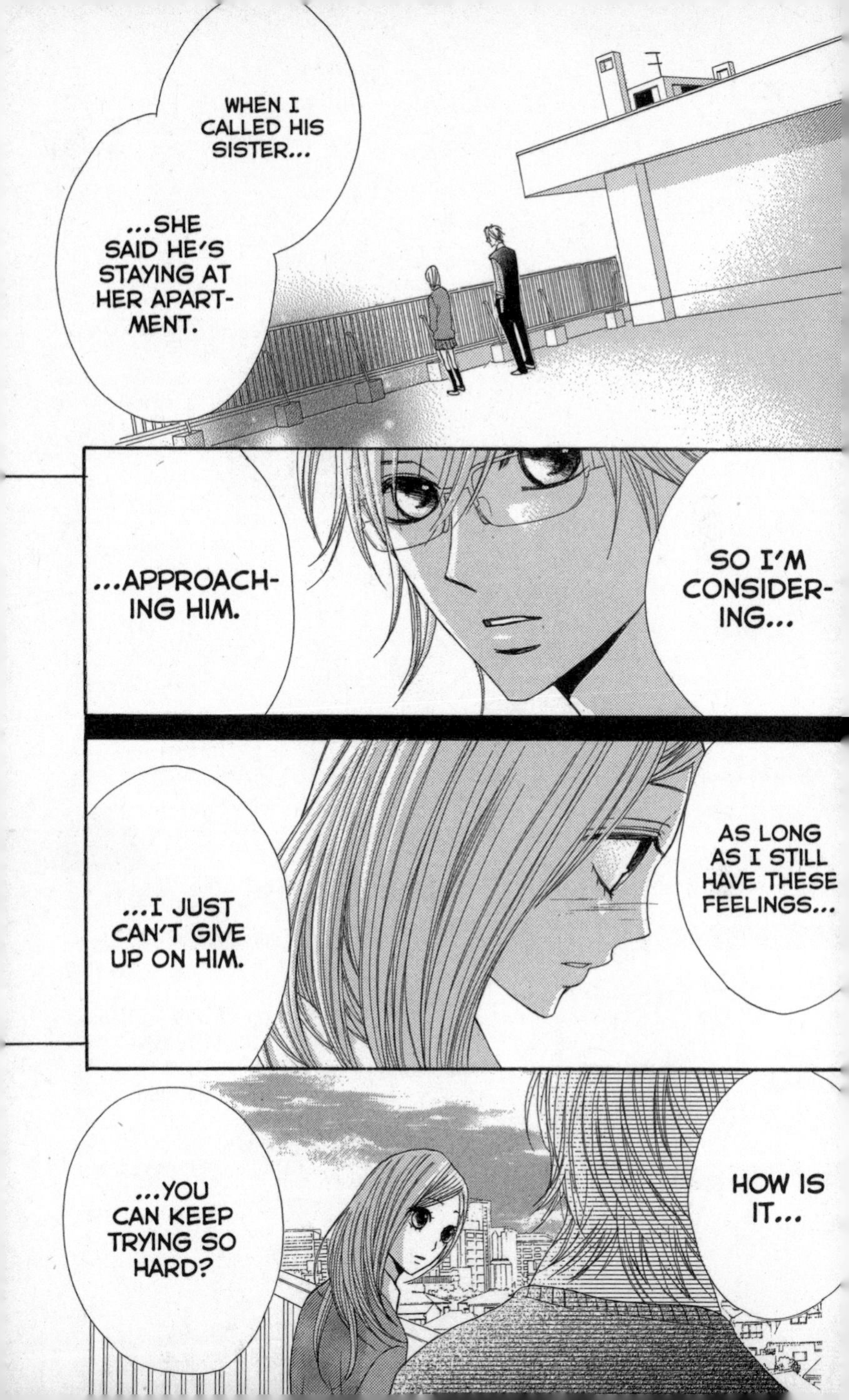
WHEN I CALLED HIS SISTER...
...SHE SAID HE'S STAYING AT HER APART-MENT.
SO I'M CONSIDER-ING...
...APPROACH-ING HIM.
AS LONG AS I STILL HAVE THESE FEELINGS...
...I JUST CAN'T GIVE UP ON HIM.
HOW IS IT...
...YOU CAN KEEP TRYING SO HARD?

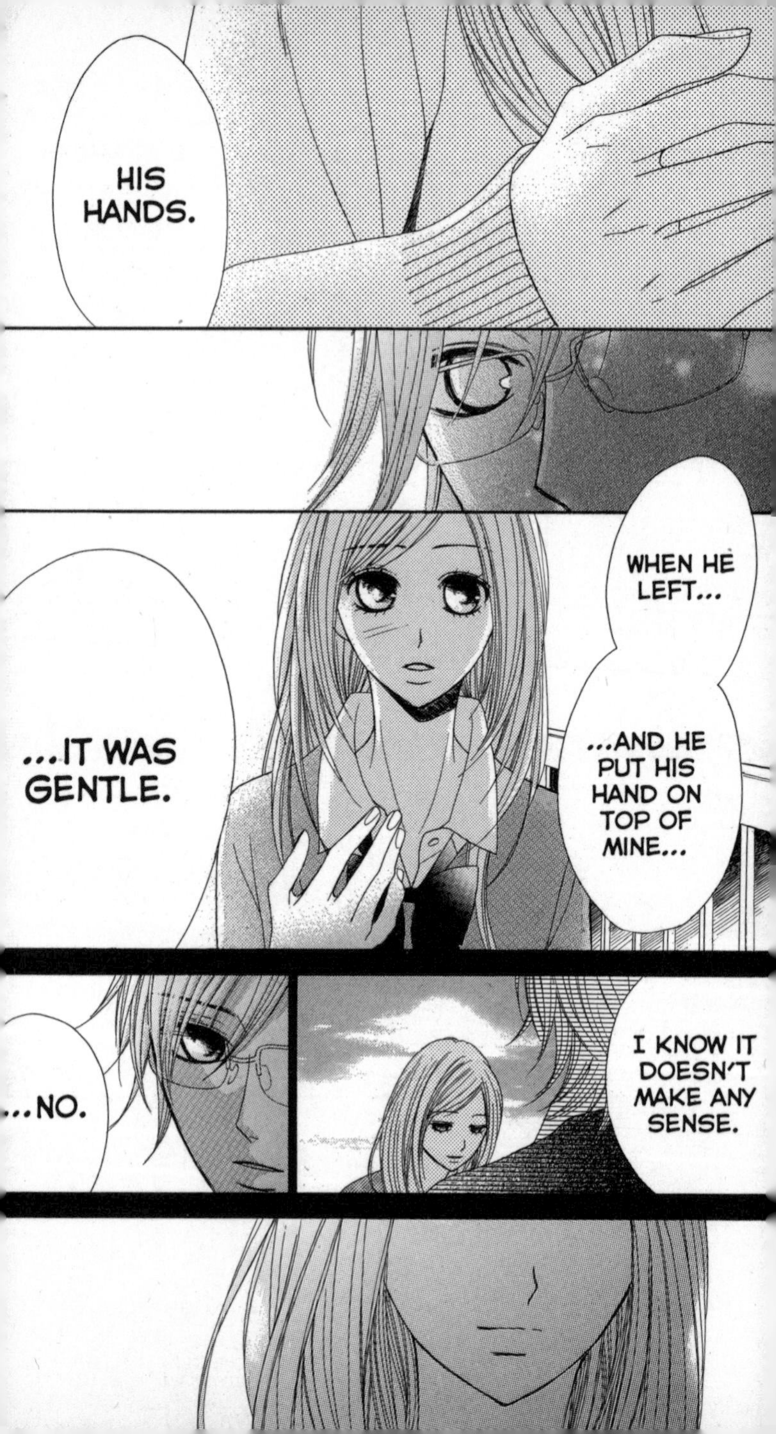
HIS HANDS.
WHEN HE LEFT...
...AND HE PUT HIS HAND ON TOP OF MINE...
...IT WAS GENTLE.
I KNOW IT DOESN'T MAKE ANY SENSE.
...NO.

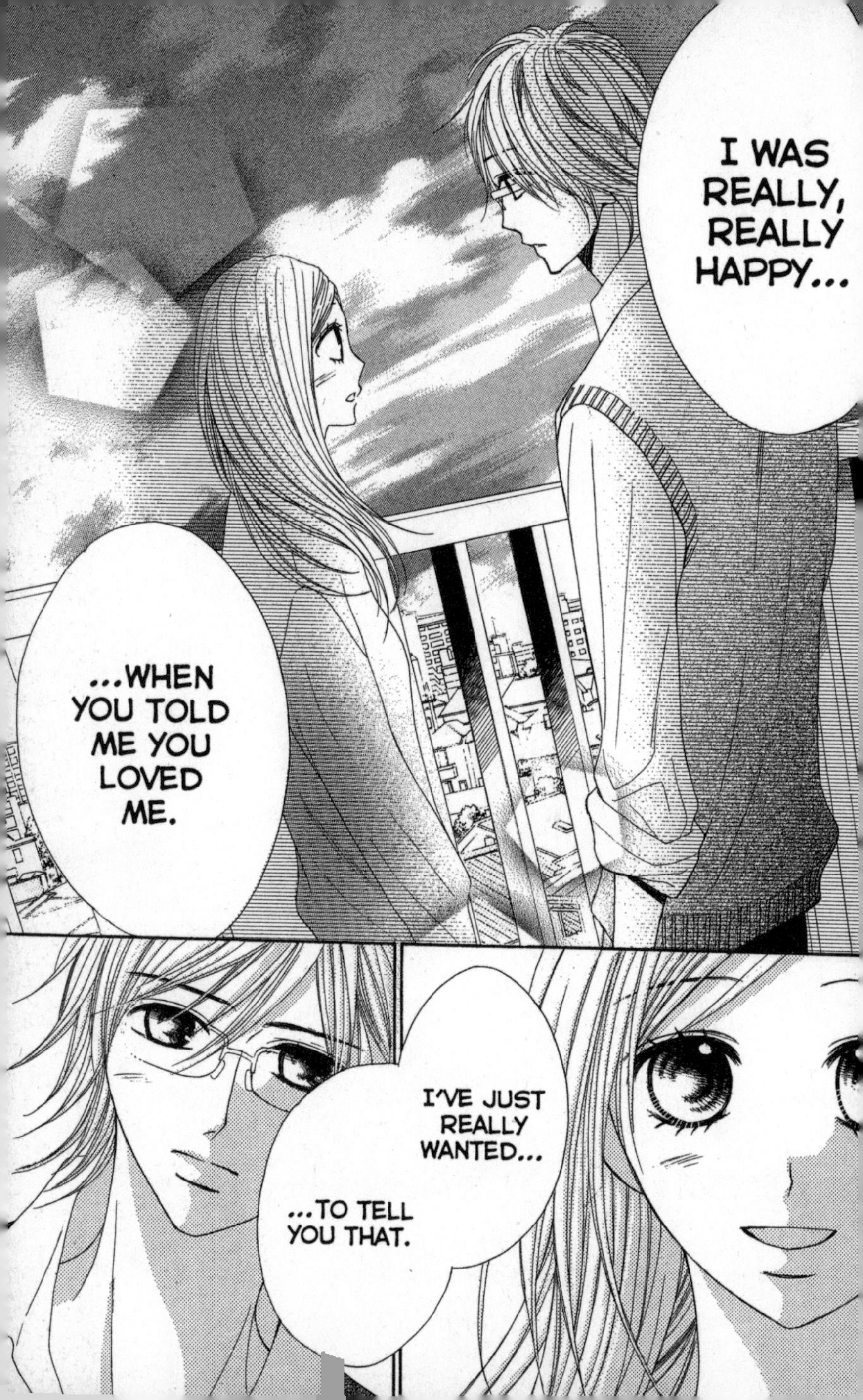
I WAS REALLY, REALLY HAPPY...
...WHEN YOU TOLD ME YOU LOVED ME.
I'VE JUST REALLY WANTED...
...TO TELL YOU THAT.

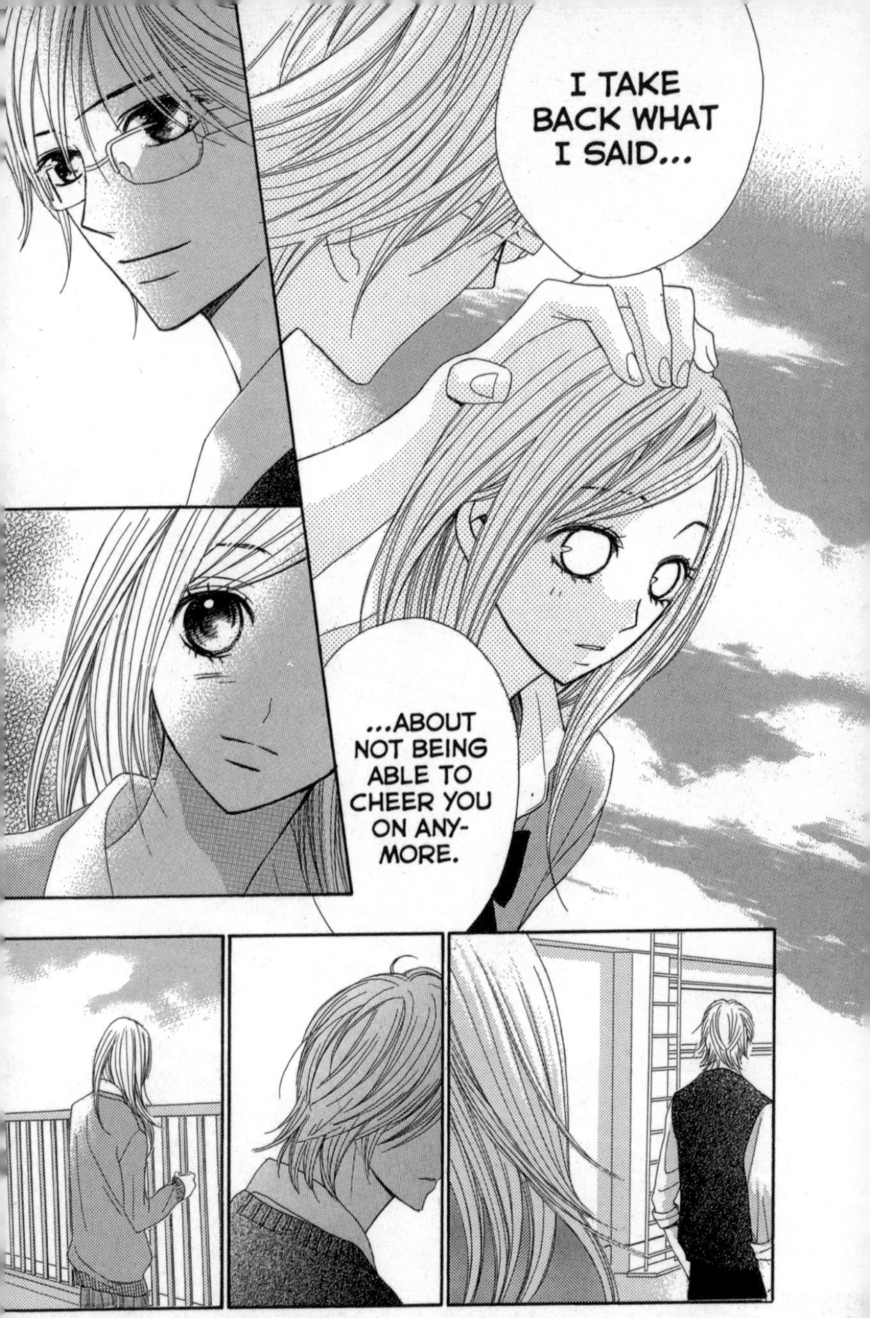
I TAKE BACK WHAT I SAID...
...ABOUT NOT BEING ABLE TO CHEER YOU ON ANY-MORE.

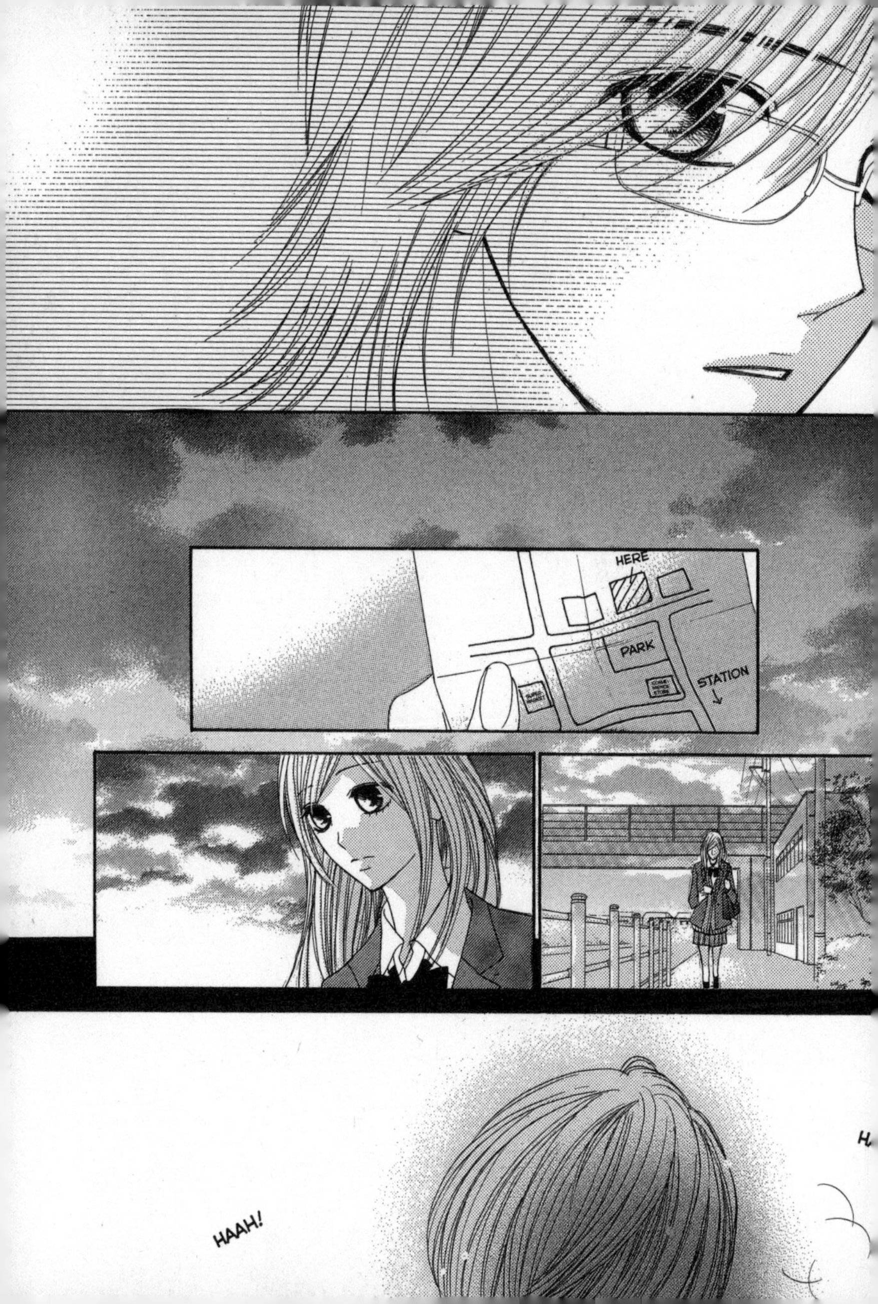
HERE
PARK
STATION
HAAH!

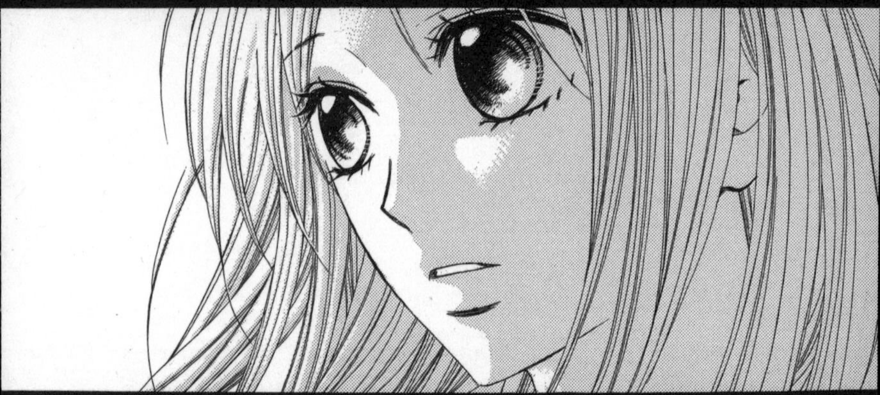

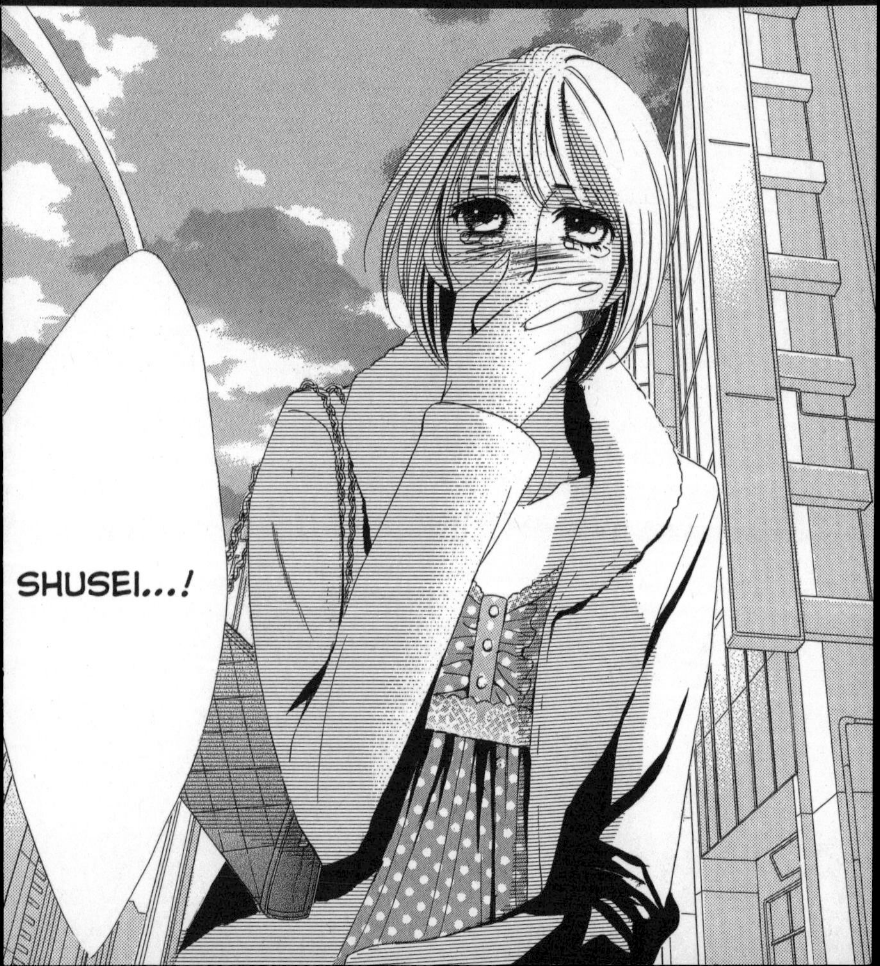
SHUSEI...!

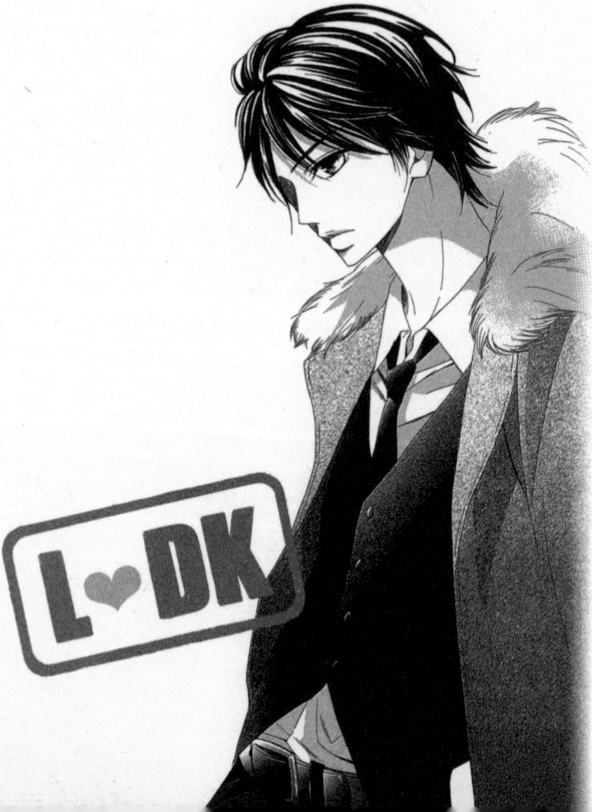
L♥DK

#24 Fighting Hosts

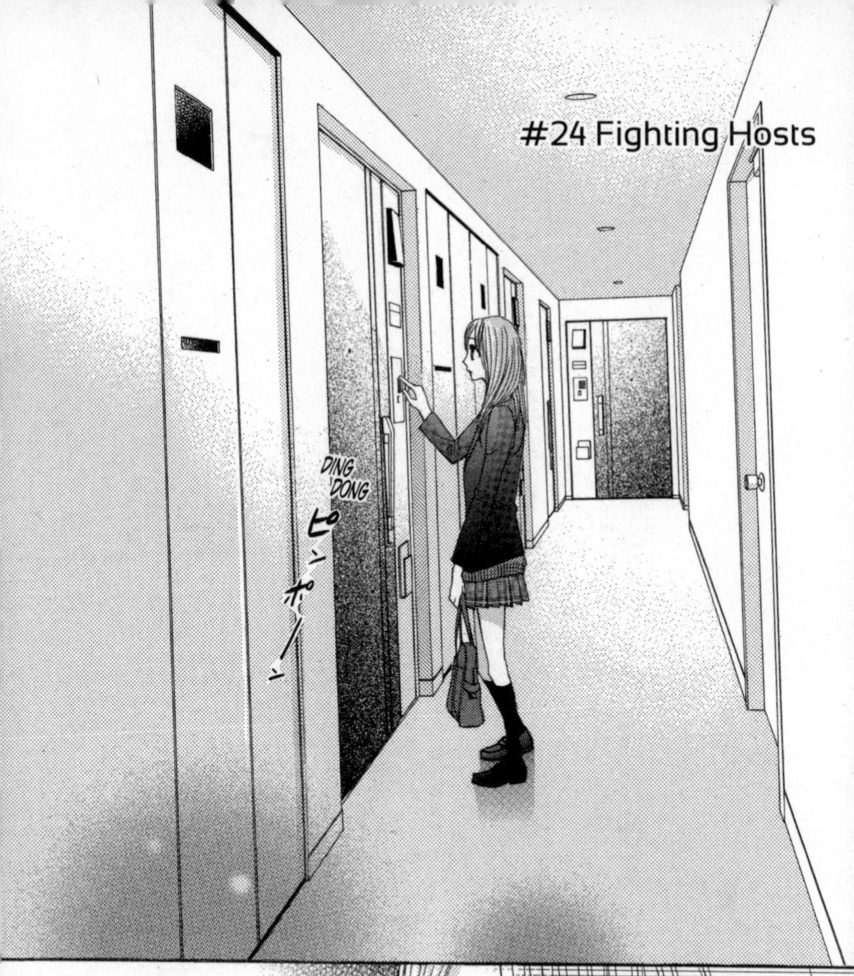
DING DONG

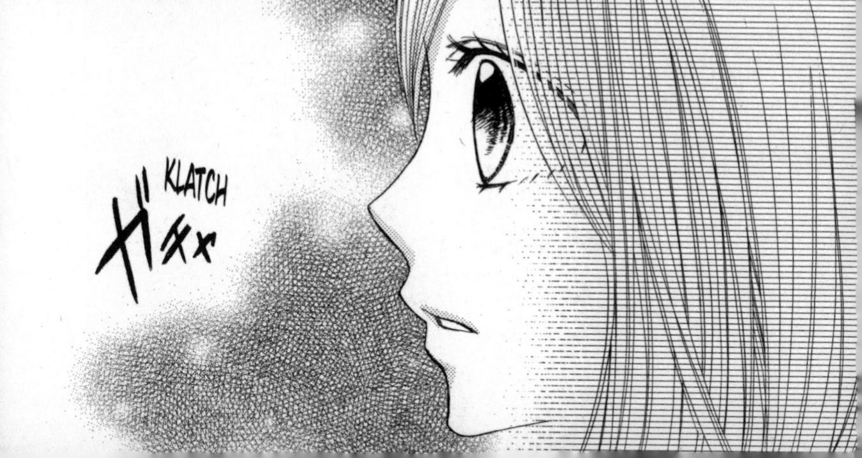
KLATCH

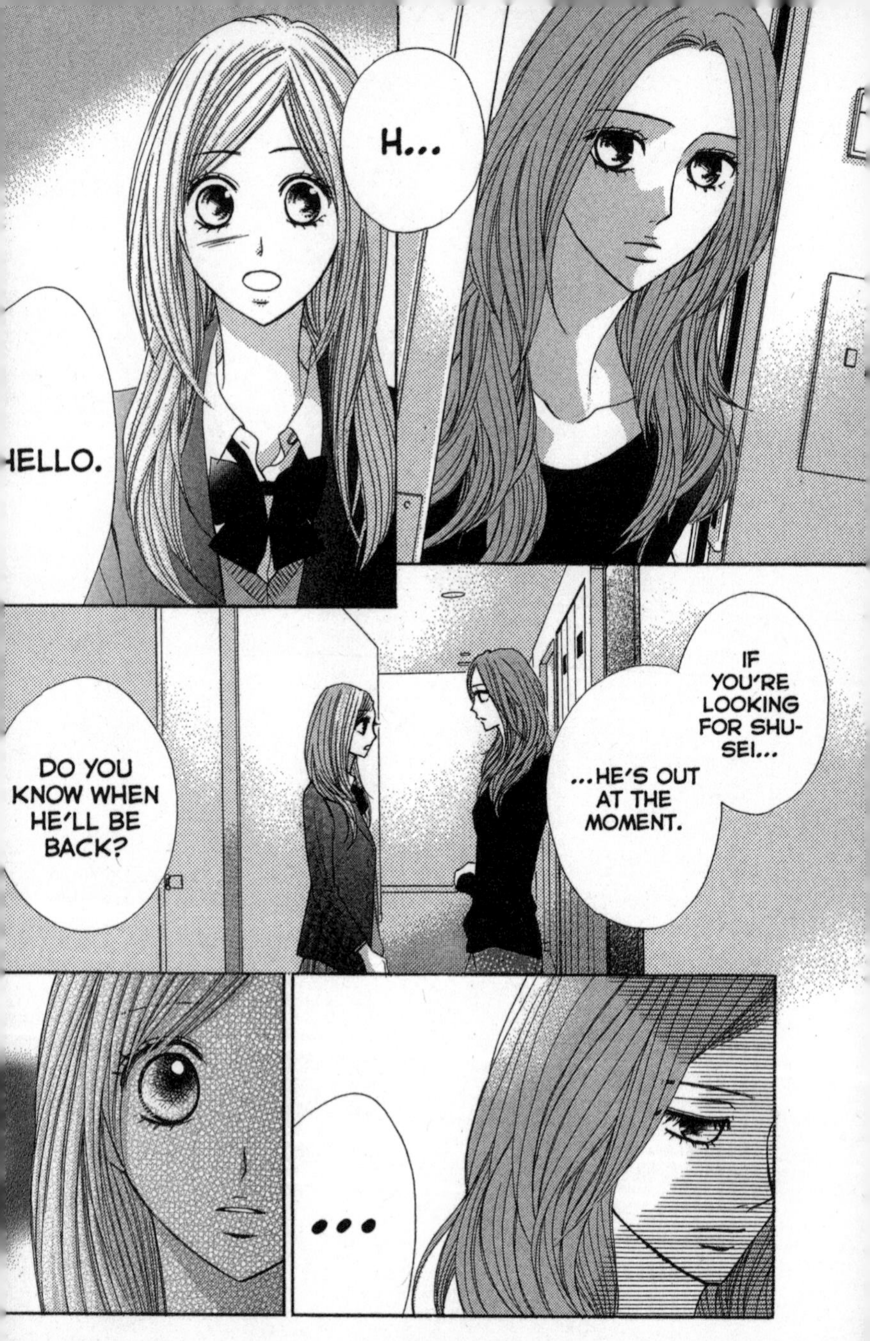
HELLO.
H...
IF YOU'RE LOOKING FOR SHU-SEI...
...HE'S OUT AT THE MOMENT.
DO YOU KNOW WHEN HE'LL BE BACK?
...

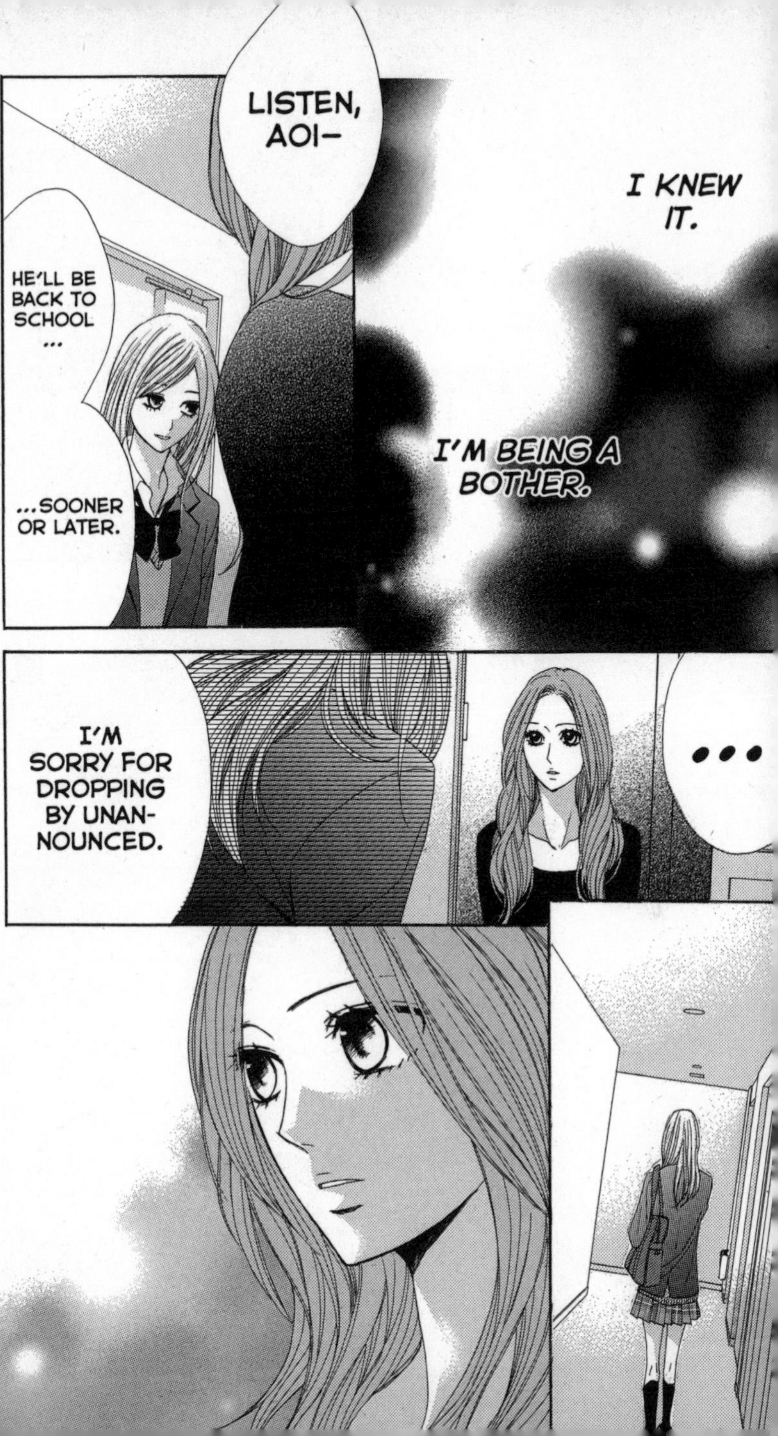
LISTEN, AOI–
HE'LL BE BACK TO SCHOOL ...
...SOONER OR LATER.
I KNEW IT.
I'M BEING A BOTHER.
...
I'M SORRY FOR DROPPING BY UNANNOUNCED.

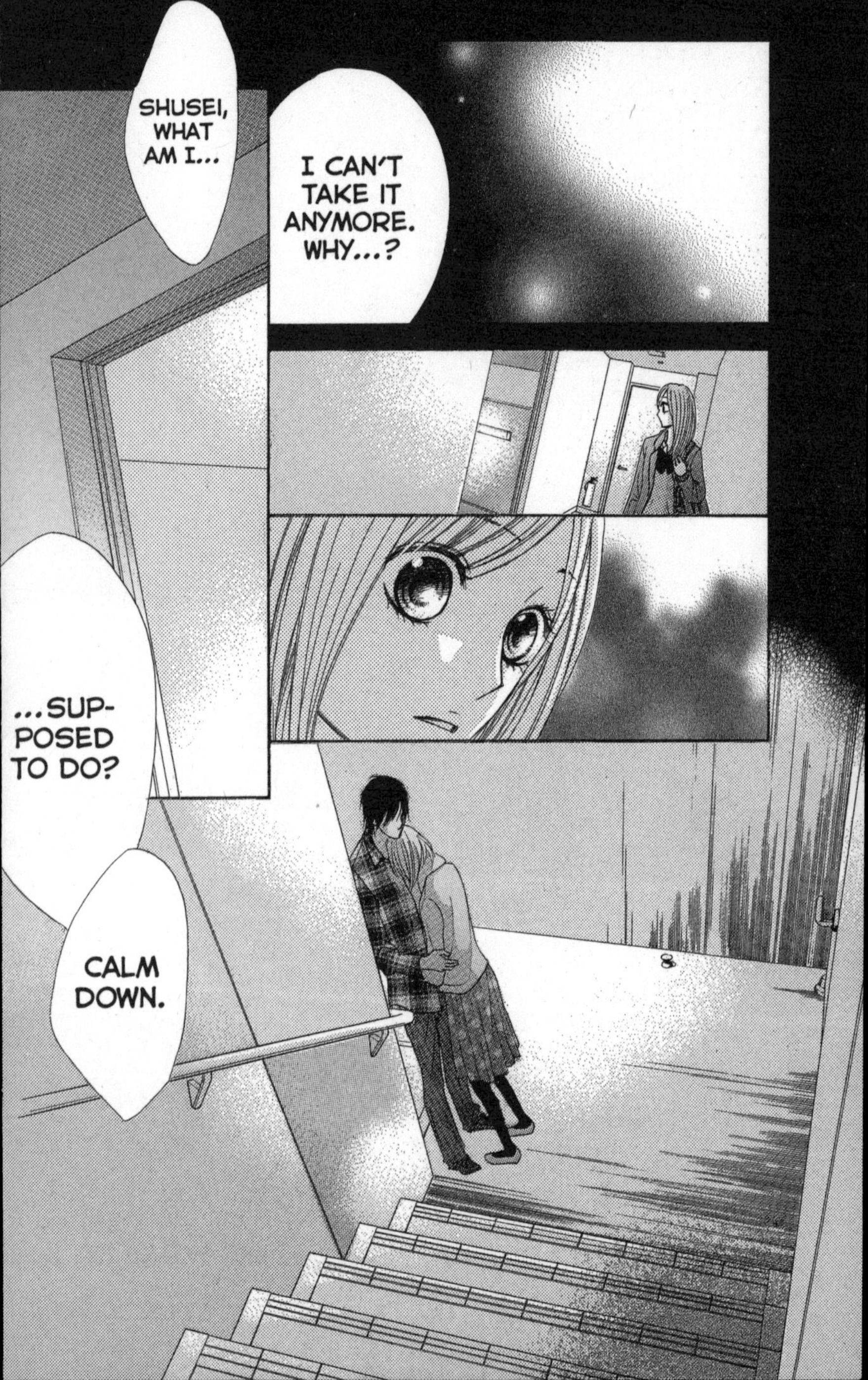
I CAN'T TAKE IT ANYMORE. WHY...?
SHUSEI, WHAT AM I...
...SUP-POSED TO DO?
CALM DOWN.

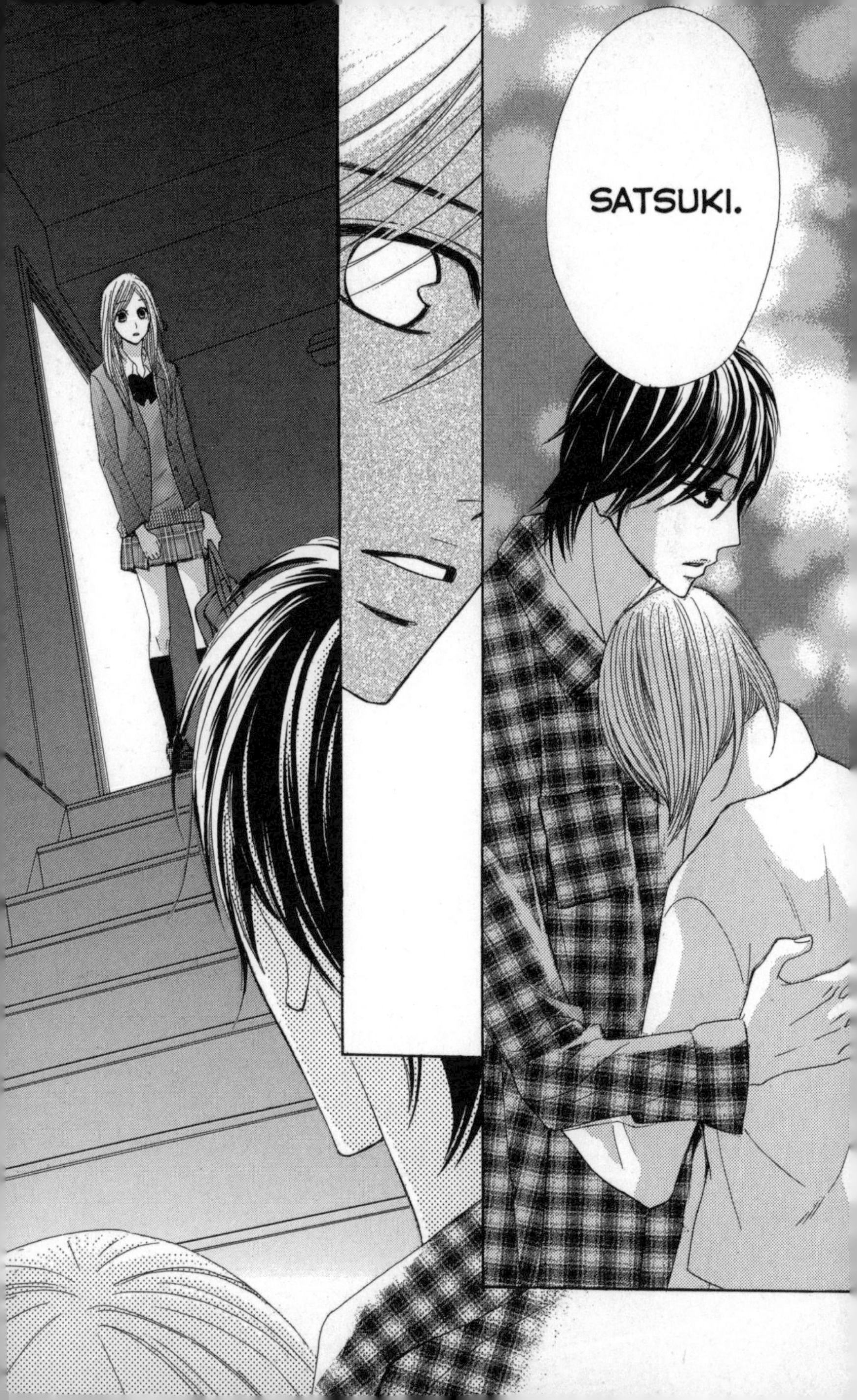
SATSUKI.

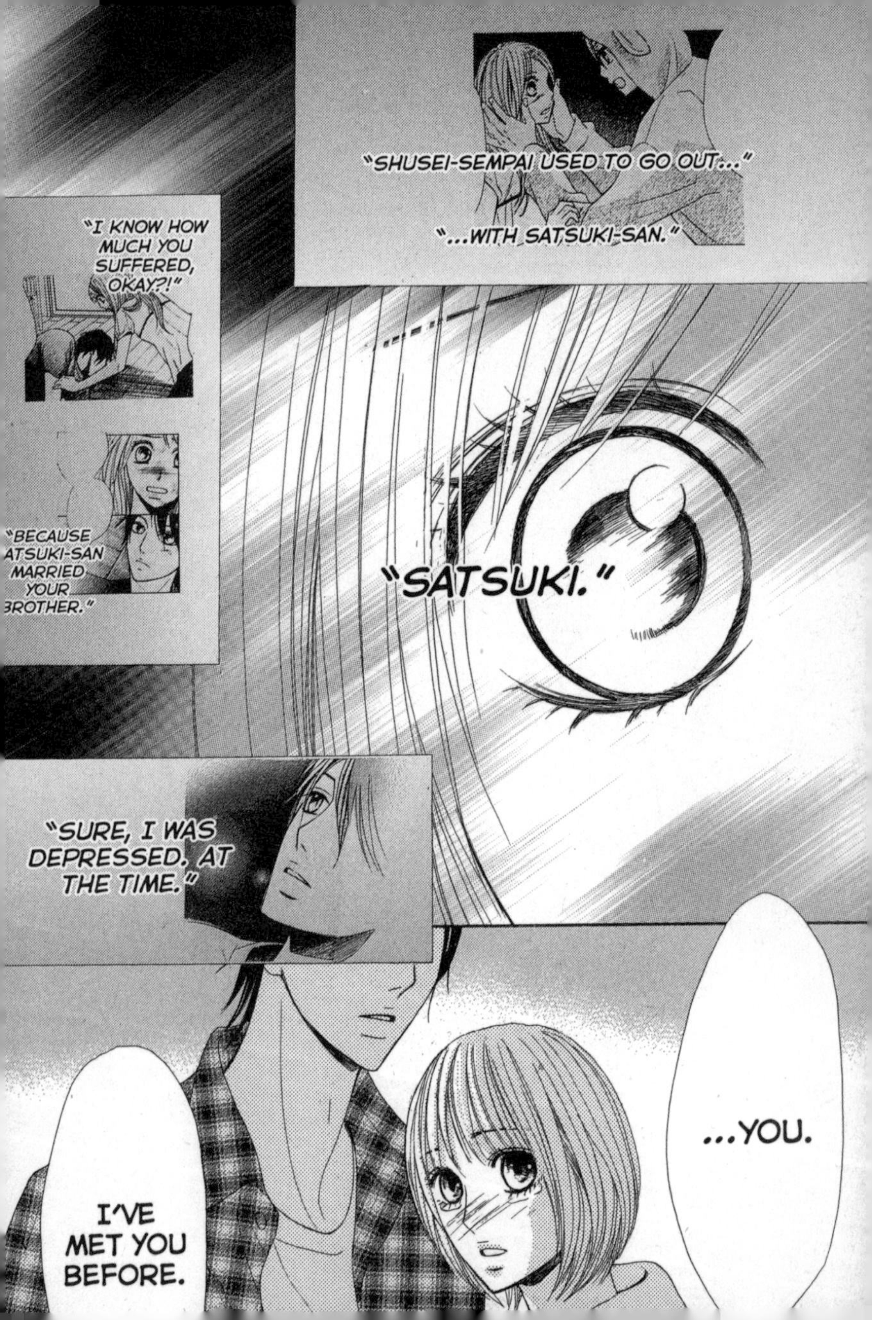
"SHUSEI-SEMPAI USED TO GO OUT..."
"...WITH SATSUKI-SAN."
"I KNOW HOW MUCH YOU SUFFERED, OKAY?!"
"BECAUSE ATSUKI-SAN MARRIED YOUR BROTHER."
"SATSUKI."
"SURE, I WAS DEPRESSED. AT THE TIME."
...YOU.
I'VE MET YOU BEFORE.

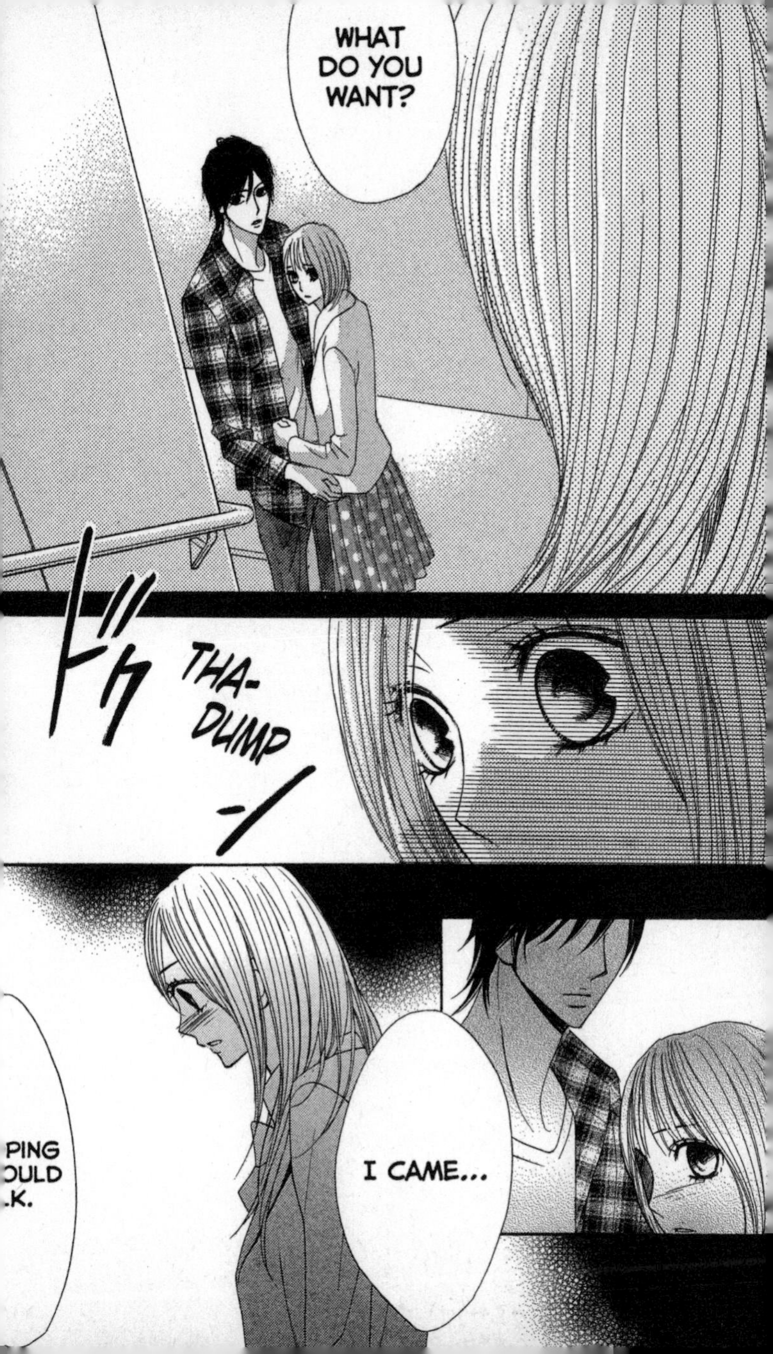
WHAT DO YOU WANT?
THA-DUMP
I CAME...
PING
OULD
.K.

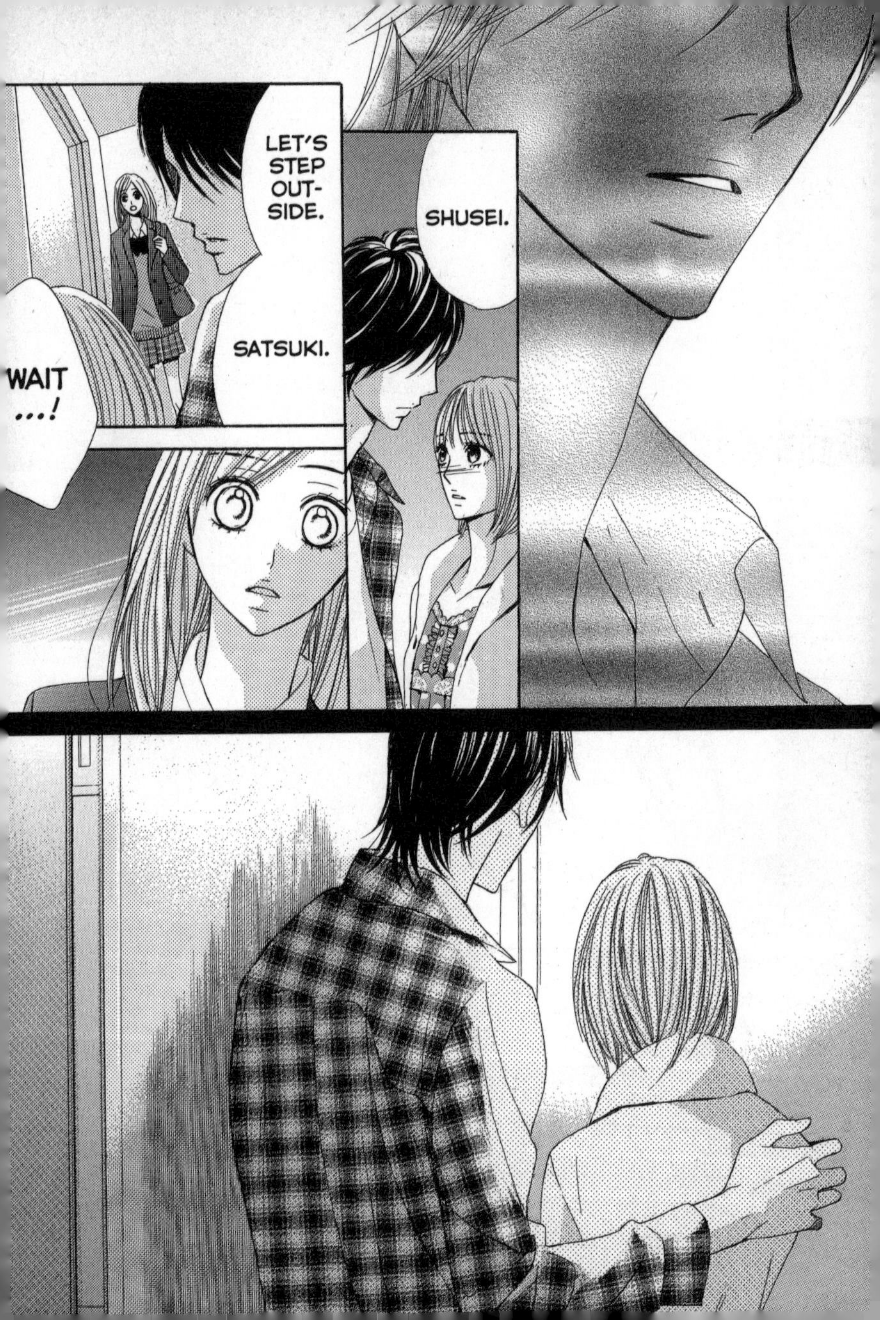
SHUSEI.
LET'S STEP OUT-SIDE.
SATSUKI.
WAIT ...!

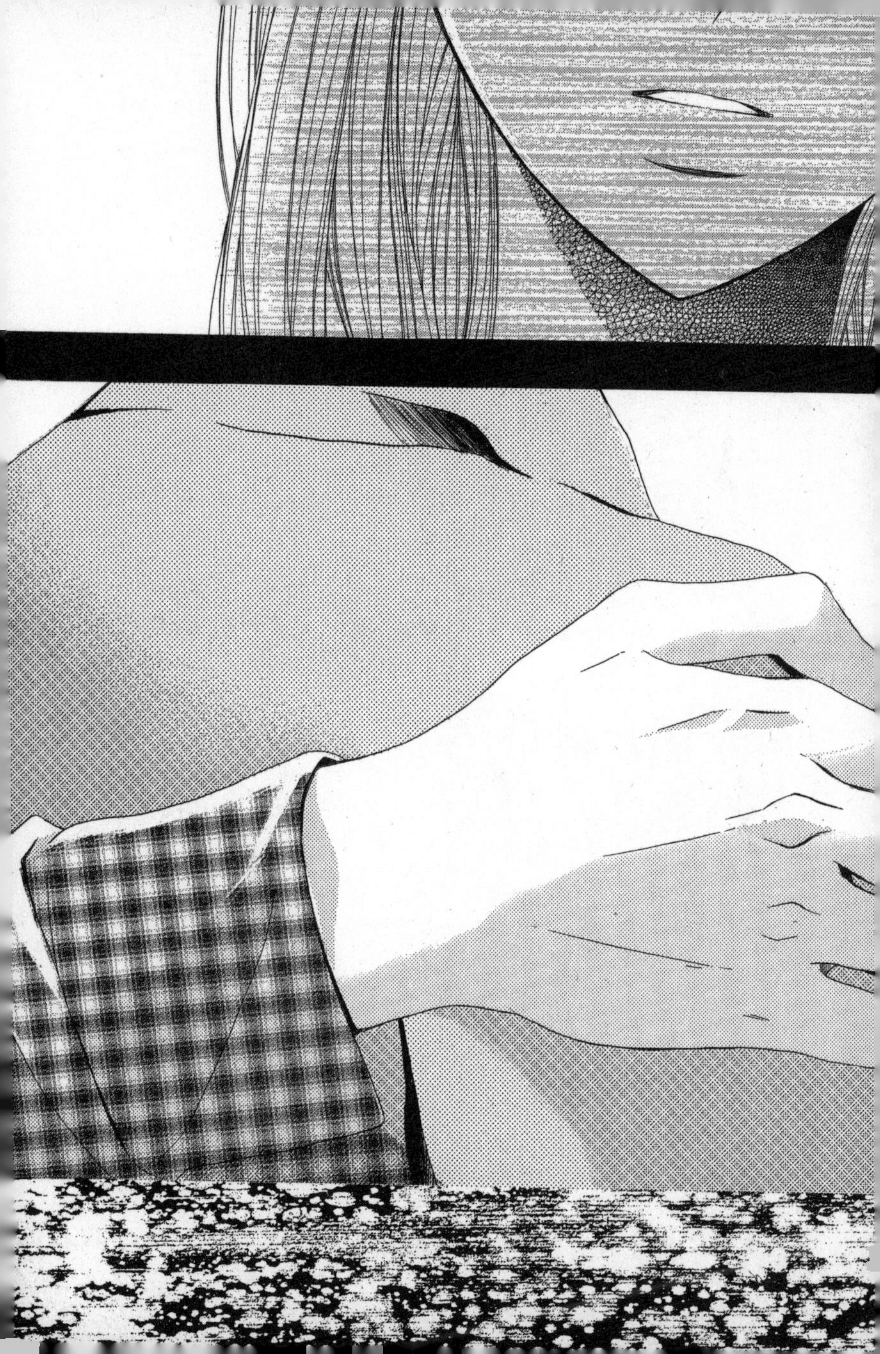

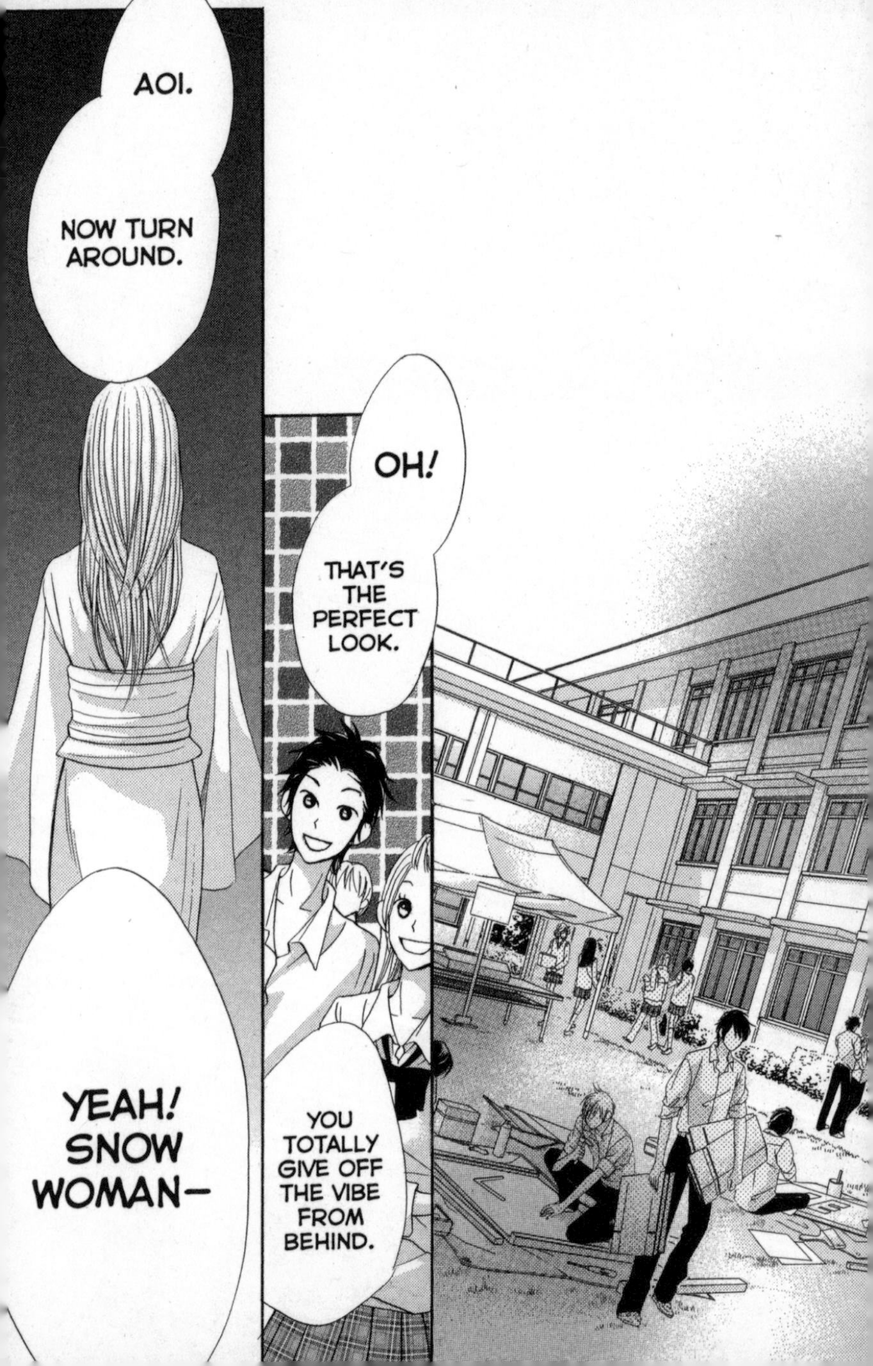
OH!
THAT'S THE PERFECT LOOK.
YOU TOTALLY GIVE OFF THE VIBE FROM BEHIND.
AOI.
NOW TURN AROUND.
YEAH! SNOW WOMAN—

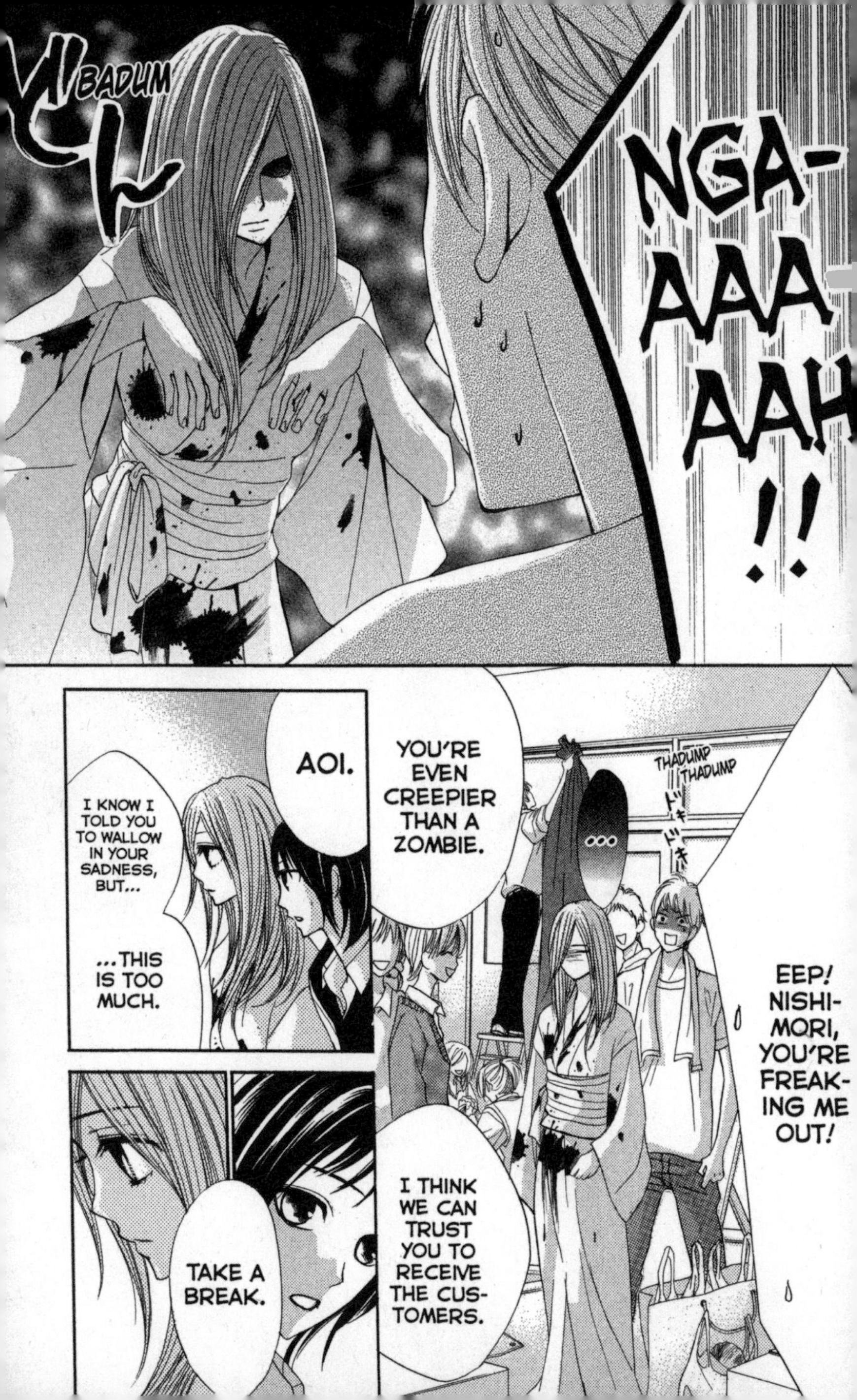
NGA-AAA-AAH!!
BADUM
THADUMP THADUMP
EEP! NISHIMORI, YOU'RE FREAKING ME OUT!
AOI.
YOU'RE EVEN CREEPIER THAN A ZOMBIE.
I KNOW I TOLD YOU TO WALLOW IN YOUR SADNESS, BUT...
...THIS IS TOO MUCH.
I THINK WE CAN TRUST YOU TO RECEIVE THE CUSTOMERS.
TAKE A BREAK.

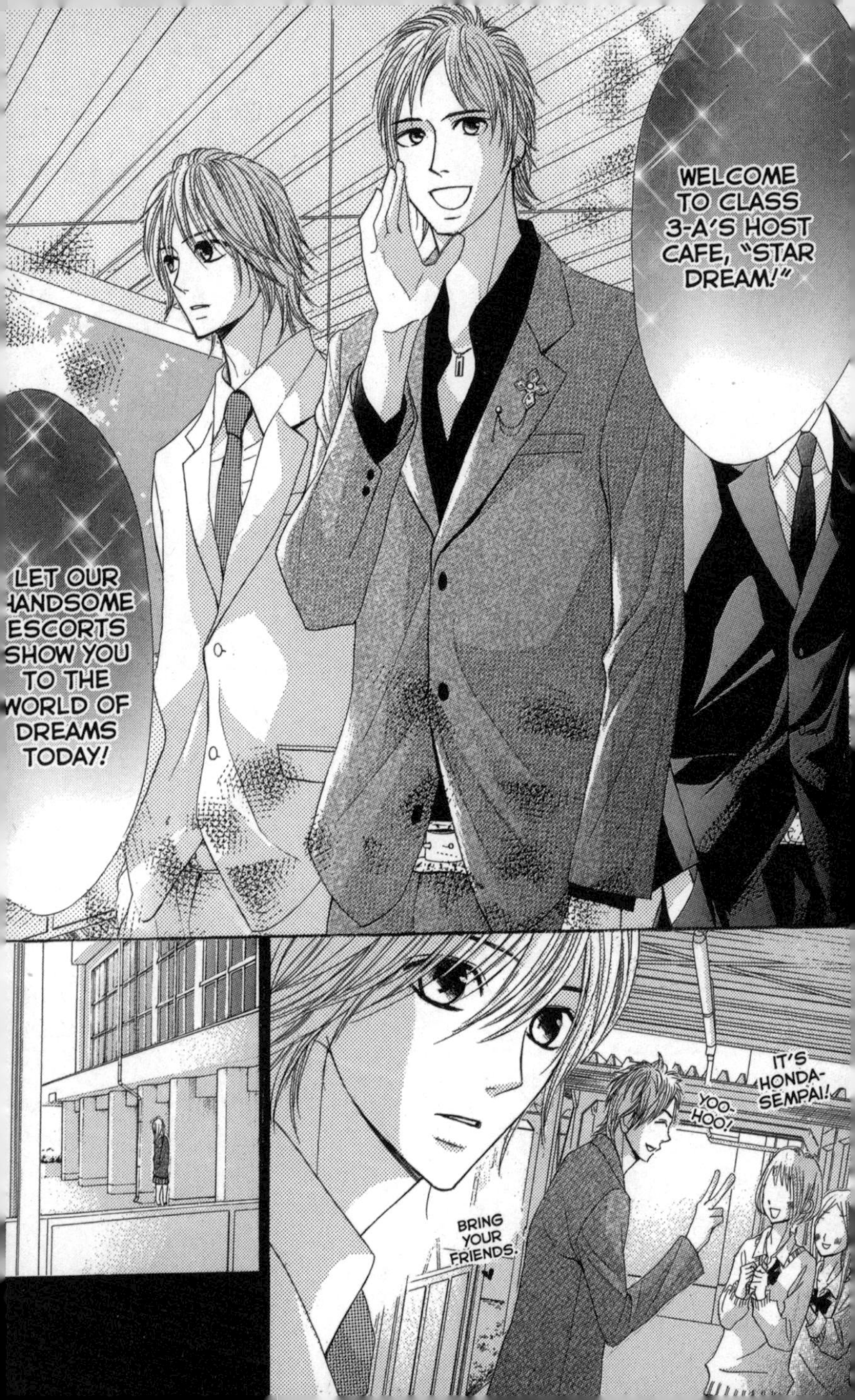
WELCOME TO CLASS 3-A'S HOST CAFE, "STAR DREAM!"
LET OUR HANDSOME ESCORTS SHOW YOU TO THE WORLD OF DREAMS TODAY!
IT'S HONDA-SEMPAI!
YOO-HOO!
BRING YOUR FRIENDS.

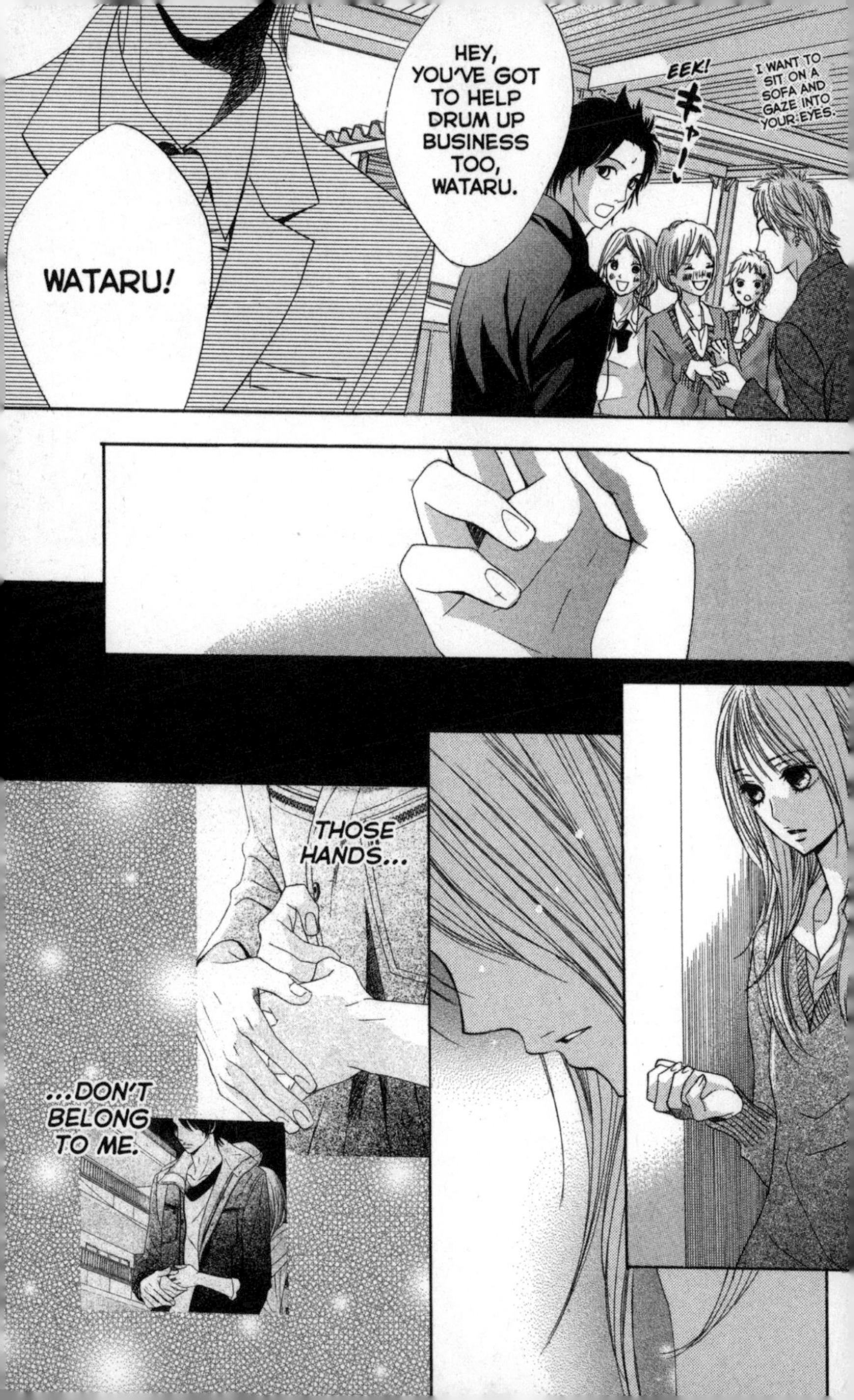
I WANT TO SIT ON A SOFA AND GAZE INTO YOUR EYES.
EEK!
キャー
HEY, YOU'VE GOT TO HELP DRUM UP BUSINESS TOO, WATARU.
WATARU!
THOSE HANDS...
...DON'T BELONG TO ME.

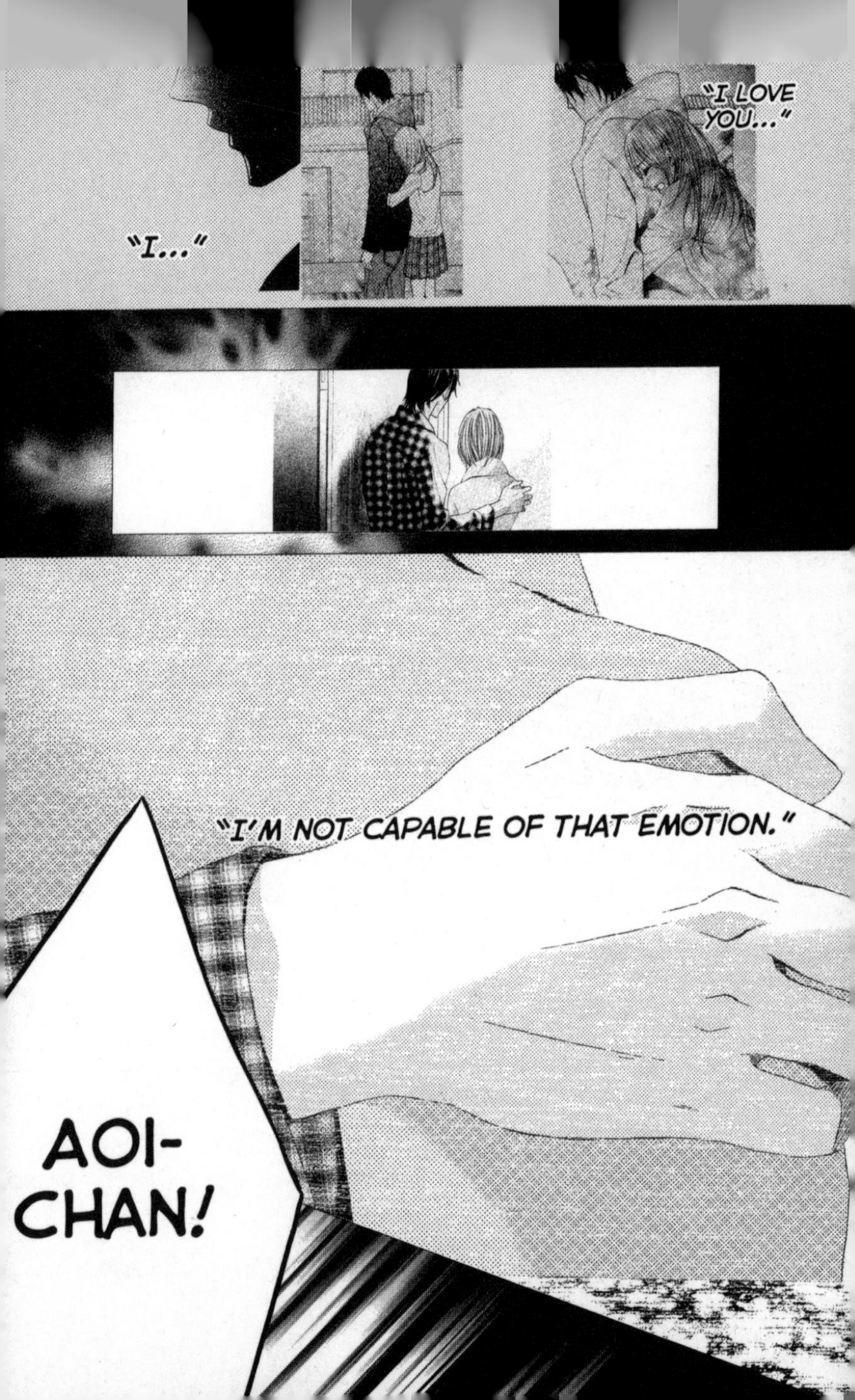
"I LOVE YOU..."
"I..."
"I'M NOT CAPABLE OF THAT EMOTION."
AOI-CHAN!

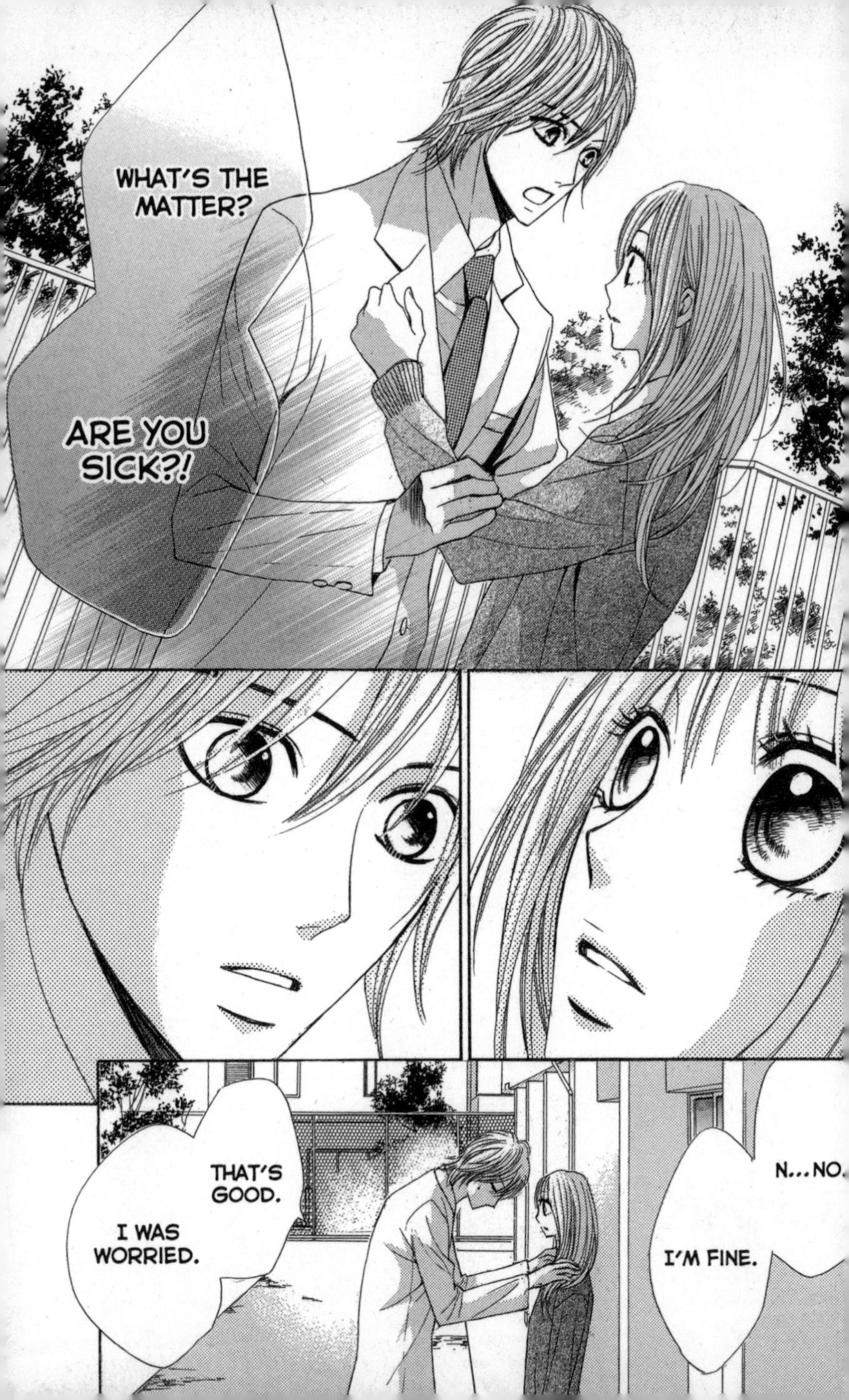
WHAT'S THE MATTER?
ARE YOU SICK?!
N...NO.
I'M FINE.
THAT'S GOOD.
I WAS WORRIED.

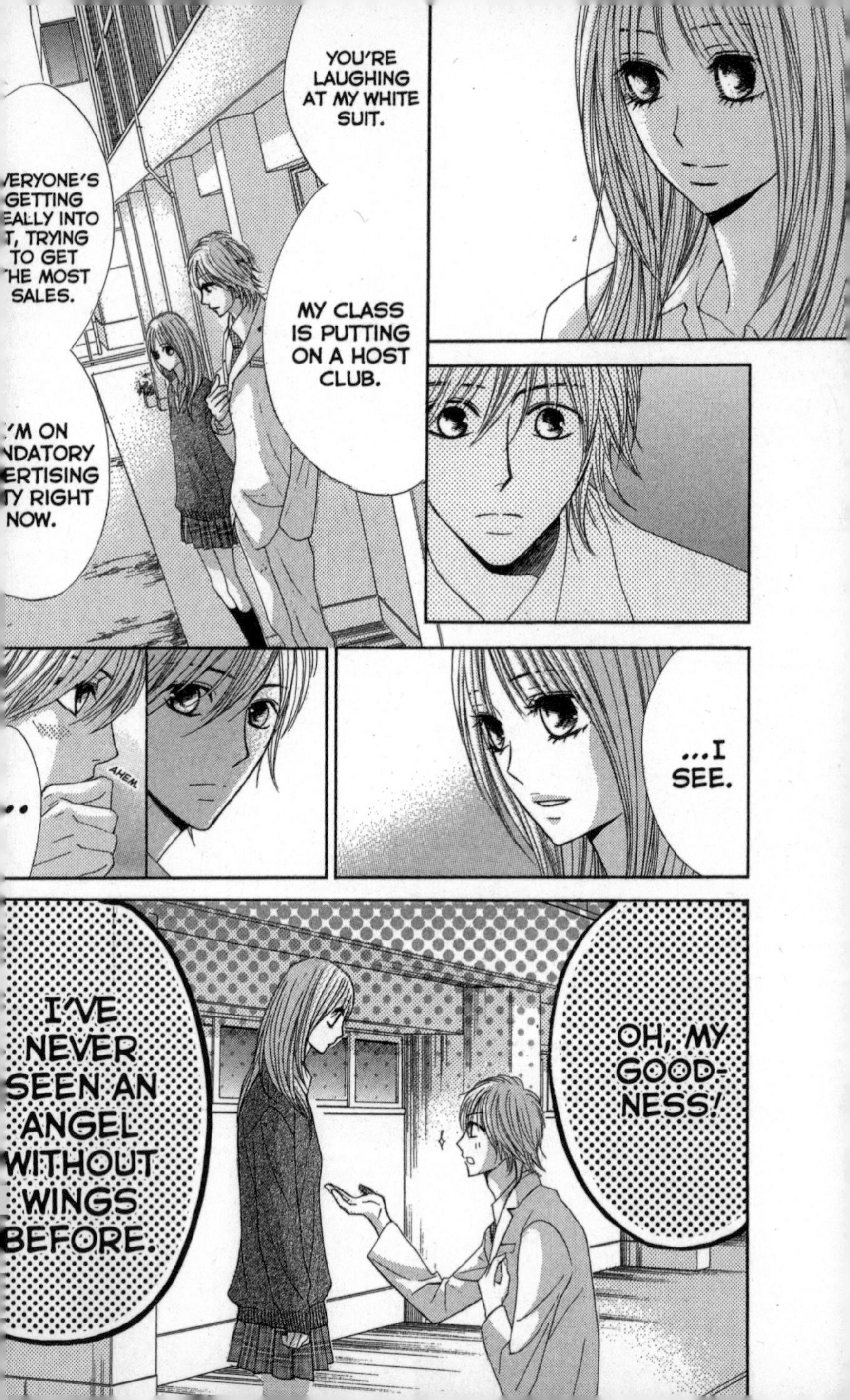
YOU'RE LAUGHING AT MY WHITE SUIT.
MY CLASS IS PUTTING ON A HOST CLUB.
ERYONE'S GETTING EALLY INTO T, TRYING TO GET HE MOST SALES.
'M ON NDATORY ERTISING TY RIGHT NOW.
...I SEE.
AHEM.
..
OH, MY GOOD-NESS!
I'VE NEVER SEEN AN ANGEL WITHOUT WINGS BEFORE.

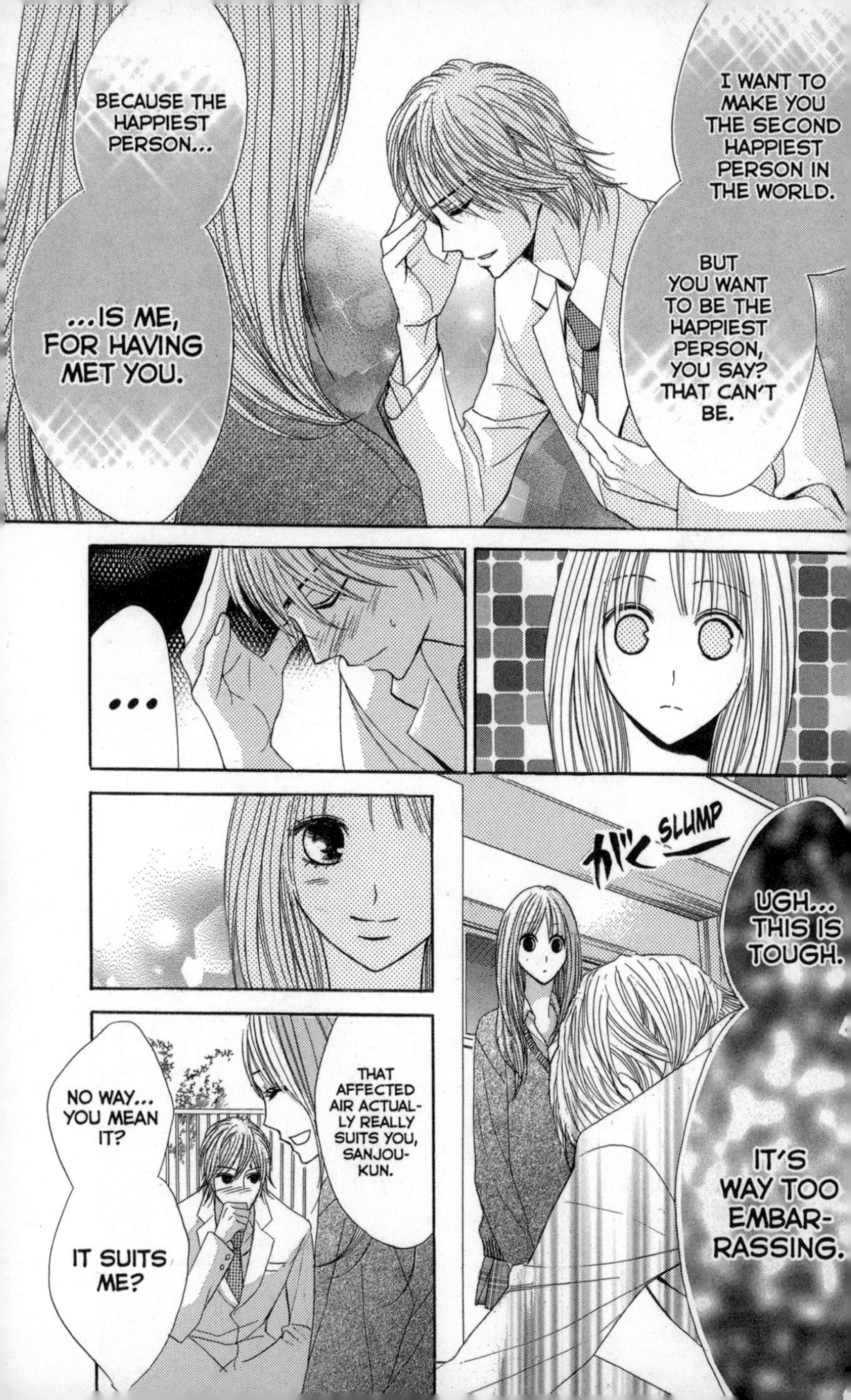
I WANT TO MAKE YOU THE SECOND HAPPIEST PERSON IN THE WORLD.
BUT YOU WANT TO BE THE HAPPIEST PERSON, YOU SAY? THAT CAN'T BE.
BECAUSE THE HAPPIEST PERSON...
...IS ME, FOR HAVING MET YOU.
...
がく SLUMP
UGH... THIS IS TOUGH.
IT'S WAY TOO EMBARRASSING.
THAT AFFECTED AIR ACTUALLY REALLY SUITS YOU, SANJOU-KUN.
NO WAY... YOU MEAN IT?
IT SUITS ME?

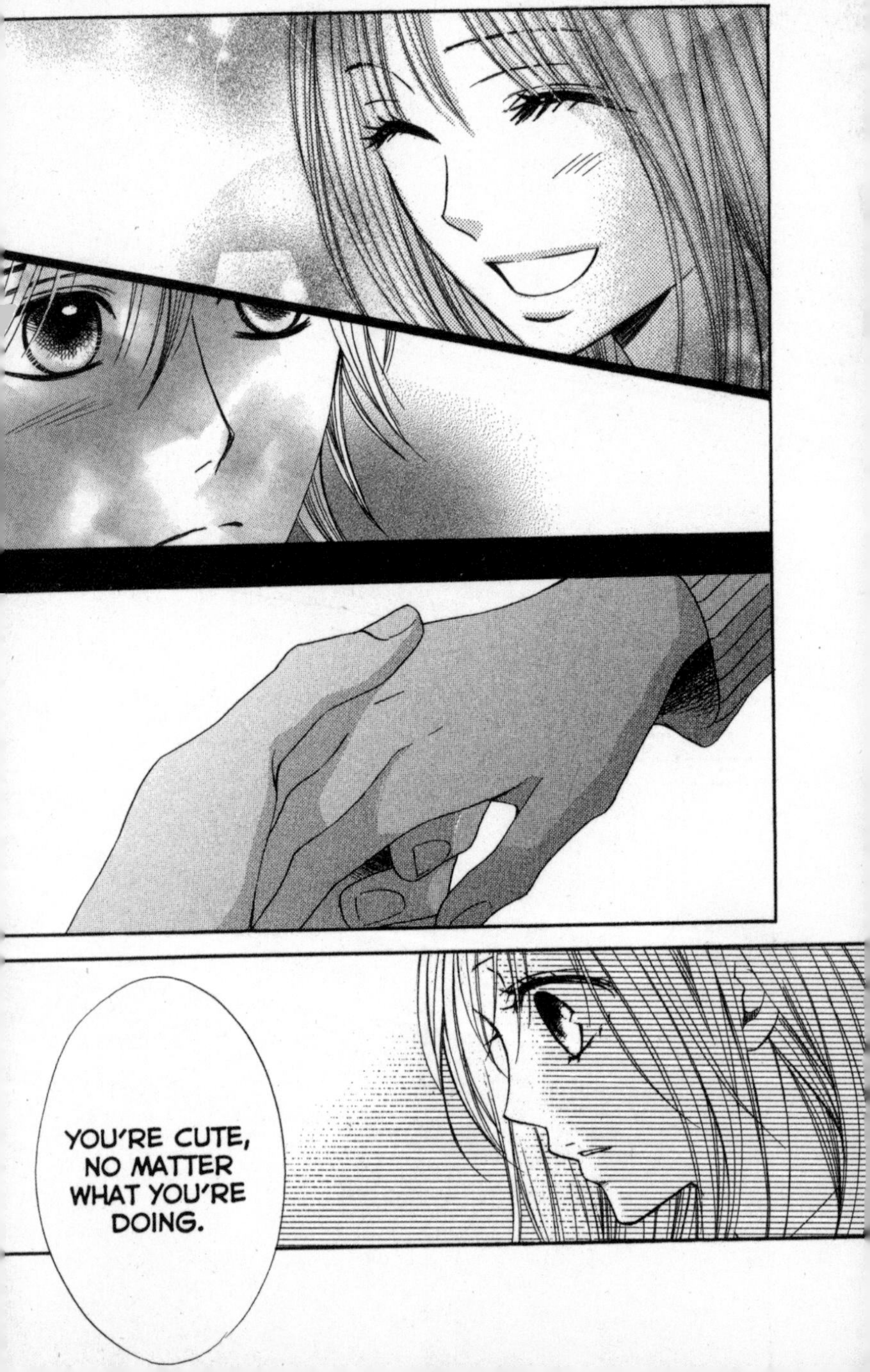
YOU'RE CUTE, NO MATTER WHAT YOU'RE DOING.

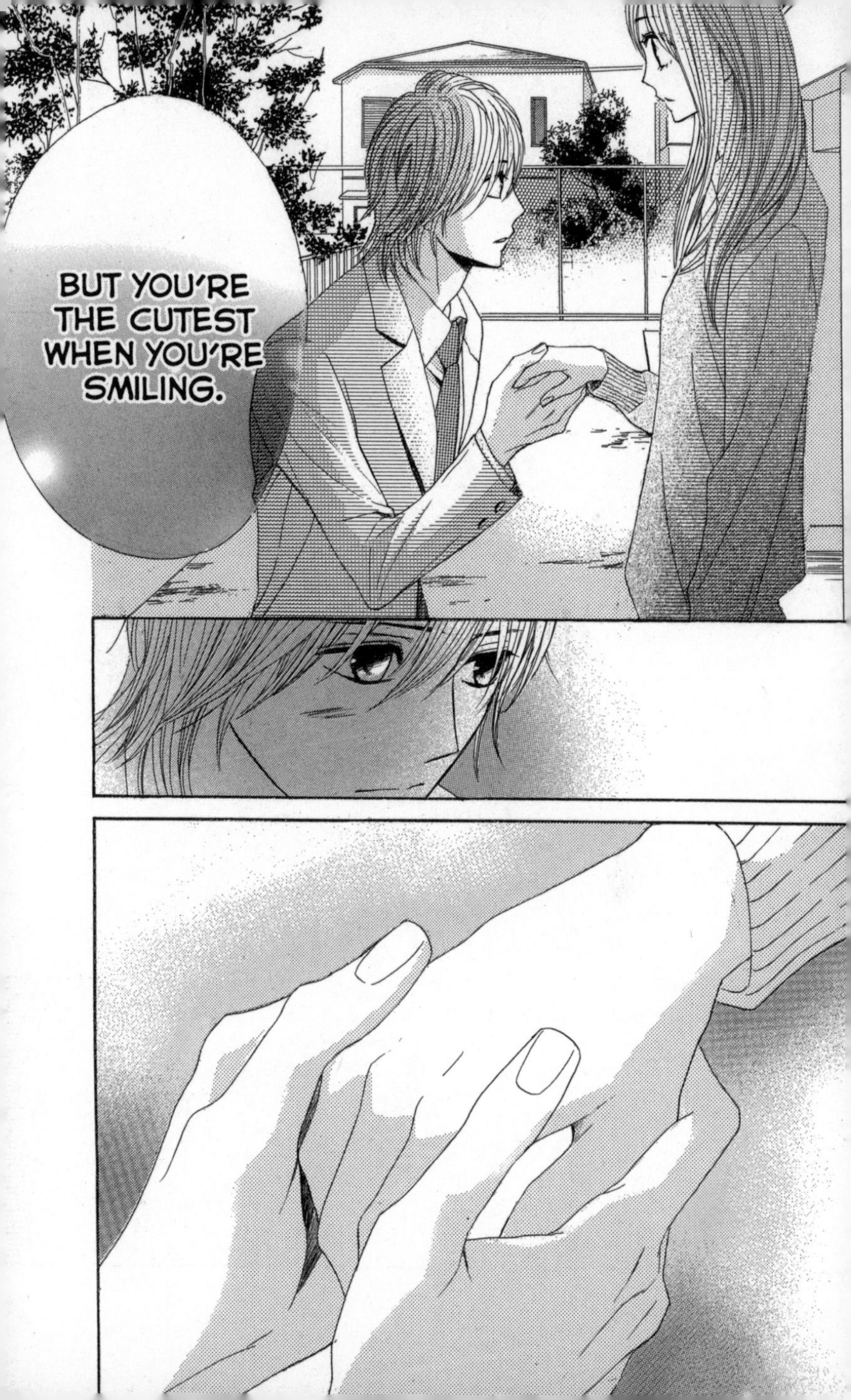
BUT YOU'RE THE CUTEST WHEN YOU'RE SMILING.

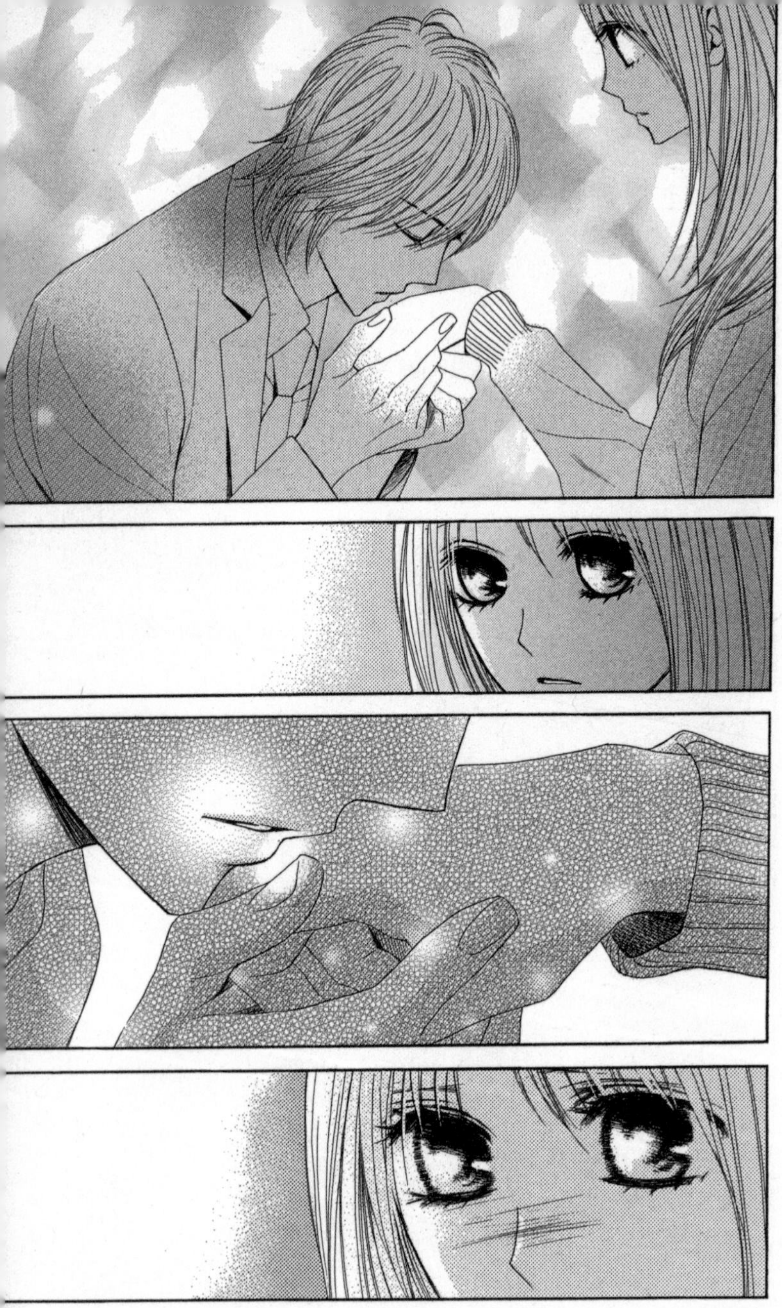

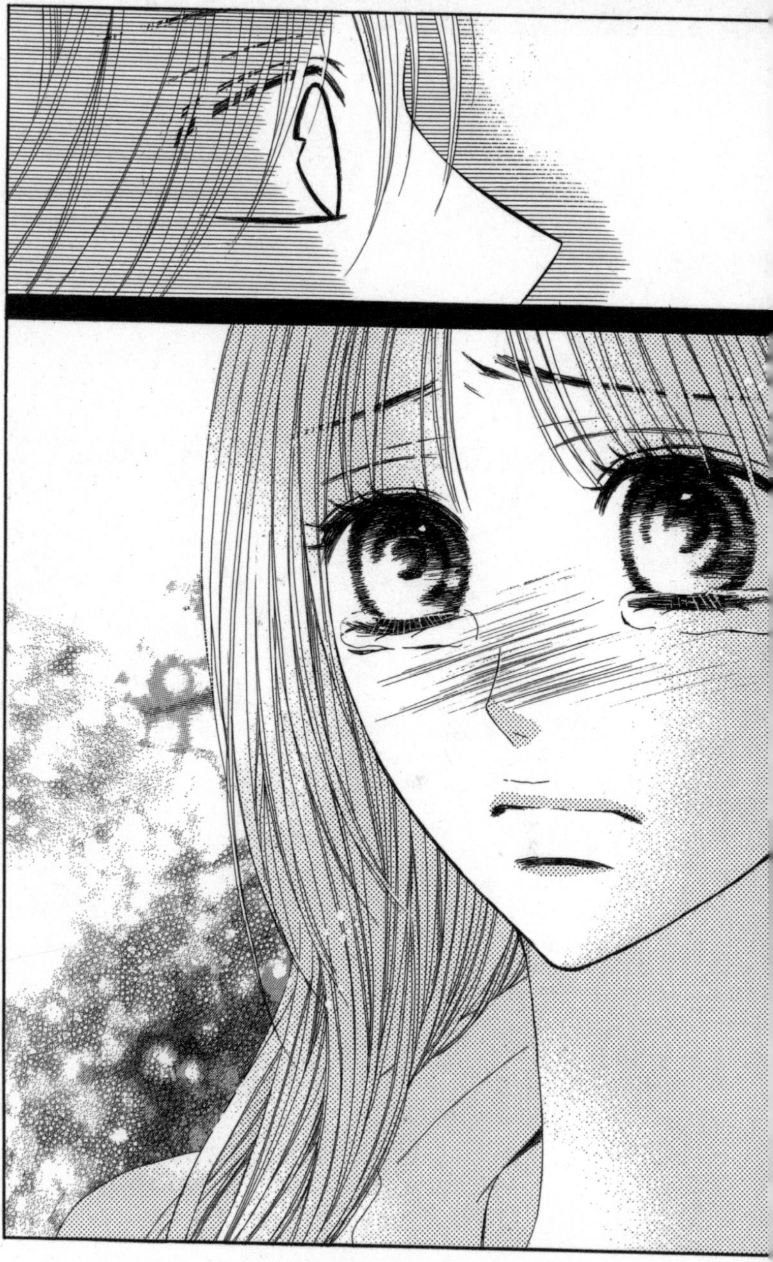

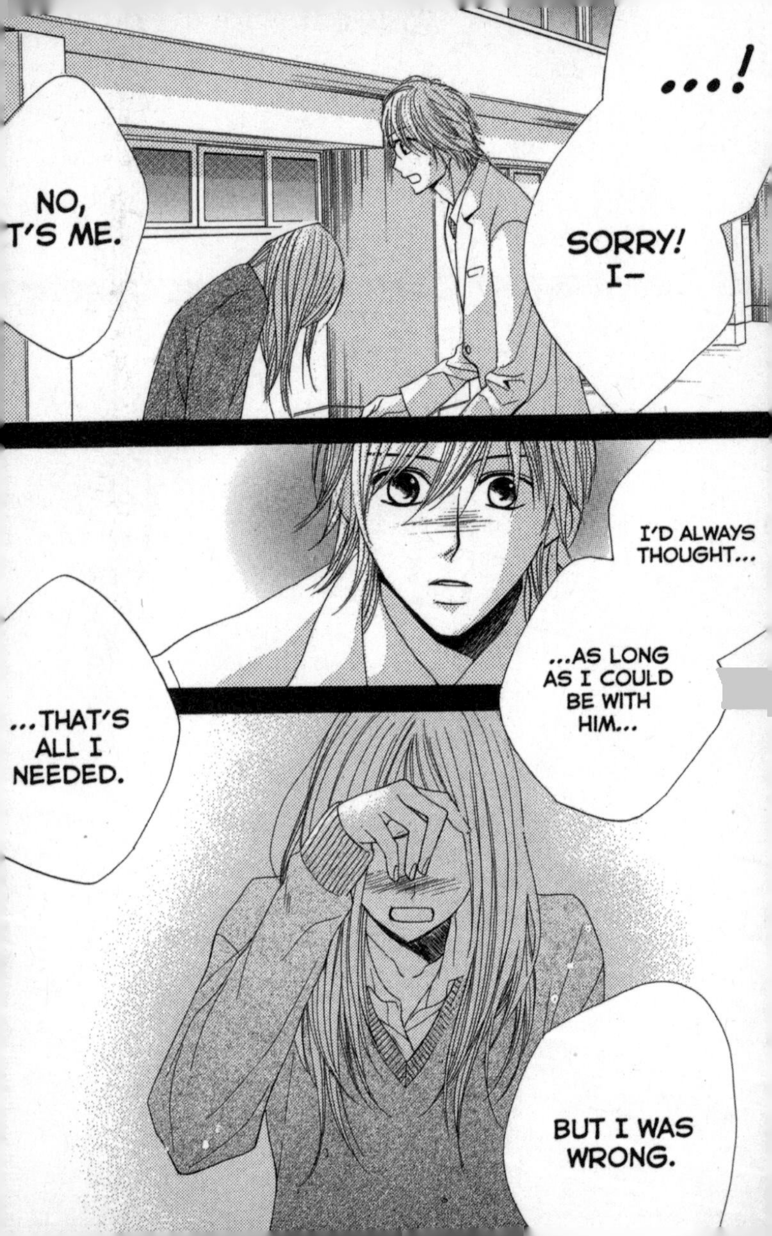
...!
SORRY! I–
NO, T'S ME.
I'D ALWAYS THOUGHT...
...AS LONG AS I COULD BE WITH HIM...
...THAT'S ALL I NEEDED.
BUT I WAS WRONG.

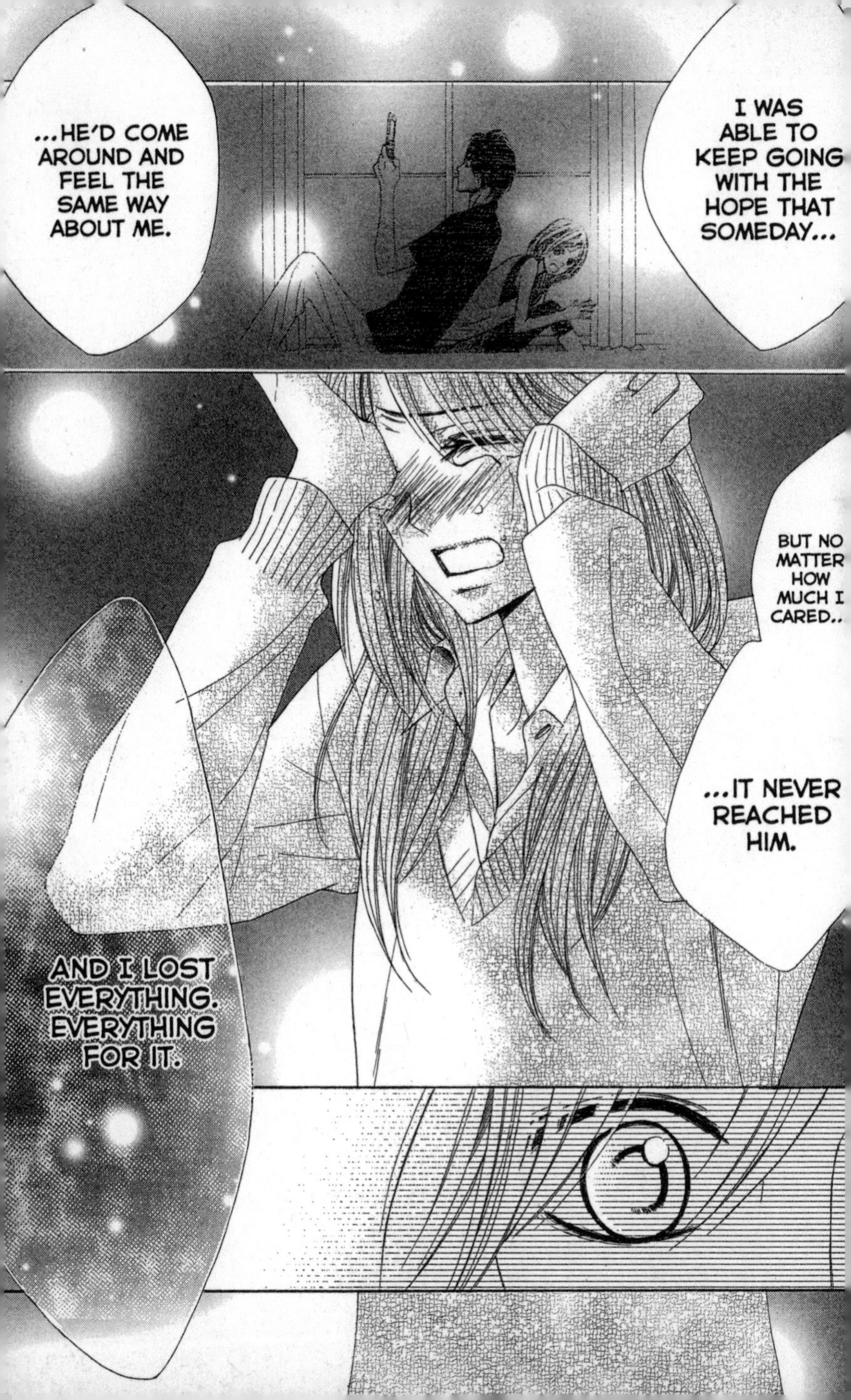
I WAS ABLE TO KEEP GOING WITH THE HOPE THAT SOMEDAY...
...HE'D COME AROUND AND FEEL THE SAME WAY ABOUT ME.
BUT NO MATTER HOW MUCH I CARED..
...IT NEVER REACHED HIM.
AND I LOST EVERYTHING. EVERYTHING FOR IT.

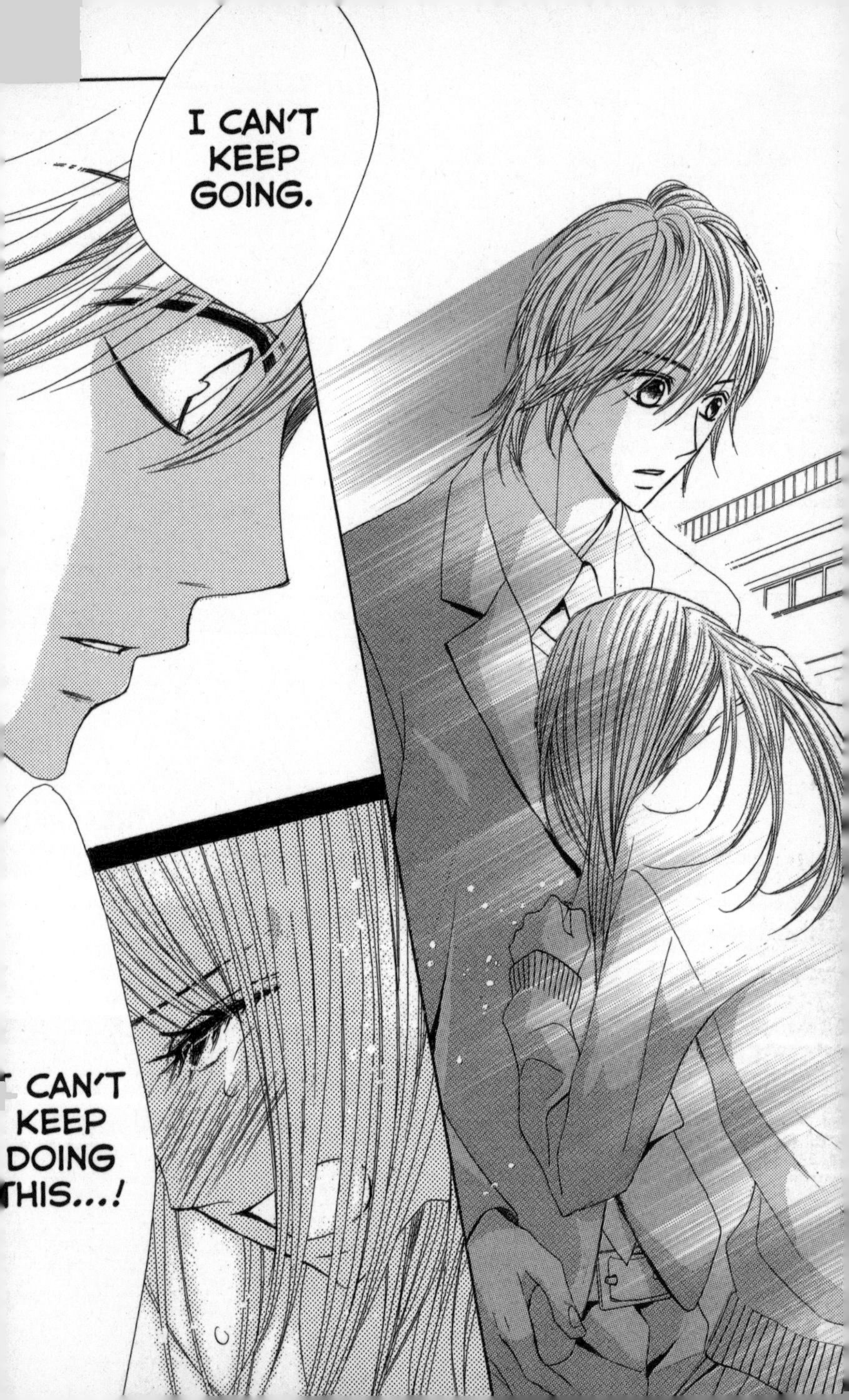
I CAN'T KEEP GOING.
CAN'T KEEP DOING THIS...!

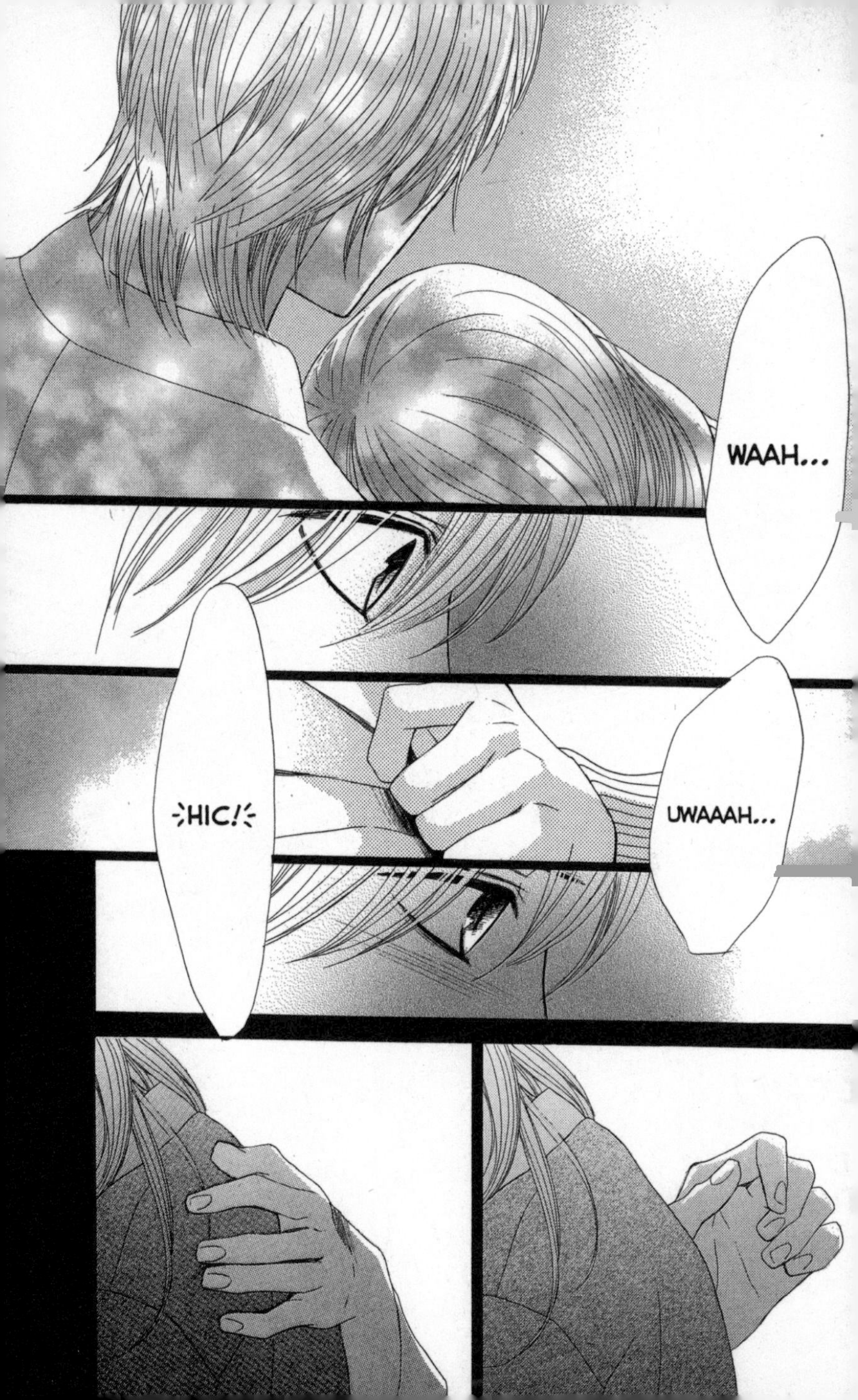
WAAH...
UWAAAH...
HIC!

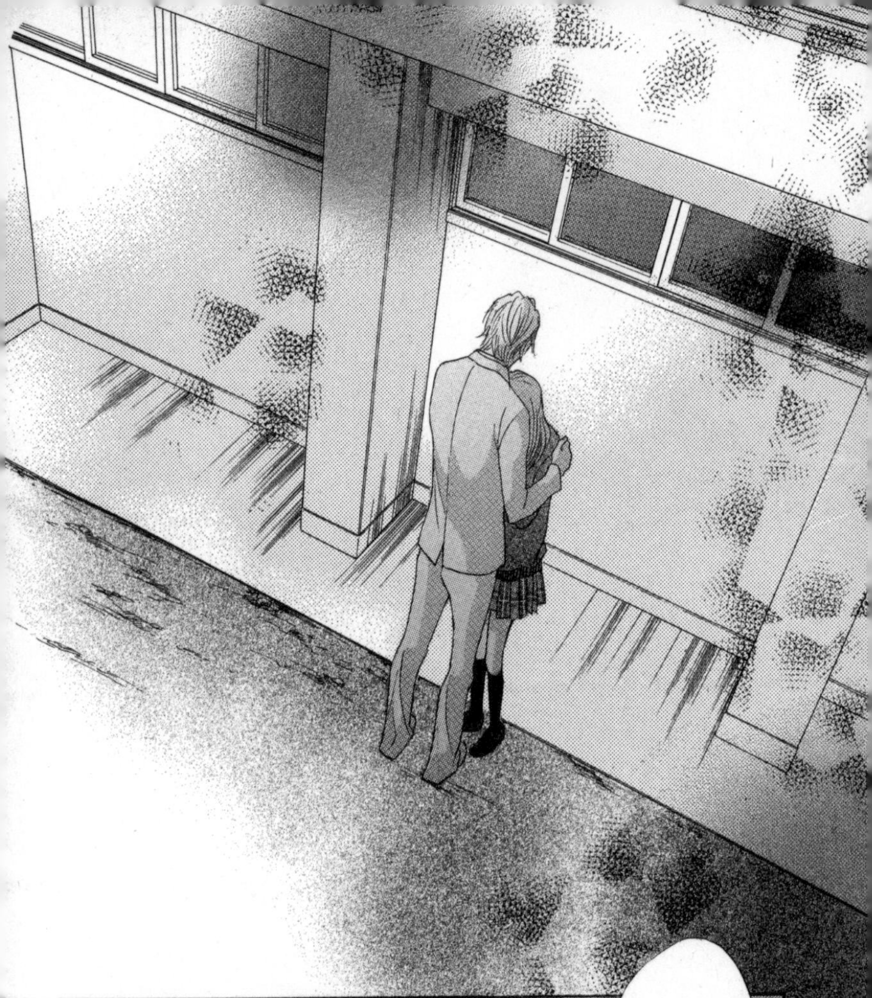

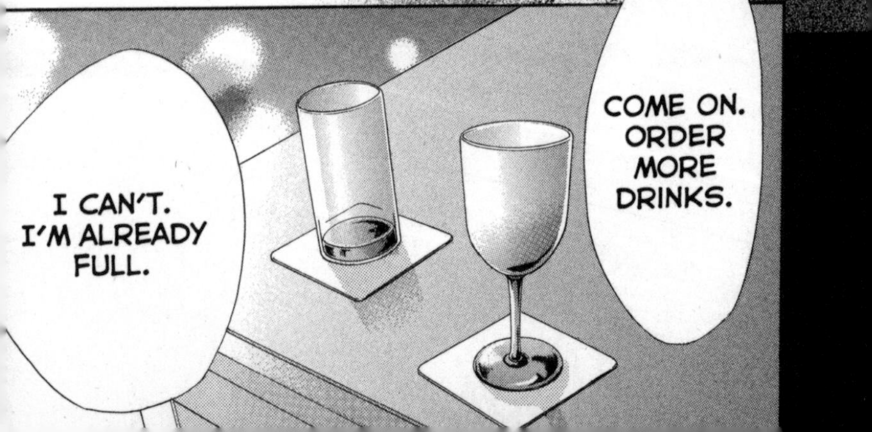
COME ON. ORDER MORE DRINKS.
I CAN'T. I'M ALREADY FULL.

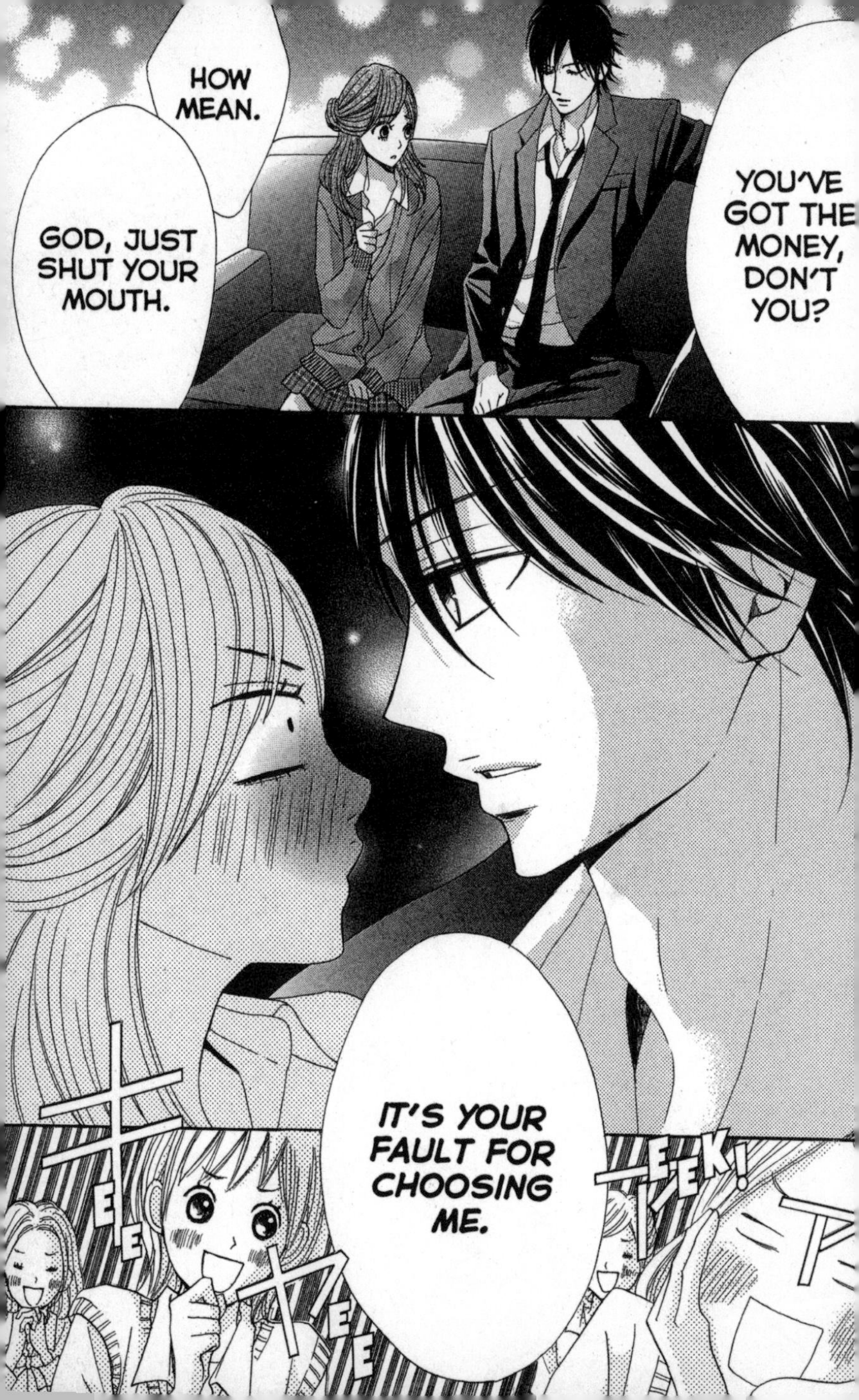
YOU'VE GOT THE MONEY, DON'T YOU?
HOW MEAN.
GOD, JUST SHUT YOUR MOUTH.
IT'S YOUR FAULT FOR CHOOSING ME.
EEK!

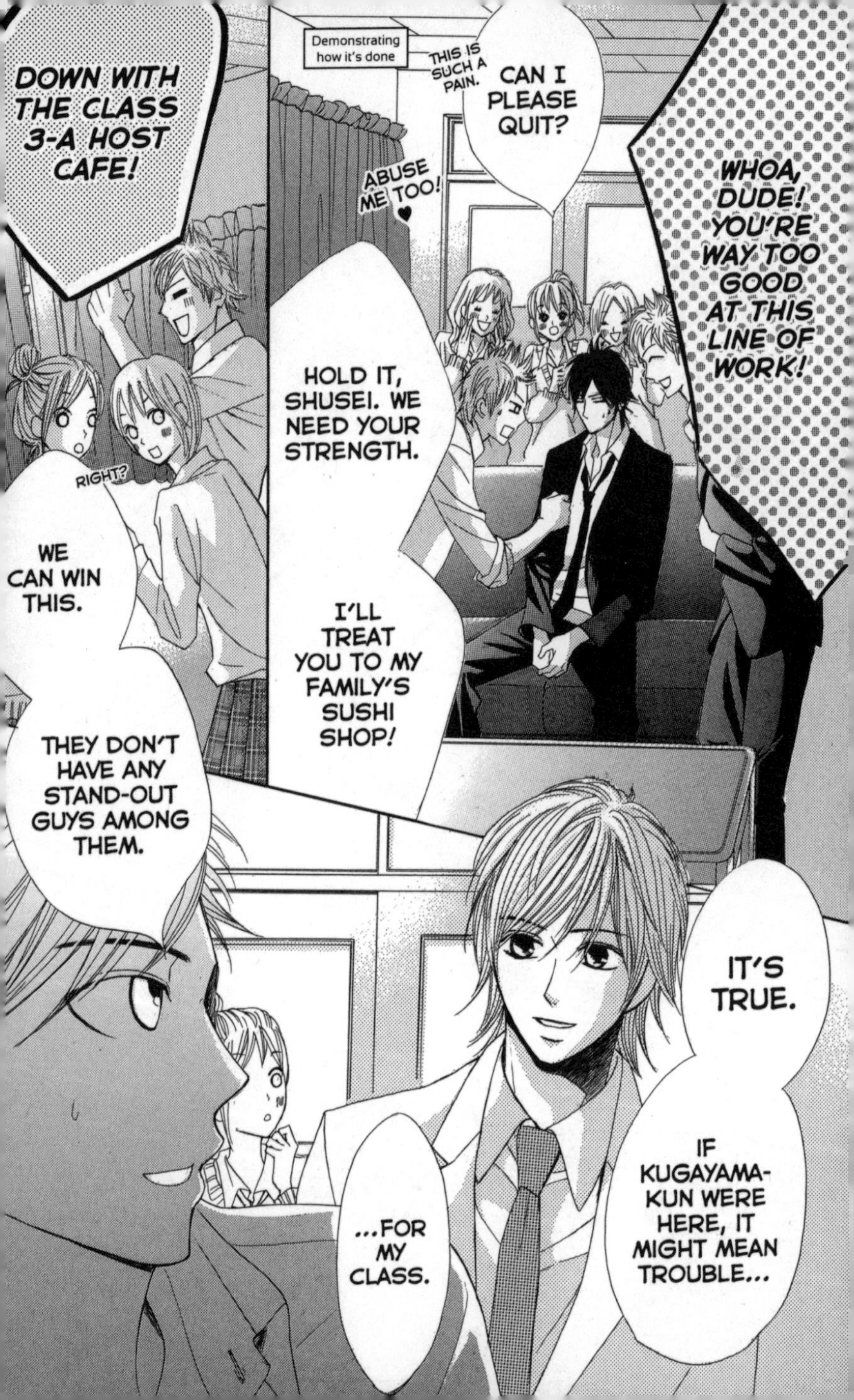

WHOA, DUDE! YOU'RE WAY TOO GOOD AT THIS LINE OF WORK!
Demonstrating how it's done
THIS IS SUCH A PAIN.
CAN I PLEASE QUIT?
ABUSE ME TOO! ♥
HOLD IT, SHUSEI. WE NEED YOUR STRENGTH.
I'LL TREAT YOU TO MY FAMILY'S SUSHI SHOP!
DOWN WITH THE CLASS 3-A HOST CAFE!
RIGHT?
WE CAN WIN THIS.
THEY DON'T HAVE ANY STAND-OUT GUYS AMONG THEM.
IT'S TRUE.
IF KUGAYAMA-KUN WERE HERE, IT MIGHT MEAN TROUBLE...
...FOR MY CLASS.

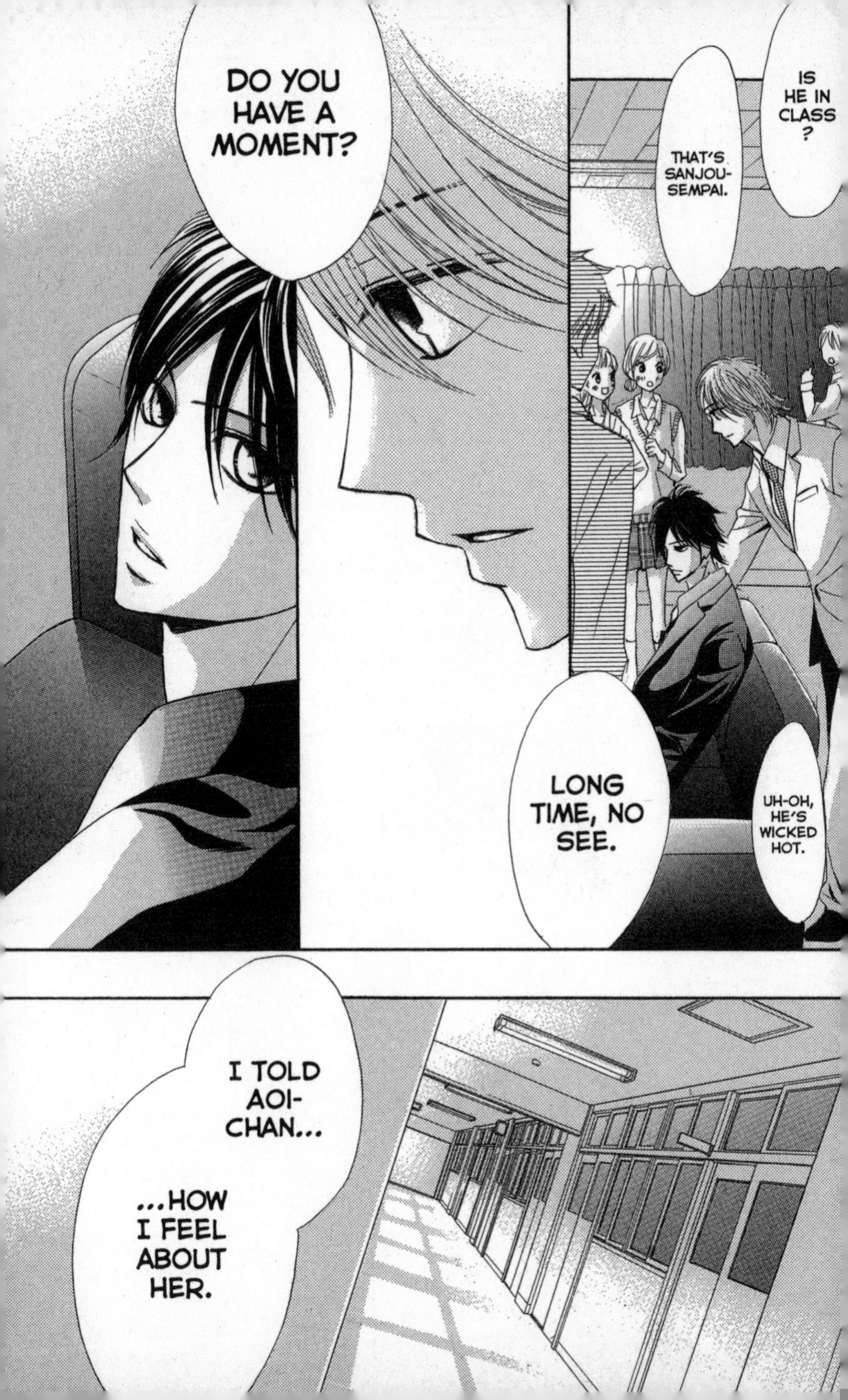
IS HE IN CLASS?
THAT'S SANJOU-SEMPAI.
UH-OH, HE'S WICKED HOT.
LONG TIME, NO SEE.
DO YOU HAVE A MOMENT?
I TOLD AOI-CHAN...
...HOW I FEEL ABOUT HER.

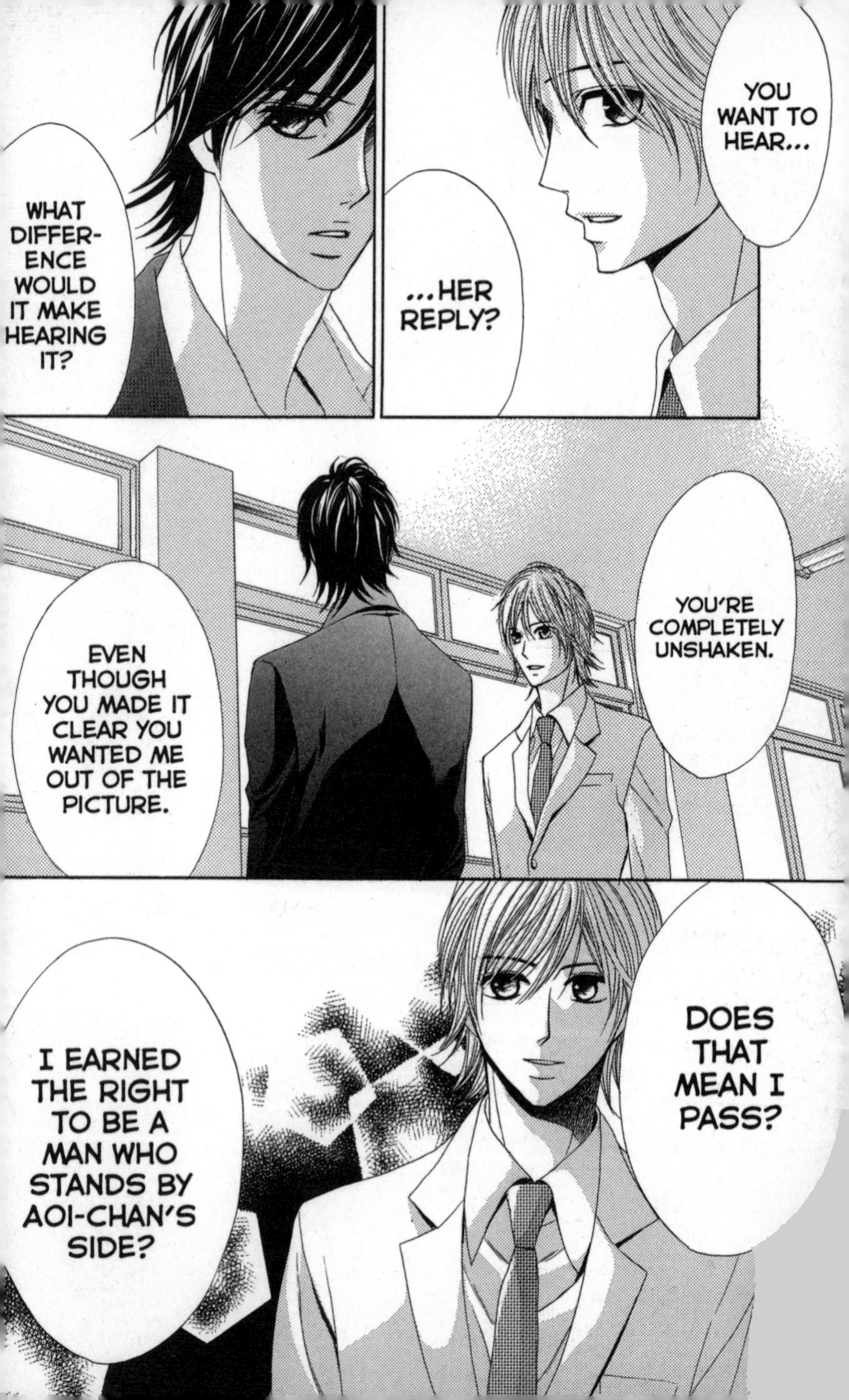
YOU WANT TO HEAR...
...HER REPLY?
WHAT DIFFERENCE WOULD IT MAKE HEARING IT?
YOU'RE COMPLETELY UNSHAKEN.
EVEN THOUGH YOU MADE IT CLEAR YOU WANTED ME OUT OF THE PICTURE.
DOES THAT MEAN I PASS?
I EARNED THE RIGHT TO BE A MAN WHO STANDS BY AOI-CHAN'S SIDE?

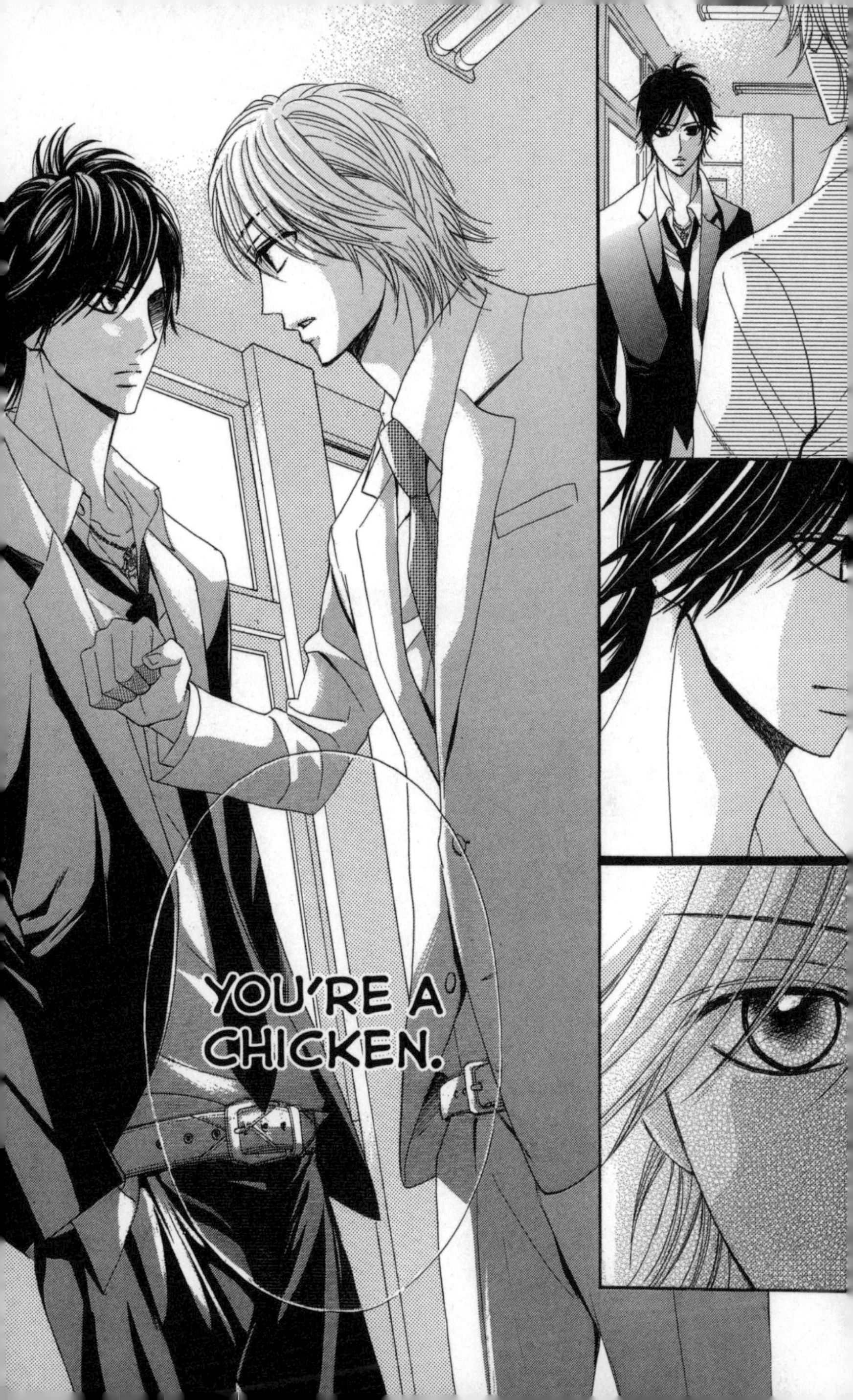
YOU'RE A CHICKEN.

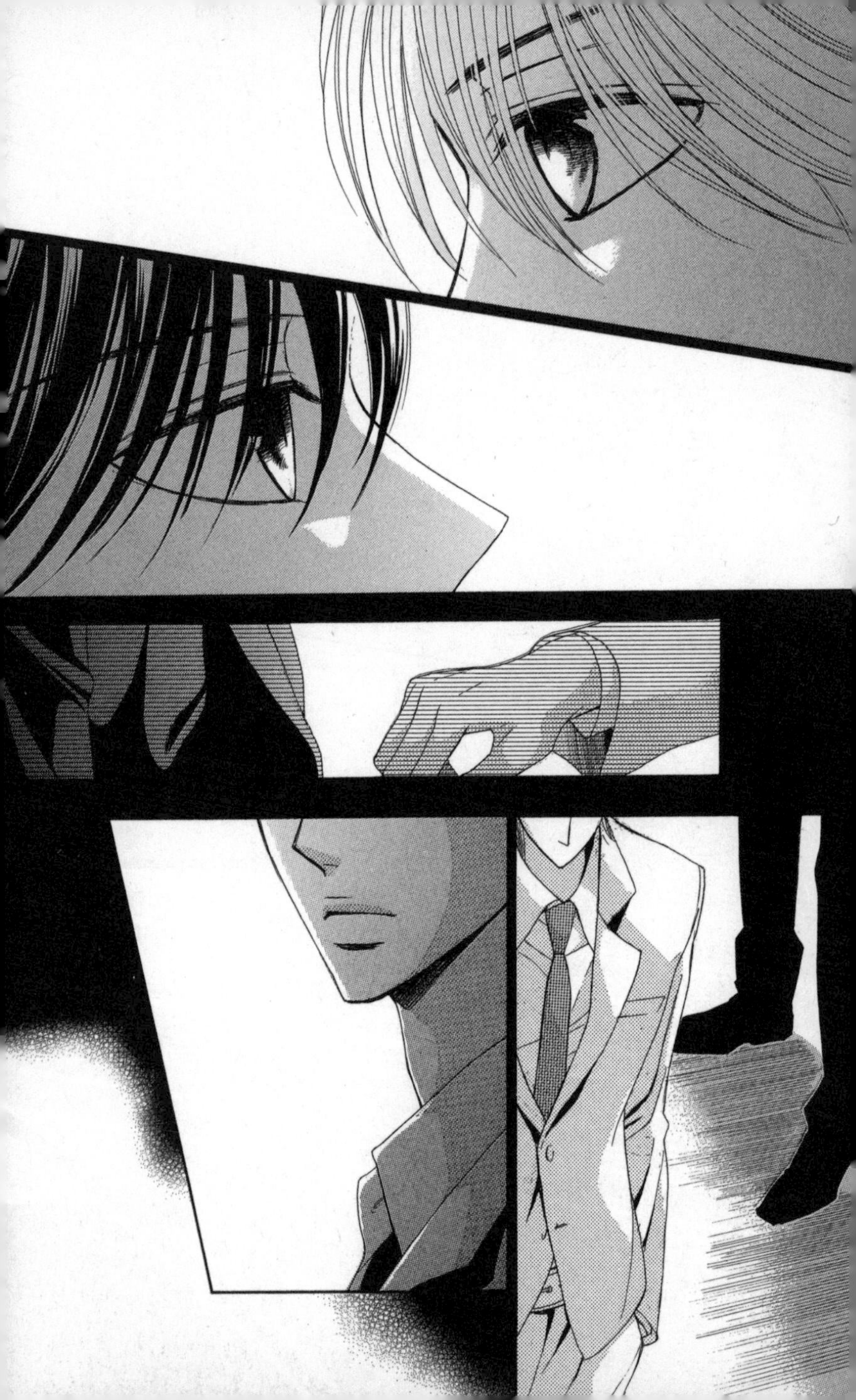

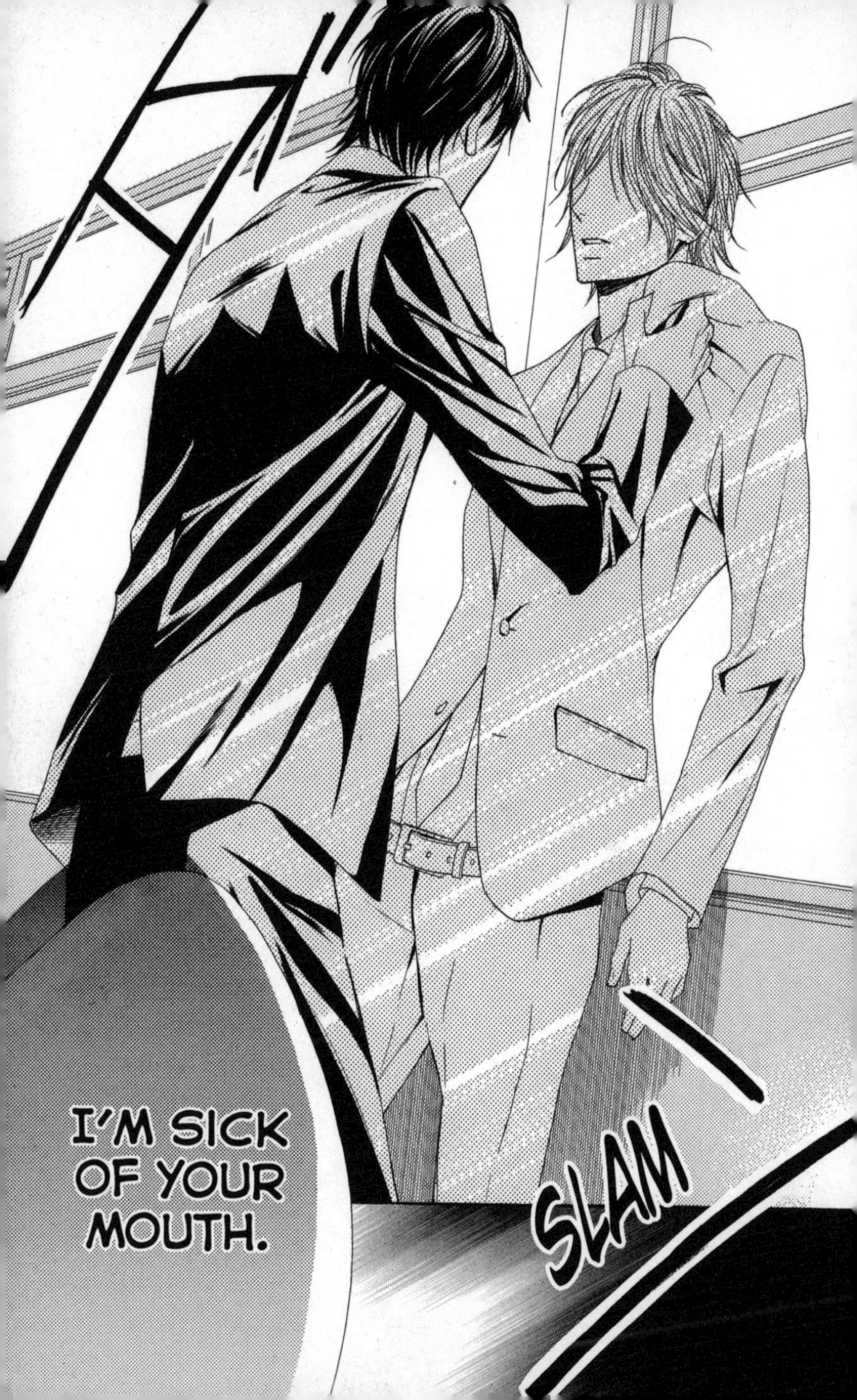
SLAM
I'M SICK OF YOUR MOUTH.

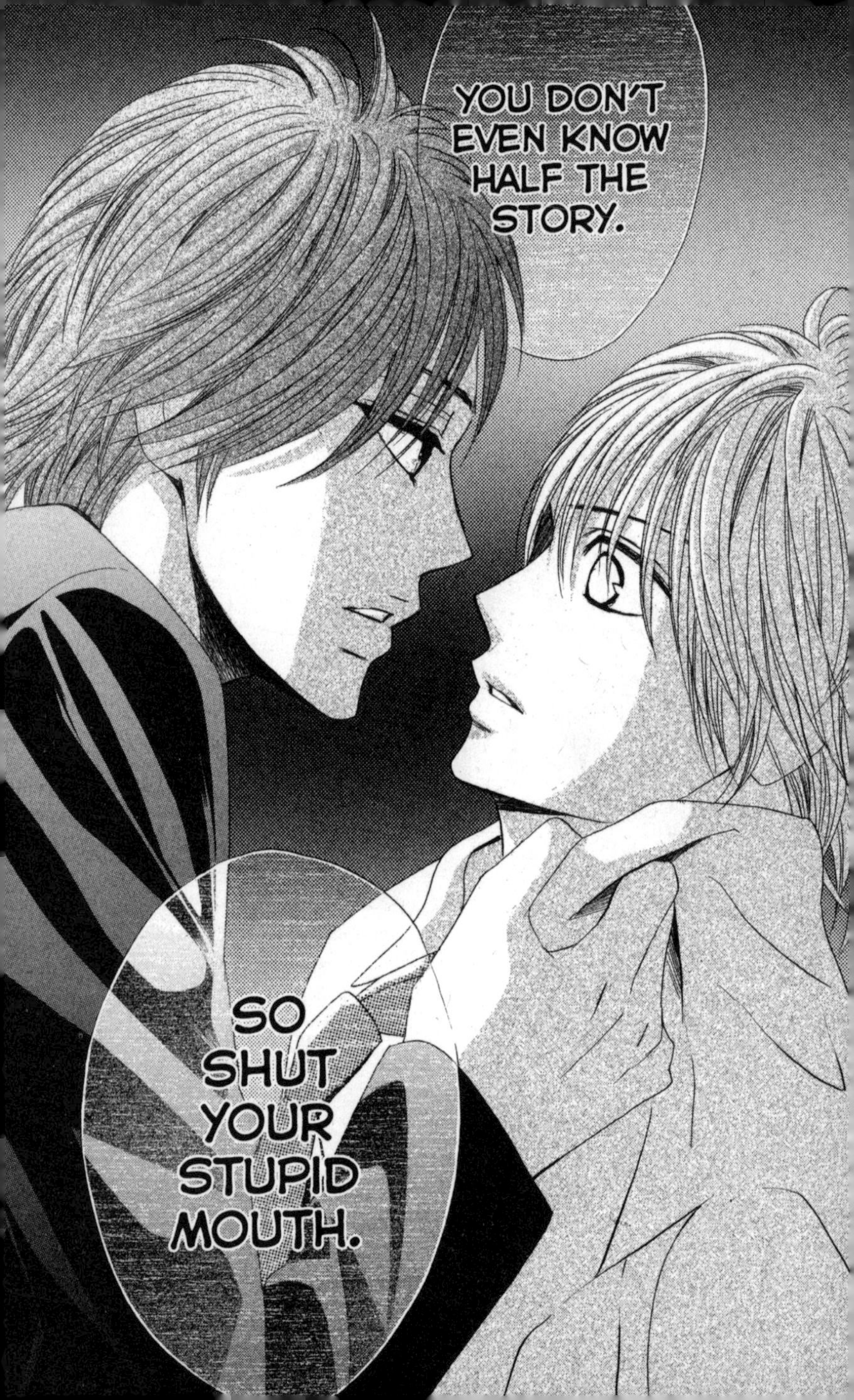
YOU DON'T EVEN KNOW HALF THE STORY.
SO SHUT YOUR STUPID MOUTH.

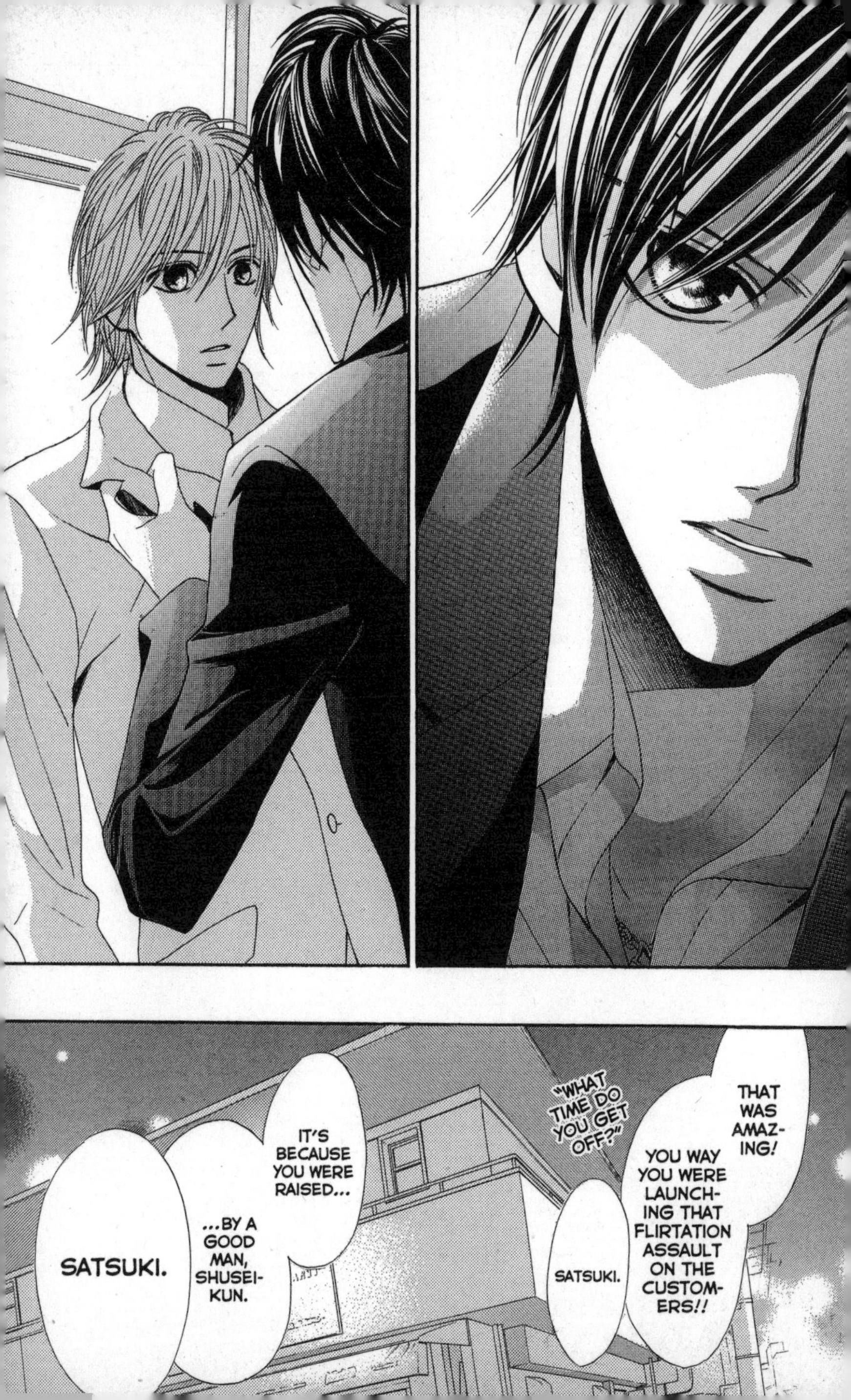
THAT WAS AMAZ-ING!
YOU WAY YOU WERE LAUNCH-ING THAT FLIRTATION ASSAULT ON THE CUSTOM-ERS!!
"WHAT TIME DO YOU GET OFF?"
SATSUKI.
IT'S BECAUSE YOU WERE RAISED...
...BY A GOOD MAN, SHUSEI-KUN.
SATSUKI.

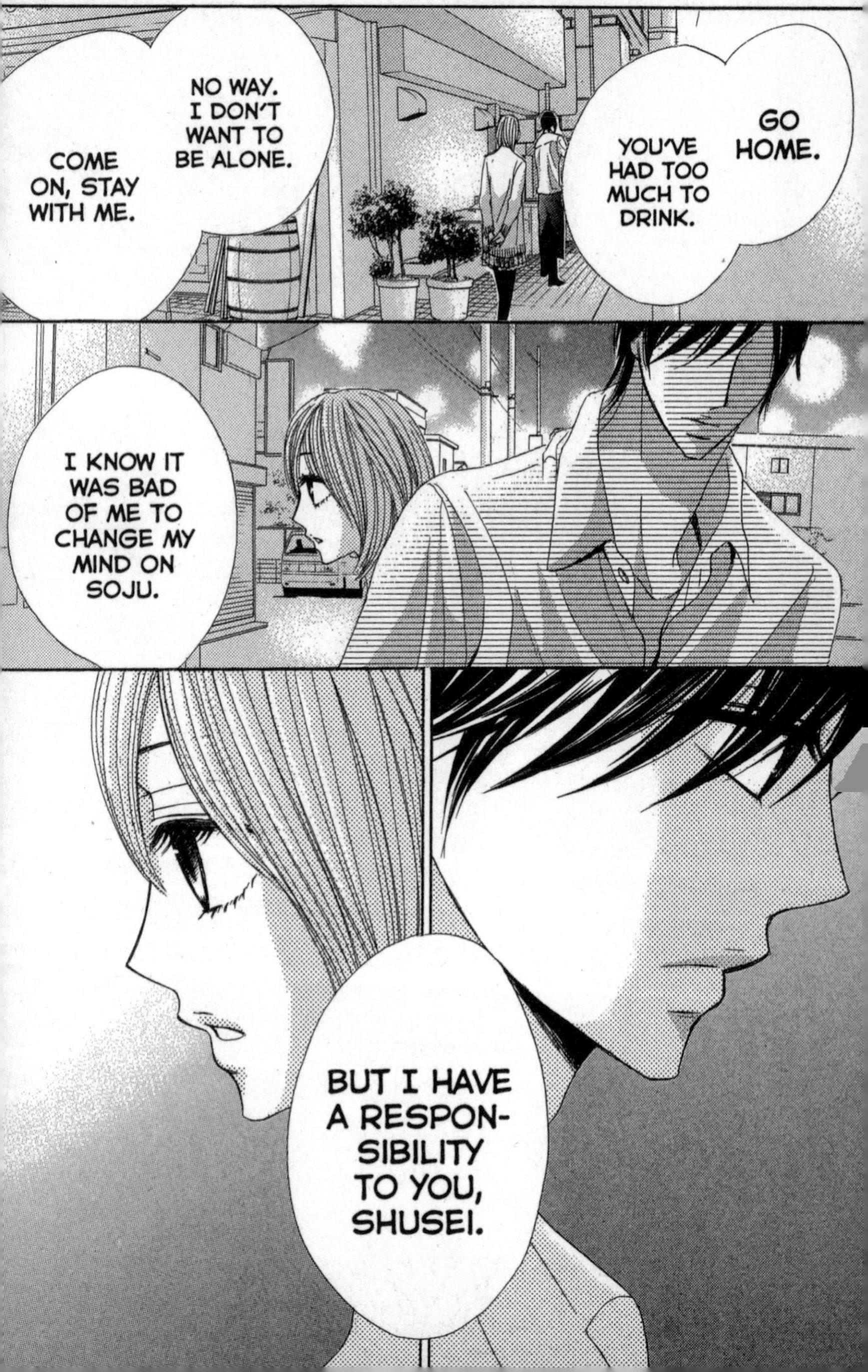
GO HOME. YOU'VE HAD TOO MUCH TO DRINK.
NO WAY. I DON'T WANT TO BE ALONE. COME ON, STAY WITH ME.
I KNOW IT WAS BAD OF ME TO CHANGE MY MIND ON SOJU.
BUT I HAVE A RESPON-SIBILITY TO YOU, SHUSEI.

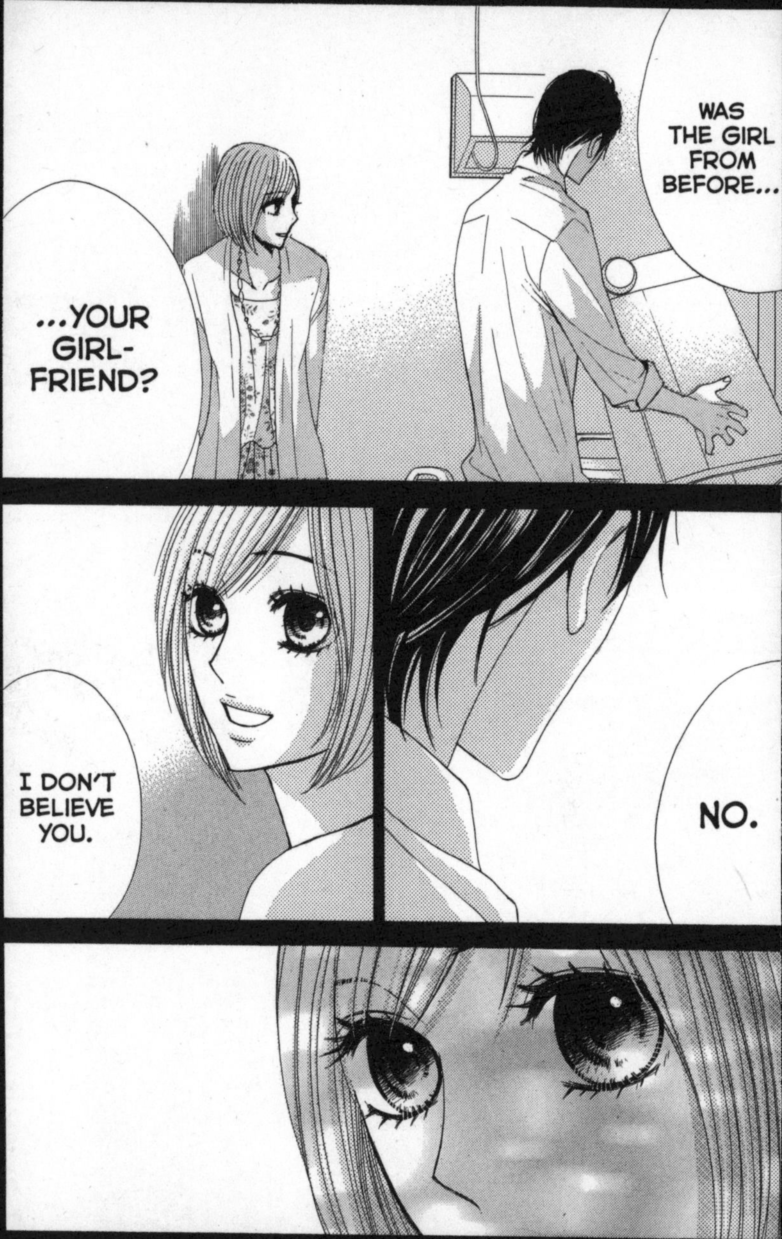
WAS THE GIRL FROM BEFORE...
...YOUR GIRL-FRIEND?
NO.
I DON'T BELIEVE YOU.

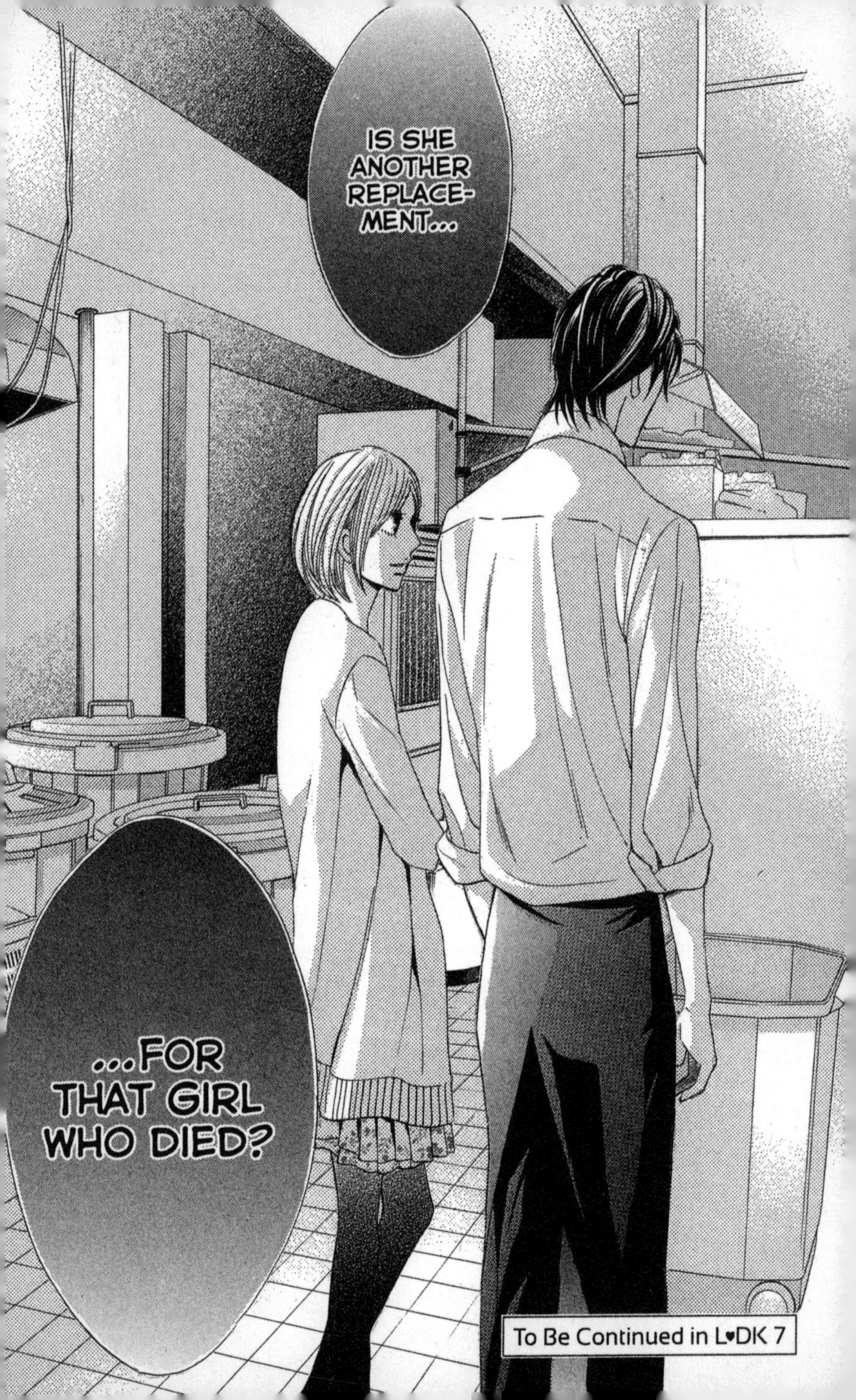
IS SHE ANOTHER REPLACEMENT...
...FOR THAT GIRL WHO DIED?
To Be Continued in L♥DK 7

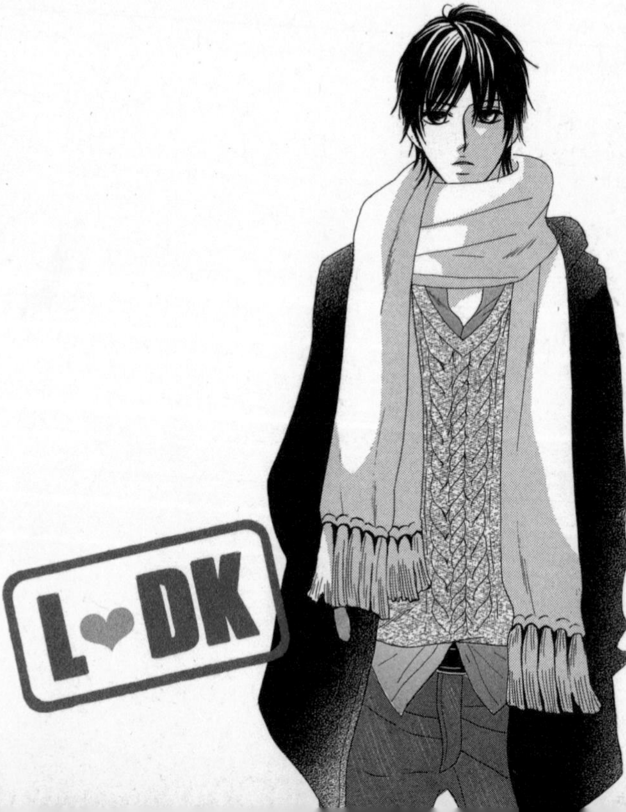
L♥DK

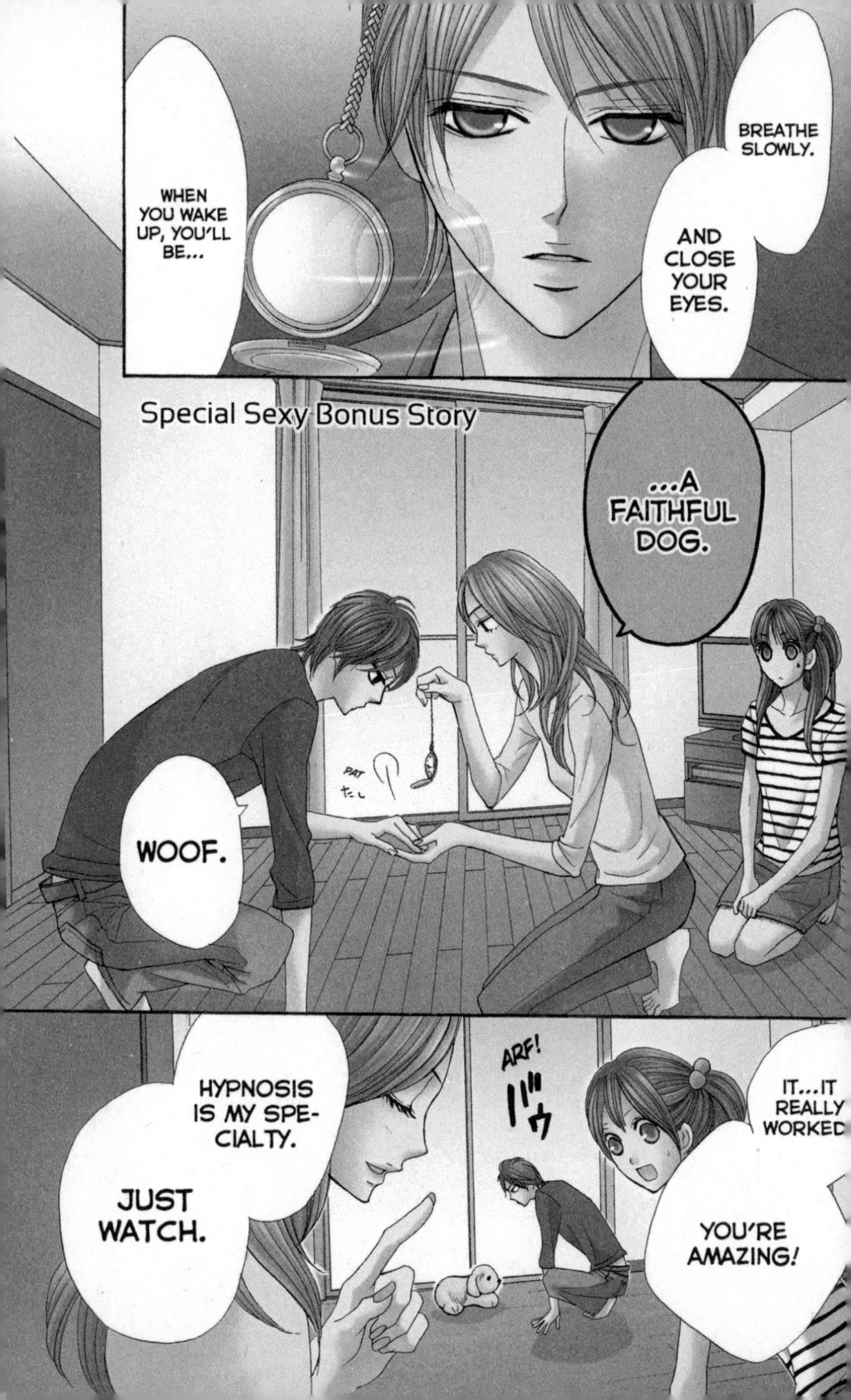
BREATHE SLOWLY.
AND CLOSE YOUR EYES.
WHEN YOU WAKE UP, YOU'LL BE...
Special Sexy Bonus Story
...A FAITHFUL DOG.
PAT
たし
WOOF.
IT...IT REALLY WORKED
YOU'RE AMAZING!
ARF!
バウ
HYPNOSIS IS MY SPECIALTY.
JUST WATCH.

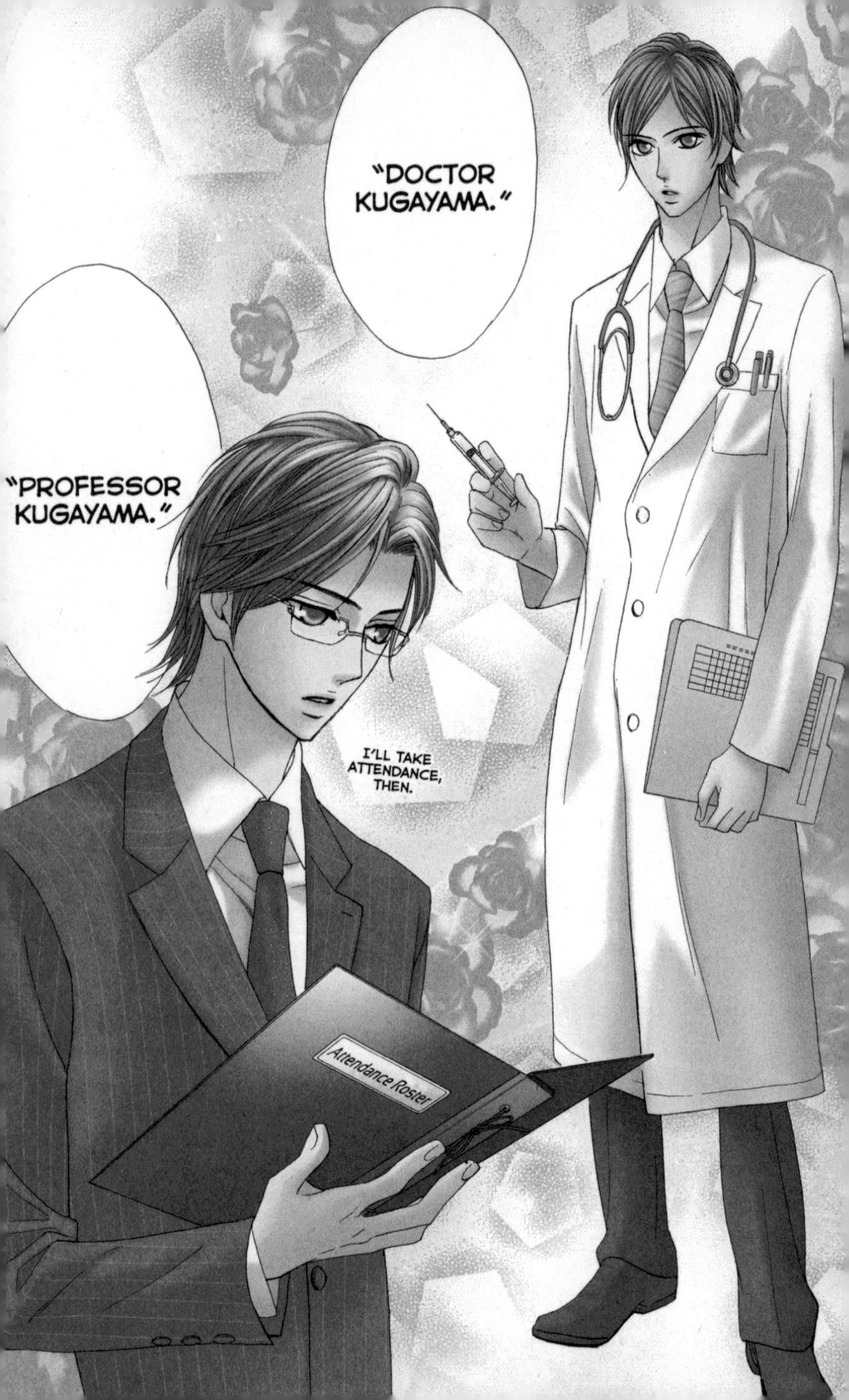
"DOCTOR KUGAYAMA."
"PROFESSOR KUGAYAMA."
I'LL TAKE ATTENDANCE, THEN.
Attendance Roster

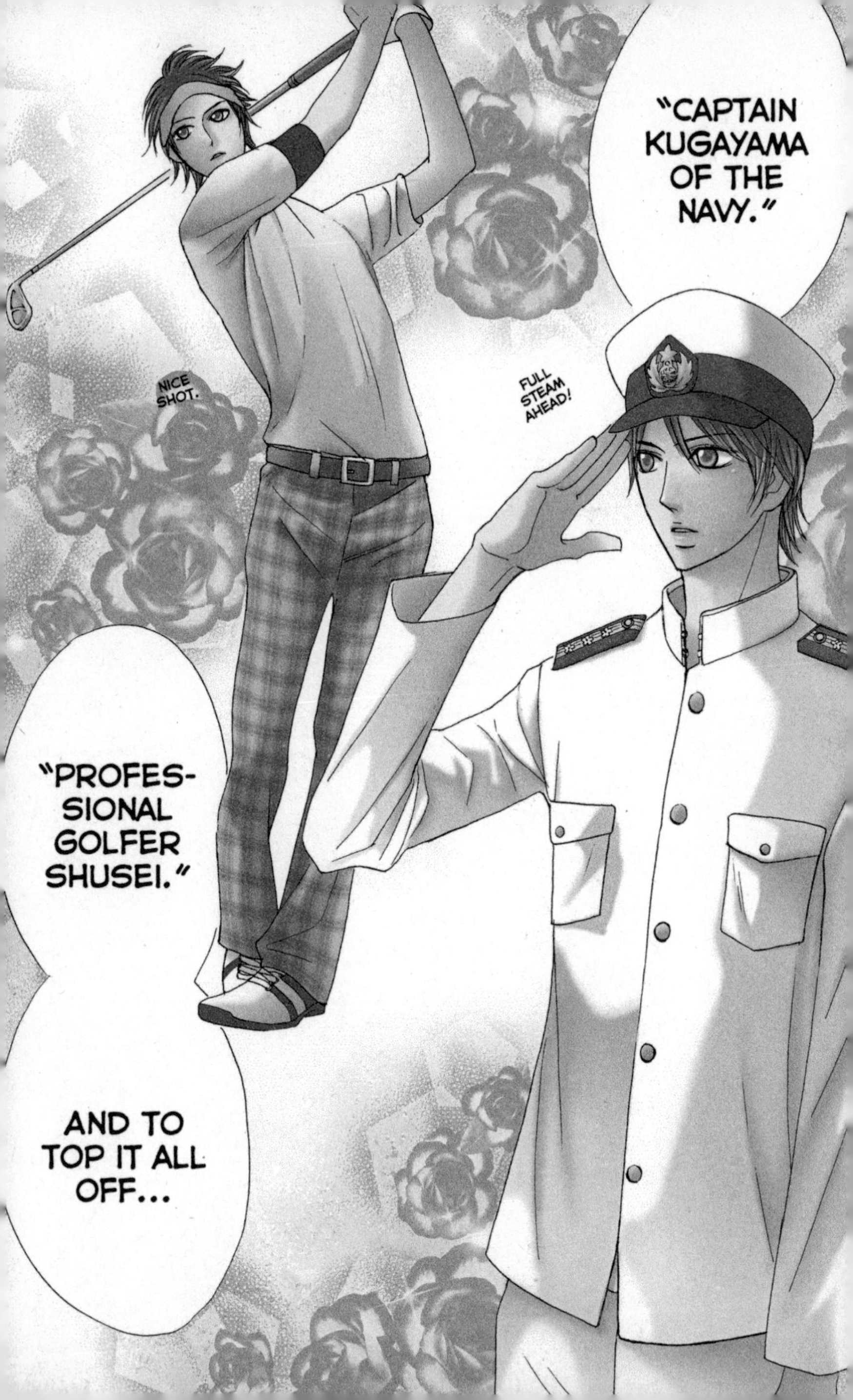
"CAPTAIN KUGAYAMA OF THE NAVY."
FULL STEAM AHEAD!
NICE SHOT.
"PROFES-SIONAL GOLFER SHUSEI."
AND TO TOP IT ALL OFF...

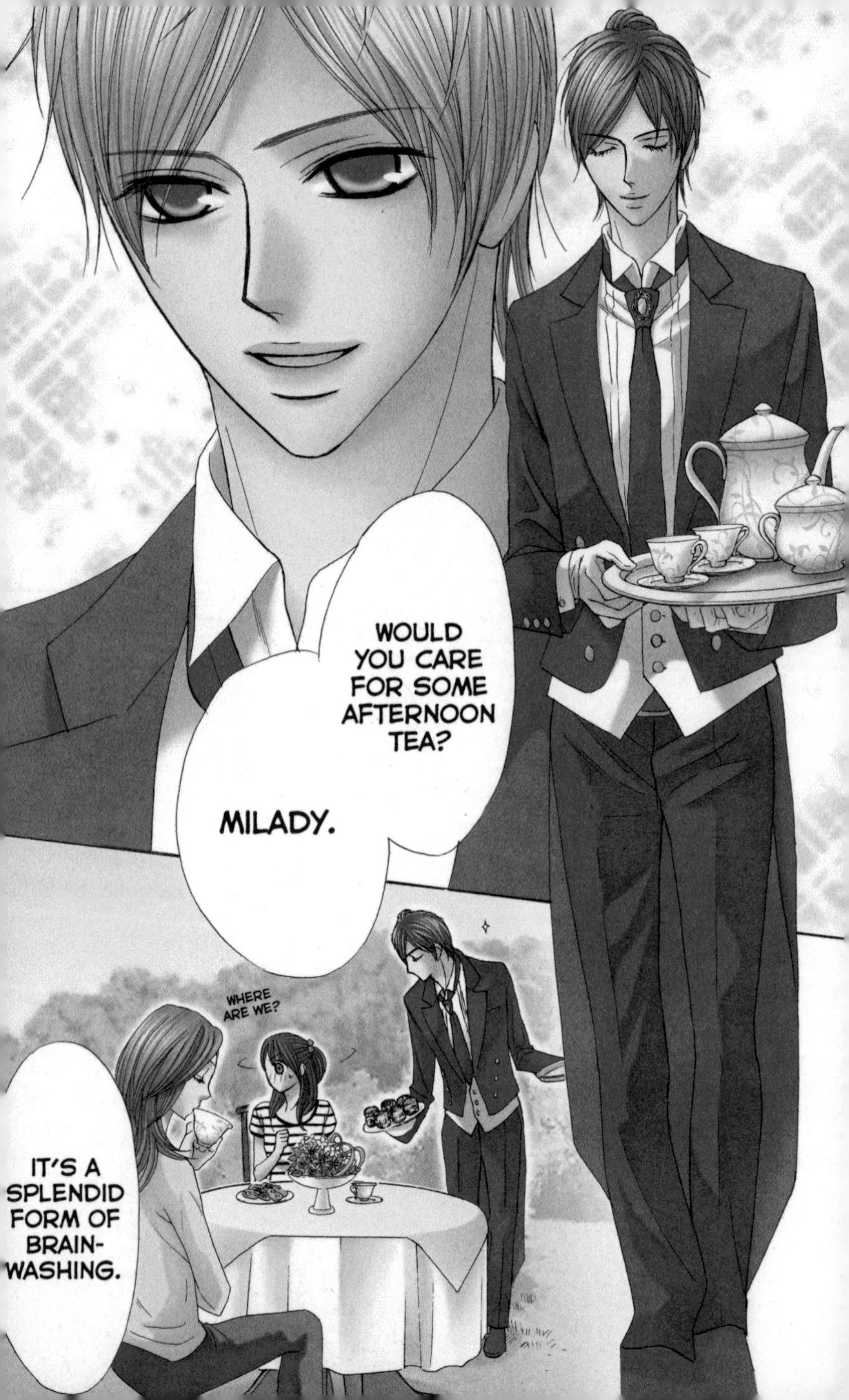
WOULD YOU CARE FOR SOME AFTERNOON TEA?
MILADY.
WHERE ARE WE?
IT'S A SPLENDID FORM OF BRAIN-WASHING.

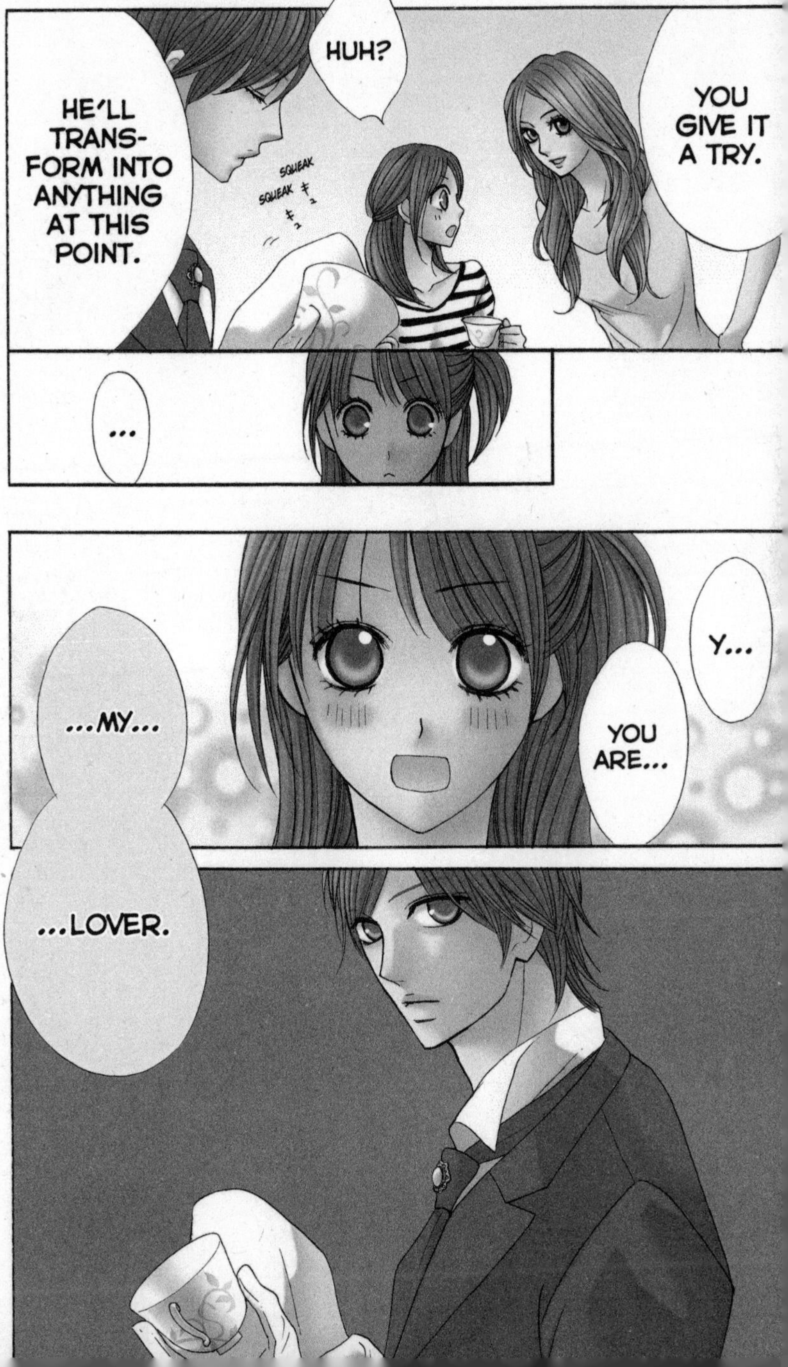
YOU GIVE IT A TRY.
HUH?
SQUEAK SQUEAK
HE'LL TRANSFORM INTO ANYTHING AT THIS POINT.
...
Y...
YOU ARE...
...MY...
...LOVER.

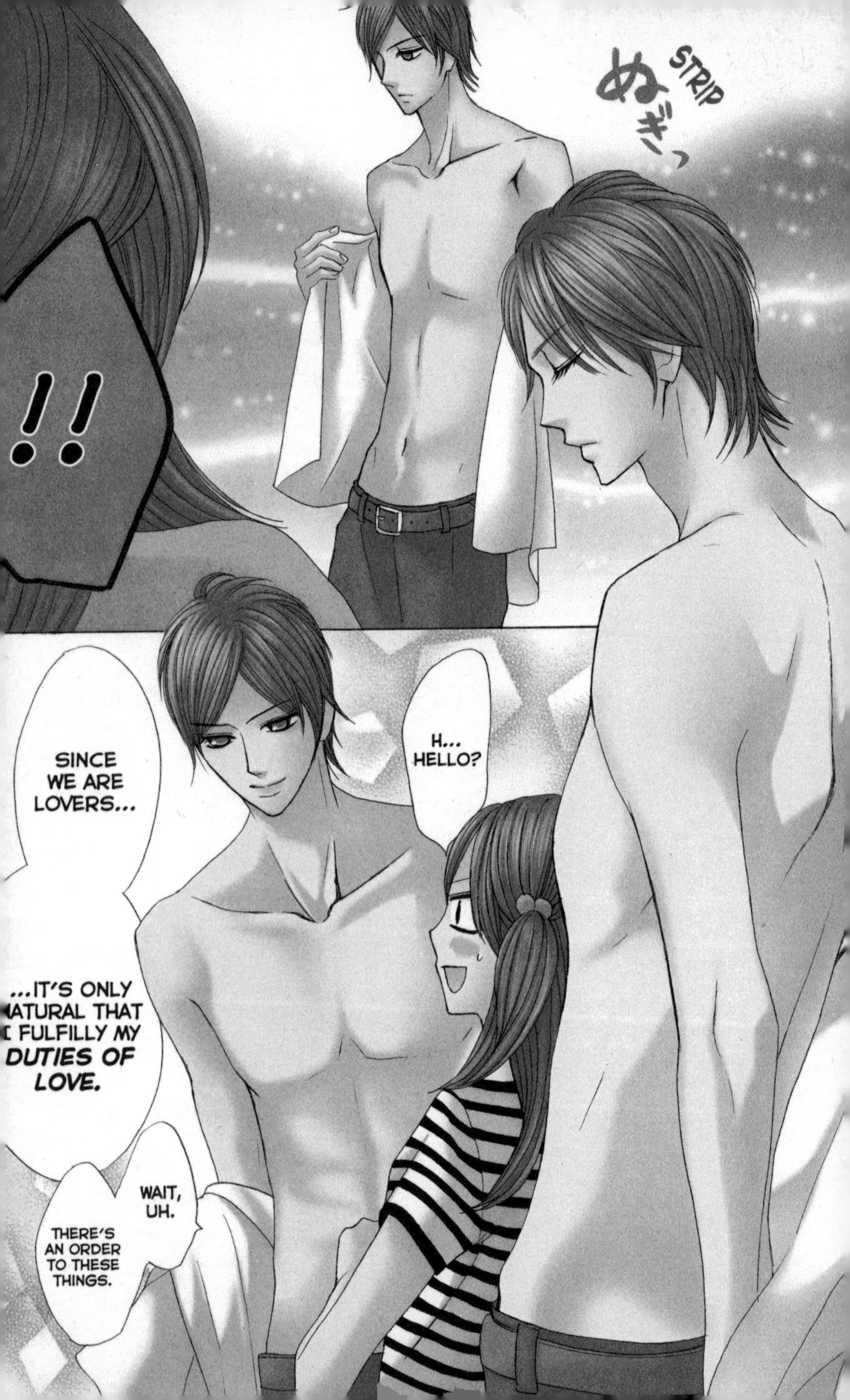
STRIP
ぬぎっ
!!
H... HELLO?
SINCE WE ARE LOVERS...
...IT'S ONLY NATURAL THAT I FULFILLY MY DUTIES OF LOVE.
WAIT, UH.
THERE'S AN ORDER TO THESE THINGS.

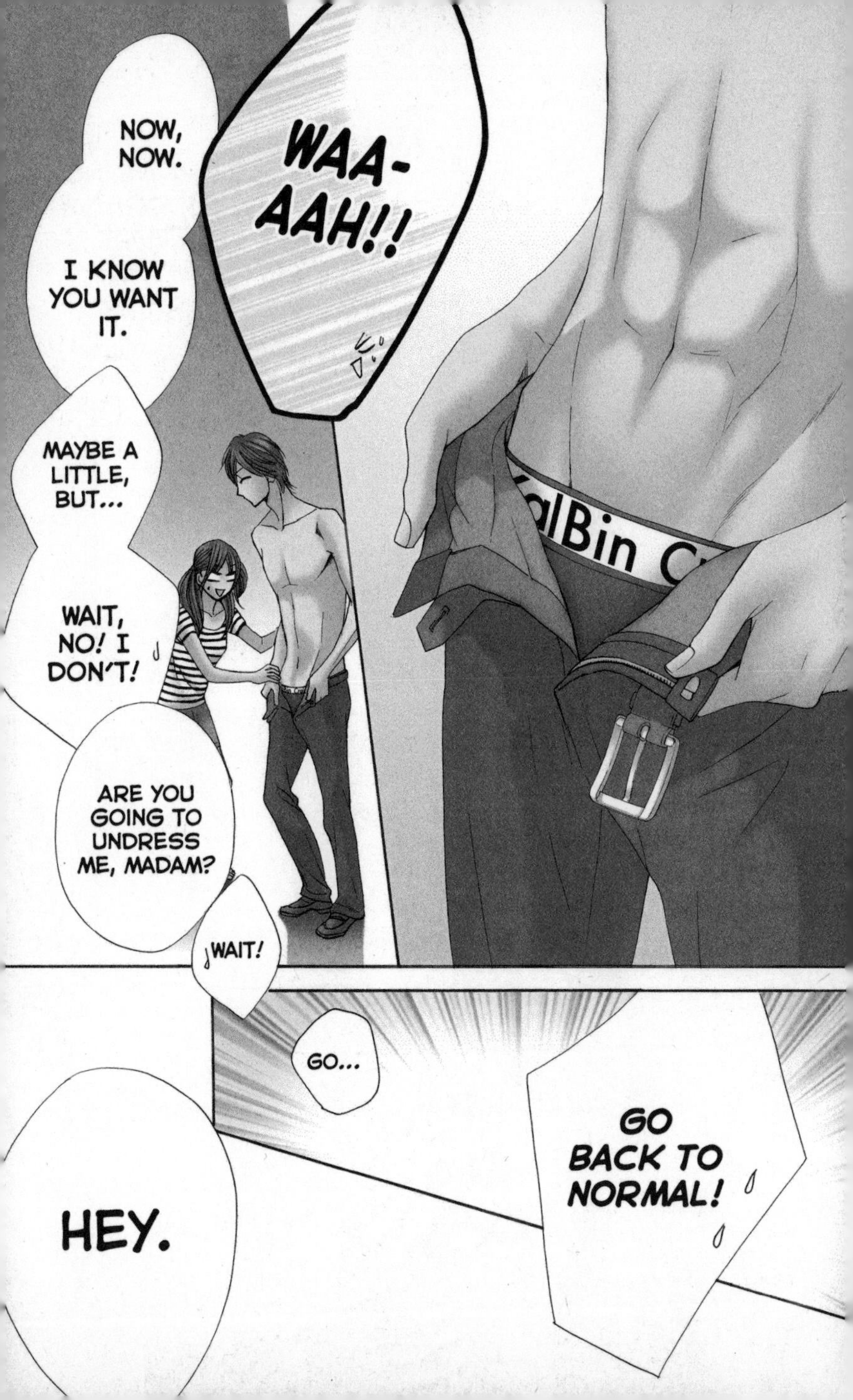
WAA-AAH!!
NOW, NOW.
I KNOW YOU WANT IT.
MAYBE A LITTLE, BUT...
WAIT, NO! I DON'T!
ARE YOU GOING TO UNDRESS ME, MADAM?
WAIT!
GO...
GO BACK TO NORMAL!
HEY.

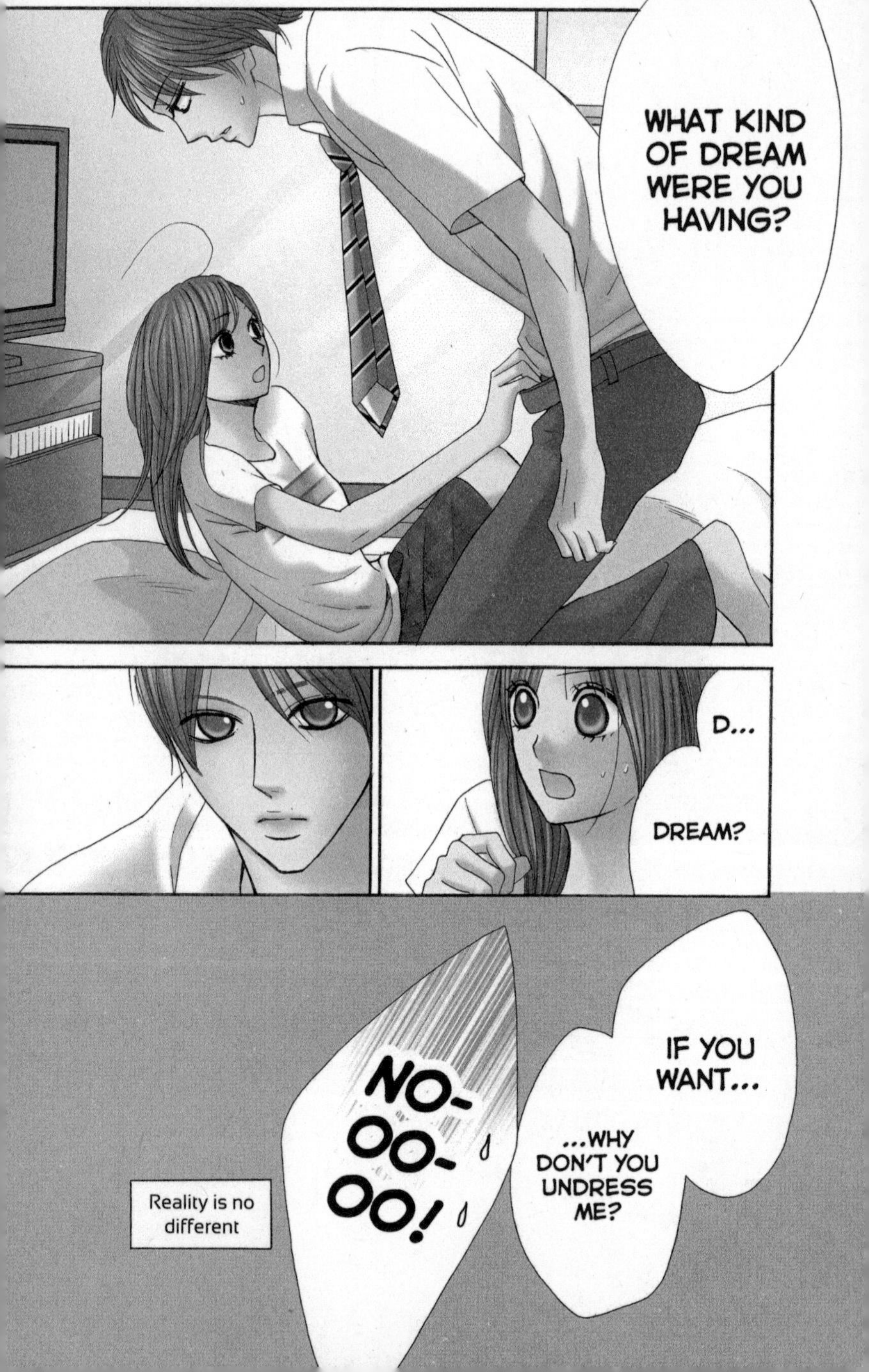
WHAT KIND OF DREAM WERE YOU HAVING?
D...
DREAM?
IF YOU WANT...
...WHY DON'T YOU UNDRESS ME?
NO-OO-OO!
Reality is no different

L♥DK

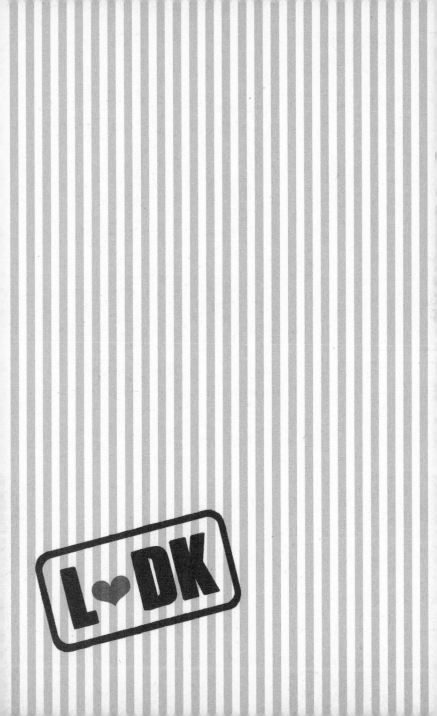

special thanks

K.Hamano
N.Imai
S.Sato
Y.Negishi
I.Kozakura

my family
my friends

M.Morita
A.Ichikawa
A.Yamamoto

AND YOU

Ayu Watanabe
Mar.2011

Everyday Essentials, Item 6
Konbu & Plum-flavored Sweets

As someone prone to midnight snacking, I am very thankful for these items. Since they're low-calorie, I always overindulge in them. Only after I've eaten through an entire bag in three minutes do I come back to myself.

Translation Notes

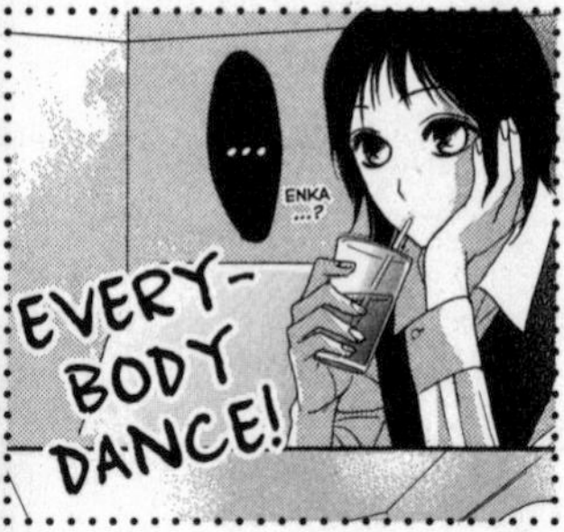
...
ENKA ...?
EVERY-BODY DANCE!

***Enka*, page 92**
As a Japanese pop music genre, *enka* are short narrative ballads dealing with sad love, old-fashioned duty (*giri*) or sentiment (*ninjo*) and are sung in a Japanese-flavored tone peculiar to the style. The genre is roughly analogous to country western music in the United States.

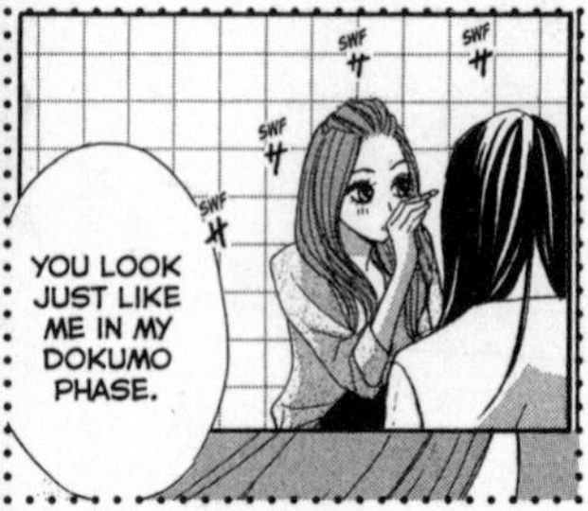
SWF
SWF
SWF
SWF
YOU LOOK JUST LIKE ME IN MY DOKUMO PHASE.

***Dokumo*, page 96**
An abbreviation for *dokusha moderu*, which literally means "reader model," *dokumo* is a term for amateur models who usually have full-time jobs aside from their occasional modelling stints. Many popular fashion icons, models and artists including Tsubasa Masuwaka and Kyary Pamyu Pamyu were *dokumo* before they made a name for themselves.

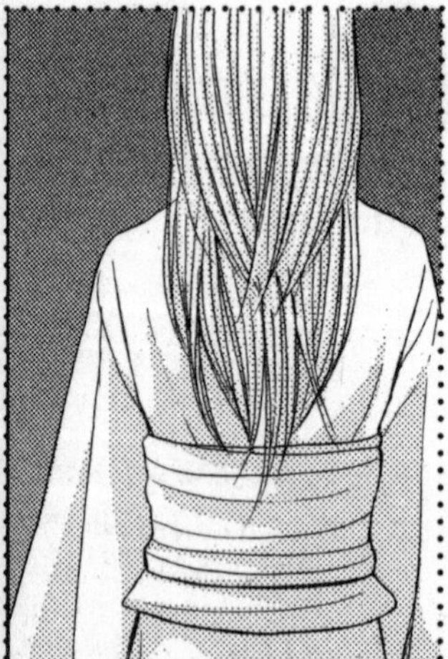

Snow Woman, page 132
The Snow Woman or *Yuki-onna* is a spirit from Japanese folklore, said to often appear during blizzards. Palely-complected and terribly beautiful, she by turns betwitches and terrifies mortals.

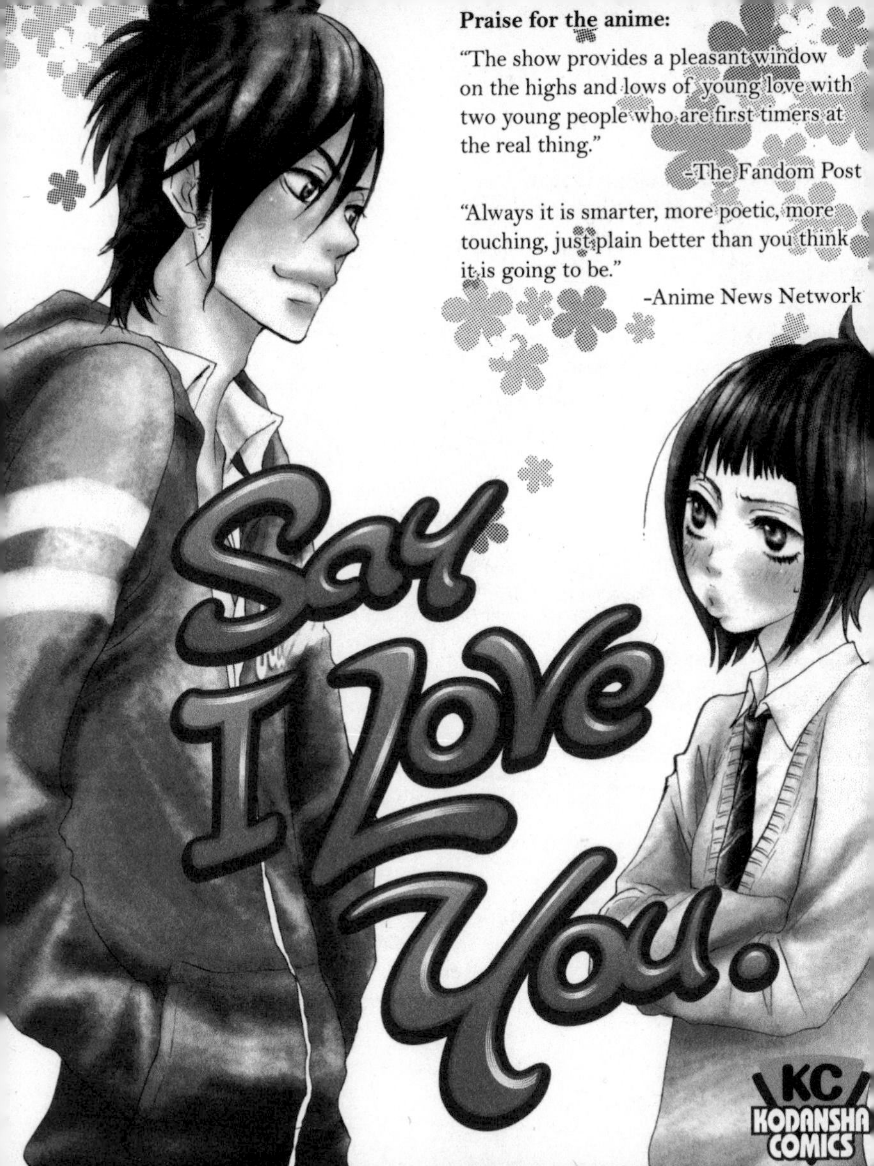
Praise for the anime:
“The show provides a pleasant window on the highs and lows of young love with two young people who are first timers at the real thing.”
-The Fandom Post
“Always it is smarter, more poetic, more touching, just plain better than you think it is going to be.”
-Anime News Network
Say I Love You.
KC
KODANSHA COMICS

Mei Tachibana has no friends — and says she doesn’t need them!

But everything changes when she accidentally roundhouse kicks the most popular boy in school! However, Yamato Kurosawa isn’t angry in the slightest—in fact, he thinks his ordinary life could use an unusual girl like Mei. But winning Mei’s trust will be a tough task. How long will she refuse to say, “I love you”?

7544

LDK volume 6 is a work of fiction. Names, characters, places, and incidents are the products of the author's imagination or are used fictitiously. Any resemblance to actual events, locales, or persons, living or dead, is entirely coincidental.

A Kodansha Comics Trade Paperback Original.

LDK volume 6 copyright © 2011 Ayu Watanabe
English translation copyright © 2016 Ayu Watanabe

All rights reserved.

Published in the United States by Kodansha Comics, an imprint of Kodansha USA Publishing, LLC, New York.

Publication rights for this English edition arranged through Kodansha Ltd., Tokyo.

First published in Japan in 2011 by Kodansha Ltd., Tokyo, as L♡DK, volume 6.

ISBN 978-1-63236-159-2

Printed in the United States of America.

www.kodanshacomics.com

9 8 7 6 5 4 3 2 1

Translation: Christine Dashiell
Lettering: Sara Linsley
Editing: Lauren Scanlan
Kodansha Comics Edition Cover Design: Phil Balsman

OCT 2016